THAT PRIDE OF RACE AND CHARACTER

That Pride of Race and Character

The Roots of Jewish Benevolence in the Jim Crow South

Caroline E. Light

NEW YORK UNIVERSITY PRESS
New York and London

NEW YORK UNIVERSITY PRESS
New York and London
www.nyupress.org

© 2014 by New York University
All rights reserved

References to Internet websites (URLs) were accurate at the time of writing. Neither the author nor New York University Press is responsible for URLs that may have expired or changed since the manuscript was prepared.

Library of Congress Cataloging-in-Publication Data
Light, Caroline E., author.
That pride of race and character : the roots of Jewish benevolence in the Jim Crow south / Caroline E. Light.
pages cm
Includes bibliographical references and index.
ISBN 978-1-4798-5453-0 (cloth : alk. paper)
1. Jews—Southern States—Social life and customs—20th century. 2. Jews—Southern States—Politics and government—20th century. 3. Benevolence. 4. Charity. 5. Kindness. 6. Jewish way of life. I. Title.
F220.J5.L54   2014
305.892'4075—dc23   2014004202

New York University Press books are printed on acid-free paper, and their binding materials are chosen for strength and durability. We strive to use environmentally responsible suppliers and materials to the greatest extent possible in publishing our books.

Manufactured in the United States of America

10 9 8 7 6 5 4 3 2 1

Also available as an ebook

CONTENTS

Acknowledgments		vii
	Introduction: Loving Kindness and Cultural Citizenship in the Jewish South	1
1	"To the Hebrews the World Is Indebted": The Southern Roots of American Jewish Benevolence	24
2	"For the Honor of the Jewish People": Gender, Race, and Immigration	55
3	"Virtue, Rectitude and Loyalty to Our Faith": Jewish Orphans and the Politics of Southern Cultural Capital	81
4	"A Very Delicate Problem": The Plight of the Southern *Agunah*	123
5	"None of My Own People": Subsidizing Jewish Motherhood in the Depression-Era South	150
6	Sex, Race, and Consumption: Southern Sephardim and the Politics of Benevolence	183
	Conclusion: Loving Kindness and Its Legacies	212
	Notes	217
	Selected Bibliography	257
	Index	273
	About the Author	278

ACKNOWLEDGMENTS

Over the years of researching and writing this book, I have incurred many debts and benefited from the tremendous generosity of friends, family, mentors, and colleagues. First and foremost, I want to thank Kathi Kern and Karla Goldman for their *un*ambivalent benevolence, for inspiring this project, for fostering my interest in American Jewish cultural history, and for helping train my eye on the multifaceted South. Thanks to Pat Cooper, for her resolute insistence that this project would one day become a book and her confidence in my ability to see it through. In the early stages of the project, I also benefited from the wisdom of my doctoral committee members: Joan Callahan, Francie Chassen-Lopez, Fon Gordon, and Gordon Hutner.

When I first began my exploration of southern Jewish history, I landed most fortuitously in the then-nascent Ida Pearle & Joseph Cuba Archives at the William Breman Jewish Heritage Museum of Atlanta, where I benefited from the exceptional generosity and support of the professional staff. I offer my sincere gratitude to Sandy Berman, archivist, friend, and expert in Jewish Atlanta, who supported this project from start to finish. Mickey Harvey and Maureen MacLaughlin helped me sort through the Archives' treasure trove of case files and images. Both of the Breman Museum's executive directors whose tenure coincided with my research, Jane Leavey and Aaron Berger, provided steady support and encouragement. Sincere thanks to Lara Dorfman, executive director of the Jewish Educational Loan Fund, and the board members who trusted me with the Atlanta Hebrew Orphans Home's confidential case files and their largely untold history.

Early research for this book received funding from the Woodrow Wilson Foundation and from the Jacob Rader Marcus American Jewish Archives in Cincinnati. Many thanks to Kevin Profitt and the other staff members at the American Jewish Archives, where I began my exploration of the New Orleans Jewish Orphans Home. Thanks to Dale Rosengarten, curator of the Jewish Heritage Collection at the College of Charleston's Addlestone Library, who introduced me to the nation's first Hebrew Benevolent Society seal and helped me uncover its fascinating history. Ned Goldberg, director of New Orleans Jewish Children's Regional Services, the organization that started as the first southern Jewish orphan home, granted me unrestricted access to his collection of images of the home's early days. I am grateful to David Geffen and Joel Ziff, who shared the fascinating unpublished autobiography of their grandfather, Rabbi Tobias Geffen.

I am deeply grateful to the many intellectually generous people who read drafts of chapters—often more than once—discussed the project with me, and offered sage advice and encouragement: Steve Beeber, Robin Bernstein, Kimberly Juanita Brown, Kirsten Delegard, Katharine DuBois, Susan Faludi, Melanie Beals Goan, Wahneema Lubiano, Susan Marine, Tamera Marko, Virginia Noble, William Norrett, Jennifer Pettit, Meredith Reiches, Elizabeth Reis, Kate Stanton, Susan Thorne, Marlene Trestman, Anne Mitchell Whisnant, Robyn Wiegman, and Kat Williams. Dianne Ashton, in her capacity as editor of *American Jewish History*, and two anonymous readers, helped me refine my thinking on the *agunah*—the abandoned Jewish woman—and some material from the resulting *AJH* article appears in chapter 4 of this book. Thanks to Jeanne Follansbee, my stalwart writing partner, whose expert interdisciplinary guidance enriched my critical reading of primary sources and who read so many drafts of this project that she can doubtless recite much of it by heart. I am ever grateful to Linda Schlossberg, extraordinary colleague and friend, who helped keep me focused on the finish line, reading multiple drafts and coaching me through the most challenging parts.

Throughout the course of this project, treasured friends and colleagues have provided support and encouragement in ways too numerous to count. I want to thank all my colleagues at Harvard's Program in Studies of Women, Gender, and Sexuality. I am also indebted to the following for contributing their guidance, friendship, and insights at various points along the long journey of this book: Michael Bronski, Kelly Cogswell, Elizabeth Jemison, Betsy Leondar-Wright, Christianna

Morgan, Eve Nagler, Afsaneh Najmabadi, Amy Parker, Ann Pellegrini, John Plotz, Anne Swedberg, and Aubry Threlkeld. I am grateful to Bradley Craig and Edward Michael Dussom for their excellent research assistance and encouragement.

Thanks to the fantastic editorial staff at New York University Press. I thank Jennifer Hammer, my editor, for her enthusiasm about the project and for shepherding me through the process so gracefully and efficiently. I am grateful to the three anonymous readers who offered exceptionally generous notes and suggestions. Their comments have significantly enriched the quality of this book, and I hope that I may someday thank them in person. Thanks to managing editor Dorothea Halliday and editorial assistant Constance Grady for their guidance and infinite patience and to Nicholas Taylor for performing the all-important and challenging task of copyediting.

I am fortunate to have had the steadfast support of family members and friends, who never tired (or at least never appeared to have tired) of discussing my project. Personal thanks to my Aunt Caroline (Light) Triplett and my Uncle Robert Berlin—each representing different sides of my family tree—who shared their fascination with genealogy and fondness for old primary documents. I thank my father and stepmother, Henry and Angelica Light, for being exemplars of modern benevolence, and my brother, Andrew Light, and sister, Leslie Light, for their unfaltering provision of humor and perspective. I thank my mother, Sandy Berlin Light, for giving me an appreciation for the unconventional and for teaching me to pursue success in my own way.

I dedicate this book to my family, to Jocelyn, Miriam, and Andrew Cubstead—for whom this project has been a lingering presence for as long as they can remember—and most importantly, to Matt, for over two decades of friendship, love, and laughter. This one's for you.

Introduction

Loving Kindness and Cultural Citizenship in the Jewish South

Jews have desired to fit in, to be like everyone else. The problem is that there is an excess expressed in this desire that is aptly captured in the joke that says that Jews are like everyone else, only more so.
—Laura Levitt, *Jews and Feminism*, 1997

It is impossible to write a history of the Jews of the South without re-creating the history of the South itself.
—Harry Golden, *Our Southern Landsman*, 1974

Ralph A. Sonn, Bavarian-born superintendent of the Hebrew Orphans Home of Atlanta, addressed the Board of Trustees on New Year's Eve, 1917, on the subject of aiding poor Jews within the institution's five-state region. Opened in 1889 in the up-and-coming "Gate City" of the New South, the home was designed for needy Jewish children whose parents were either deceased or unable to care for them. Most of its 111 young charges were sons and daughters of the immigrants who had made the South their home in the late nineteenth and early twentieth century, many having fled the pogroms of Russia to establish a permanent home in the "golden land" of America.[1] It was up to Sonn and the other comparatively privileged and acculturated members of the Orphans Home Board to ensure that these future Jewish citizens did not become wards of Christian institutions or burdens to the public purse. In his speech, Sonn disparaged what he perceived as a "conservative" tendency to "let good enough alone." Invoking the familiar wooden fence posts that surrounded many of the nearby middle-class homes in Atlanta's growing

Jewish community, Sonn declared, "If you leave a white post alone, it will soon be a black post." He continued, "If you particularly want it to be white you must be always painting it again . . . What does not go forward does not stand still, it goes backward."[2]

Delivered two and half years after Leo Frank's death by lynching in August 1915, Sonn's metaphor in black and white was no epistemological accident. He and the other Jews of Atlanta lived in the shadow of the scandal that ensued when Frank, a Texas-born and Cornell-educated Jew of German descent, was accused and found guilty of murdering thirteen-year-old Mary Phagan, one of many young, poor white girls who worked under his supervision at the National Pencil Factory.[3] The violent outcome of Frank's trial broadcast to the southern Jewish community and beyond the ease with which Jewishness might translate to racial and sexual deviance, as public characterizations of Frank as a "Jew Pervert" and "lascivious simian," driven to violence by his lust for a white, gentile girl, took on a close resemblance to pervasive depictions of the mythological "black beast" rapist.[4]

The place of Jewish citizens was far from secure, and after Frank's death, many closed down their shops and left the city, fearful of retribution and an escalating wave of anti-Semitic violence.[5] Those who returned to or remained in the South were highly attuned to the need to fit into the social landscape, and they struggled to cultivate a low profile and to make Jewishness synonymous with exemplary southern citizenship. Benevolent social uplift—particularly efforts to support impoverished widows and orphans—centered on a need to ensure that fellow Jews internalized the localized racial knowledge that would enable them to adopt "American" values. Exploring the historical records and case files of charitable organizations and social uplift societies helps us untangle the ways in which southern Jews—in all their cultural and regional diversity—negotiated efforts to remain Jewish while also making a home in the South.

The rich legacy of Jewish benevolence is evident in the names of hospitals, schools, and charitable institutions spread across the contemporary American landscape, visible in all the places Jews have called home. Yet the southern origins of these civic contributions are less prominent in public memory and largely overlooked by scholars of Jewish culture and history. This book challenges northern-centric perspectives on American Jewish history by looking south to uncover the roots of Jewish benevolent traditions and to explore the ways in which region shaped a minoritized people's pursuit of belonging. For Jews living in the Jim Crow South, charity and social uplift served as a vital citizenship project, a complex give-and-take whereby relatively privileged, established Jews worked to support and educate their poor, immigrant coreligionists. Theirs was also an effort to protect collective Jewishness from association with poverty and cultural degeneration, and their work on behalf of poor brethren reveals how the lessons of regional belonging and social mobility assumed concrete form.[6] This book shows how Jewish southerners responded to the precariousness of their lives by instituting a sophisticated network of social uplift organizations to ensure that their poorest coreligionists did not endanger collective Jewish prosperity and belonging.

Through a complex dialectic of benevolence characterized by simultaneous self-interest and altruism, southern Jews navigated their relationship with regional authenticity by proving themselves to be exemplars of charity. This book argues that their exceptional performance of *gemilut hasadim*—Hebrew for "giving loving kindness"—provided the vehicle through which they negotiated the politics of belonging, particularly the cultural and symbolic properties of citizenship, in a time and place of extreme insecurity and social transformation. Ultimately, poor southern Jews' encounters with their benevolent coreligionists confirm that the history of southern Jewishness is not simply that of Jews fitting in *despite* their cultural and religious differences. Rather, this is a story of how Jewish southerners absorbed the social mores of their adoptive homeland while shaping them, in journalist Harry Golden's words, "re-creating the history of the South itself."[7]

The migration of roughly two million eastern European Jews between 1881 and 1924 sparked national anti-Semitic speculation about Jewish inassimilability, driving native-born coreligionists to step up efforts to provide material support as well as guidance on the finer points of becoming American. Jewish benevolence was thus a "categorical imperative" nationwide.[8] Yet, in the post-Reconstruction South, the effort to take care of impoverished coreligionists was amplified at the crossroads of economic turmoil, profound shifts in the way racial differences were known, and violent policing of the color line, creating for southern Jews a compulsion to excel in the performance of charity or else fall prey to the region's most lethal exclusions.

The approximately twenty-five thousand Jews who called the South home in the late nineteenth century saw their social stability and authenticity shaken by the arrival of over forty thousand immigrant coreligionists, whose poverty and cultural and religious differences called into question the ability of Jewish people to be truly southern.[9] Classified by racial taxonomists as "Caucasian," the predominantly eastern European newcomers were nevertheless foreign to the collective memories of postwar sectionalism in which modern southern white identities were grounded. Further, the new immigrants' arrival coincided with what historian Rayford Logan termed the "nadir" of southern race relations, a period spanning from the end of Reconstruction into the 1920s, during which racist violence claimed approximately three thousand African American lives.[10] As they bore witness to, participated in, and sometimes became subject to this violence, Jewish southerners internalized a sense of the region's racial and gender hierarchies that in turn helped authenticate their status as true citizens of the South.[11] This book tells the story of how the Jews of the South navigated the dangers of this crossroads by constructing a benevolent empire to provide irrefutable proof of their superior commitment to loving kindness and to cement their claims to southern authenticity.

Orphan societies and homes were among the most cherished institutional responses to the insecurity of Jewish citizenship in the South, and their archival records reveal the depth of leaders' commitment to the protection and education of the region's impoverished Jewish children. The genealogy of these orphan-protection efforts extends throughout the nineteenth century, from the 1801 formation of the Charleston Hebrew Orphans Society, to the establishment in 1856 of the Jewish Orphans Home (later renamed the Association of Relief for Hebrew Widows and Orphans) of New Orleans, to the 1889 dedication of the Hebrew Orphans Asylum (later renamed the Hebrew Orphans Home) of Atlanta. Their institutional records—including public speeches, newsletters, meeting minutes, annual reports, and social worker case files—testify to the ambivalent coexistence of selflessness and self-promotion, of altruism and opportunism that congealed at the volatile intersection of immigrant acculturation, social uplift, and regional racial norms.

An active and ongoing investment in charity has long constituted a vital component of Jewish citizenship, yet the effort took on additional urgency in spaces where anti-Semitism, anti-immigration backlash, and Jim Crow culture coexisted. This book therefore looks south to understand how charity served as an essential defense against the cultural, social, and political uncertainties of Jewish belonging. While scholars of American Jewish history have documented the range and depth of Jewish charity as a collective effort to assuage poverty and to bolster Jewish belonging, few have investigated the charitable infrastructure established by southern Jews or explored the ways in which regional culture and politics influenced the provision of charity to impoverished coreligionists.[12] Although the largest population of American Jews in 1820 was concentrated in Charleston, South Carolina, subsequent waves of Jewish immigrants settled chiefly in the North, creating a demographic disparity that influenced narratives of American Jewish history. One consequence of this imbalance was an amnesiac depiction of the North as the primary site of American Jewish life, culture, and history. The field of southern Jewish history emerged decades ago to correct this historical imbalance, and this book is part of that restorative intervention.[13]

Scholars of southern Jewish history have opened many doors onto formerly unseen sources, contextualizing Jewish life in the South by revealing, for example, the extent to which southern Jews were pioneers in the larger national movement for Reform Judaism and illuminating the participation of Jewish immigrants as rank-and-file soldiers of the Confederacy.[14] However, the intricate relationship between transnational Jewish identities and a culture in which Jim Crow segregation, economic turmoil, and state-sanctioned racial violence flourished remains under-analyzed. Some scholars assert that southern Jewish difference began and ended at population size; southern Jews lived in largely gentile communities in which they had access to fewer traditional lines of Jewish ritual and cultural continuity.[15] While demographic factors influenced the emergence of distinct southern Jewish cultural practices and folkways, post-Reconstruction modes of racial and gender etiquette, including the means of differentiating "citizens" from "noncitizens," helped set the stage on which Jewish leaders, social workers, and the recipients of their benevolence forged a path to full citizenship in the South.

In a public presentation titled "How Southern Is Southern Jewish History?" historian Eric Goldstein called for "a new paradigm for the study of southern Jewish history," one that takes into consideration the "particular social, legal and cultural framework operating in the South."[16] Given the post–Civil War prevalence of white longing for a mythologized era of unequivocal social order and white racial purity, this book explores how "the South" takes shape as a fictive historical space through which affiliations and exclusions are imagined and coded into language, memory, and social landscape.[17] If culture and shared history play a pivotal role in shaping individual citizens, "the South" is not simply a location confined by the boundaries designating the Confederate combatants in the Civil War.[18] Rather, it was (and continues to be) a set of collectively forged memories and practices, culturally and locally specific folklores and identificatory rituals that configure the lines dividing insider from outsider, citizen from stranger.[19] Southern belonging was therefore framed in a series of interimplicated and overlapping relations of power, all of which influenced Jewish efforts to exemplify good citizenship through acts of loving kindness.

Cultural Citizenship and Southern Jewish Belonging

In addition to illuminating the sophisticated network of Jewish benevolent institutions in the southern United States, this volume contributes to contemporary ethnic studies scholarship by exploring a minoritized people's multifaceted efforts to obtain access to the benefits of full citizenship. Drawing from recent work on "cultural citizenship," a concept popularized by cultural anthropologist Renato Rosaldo, this book looks beyond the rights, privileges, and protections delineated in legal structures to explore how collectively shared values, ideals, and practices shape historical actors' authenticity as members of a community. According to Rosaldo, cultural citizenship constitutes the "everyday cultural practices through which [minoritized subjects] claim space and their right to be full members of society."[20] Recent scholarship in Latino/a and Asian American studies has applied this approach in investigations of communal and individual negotiations for belonging and the complex interdependencies and fluctuating identity politics that comprise the realm of "culture."[21] The book builds on understandings of what American studies scholar Lisa Lowe calls "the collectively forged images, histories, and narratives that place, displace, and replace individuals in relation to the national polity" by illustrating how hegemonic understandings of gender and race inflected idealized notions of citizenship. I analyze the shared values, norms, and histories that, in Lowe's words, "powerfully shape who the citizenry is, where they dwell, what they remember, and what they forget."[22] Yet in a departure from Lowe's analysis of national identities and citizenship claims, this book illustrates how regional culture and collective memory shaped the boundaries of citizenship for southern Jews. For Jews living in the post-Reconstruction South, loving kindness constituted an authoritative, historically rooted assertion of collective common cause, a representational strategy that tied Jewish southerners to one another and their southern homeland while policing the boundaries between insider and outsider, citizen and stranger.

This book frames the South as a critical site of Jewish cultural production, where some of the earliest Jewish settlers first initiated the networks of charity that would help prove their entitlement to full belonging in their adoptive homeland. Without reducing the South to its tired stereotypes, the book demonstrates how a southern environment configured by a war-torn economy and a forcefully defended color line, the latter supported by "Lost Cause" ideology and pervasive mythologies of sexualized race difference, shaped the experiences and collective identity of southern Jews. Benevolent leaders' and social workers' negotiations with their needy clients—orphans, widows, abandoned wives, and impoverished families—provide insight into a minoritized people's encounter with their region's shifting ideals of belonging. In this story of acculturation, benevolence provides a lens on the multifaceted give and take of Jewish identity formation, ultimately asking how an internally variegated community negotiated a path to inclusion with an eye to the larger community's reckoning of citizenship.

The book explores and contextualizes the cultural roots of the Jewish obligation to give loving kindness to others, particularly to impoverished women and children. *Gemilut hasadim* emphasizes the individual's responsibility to others and celebrates the performance of *mitzvot*—good deeds—in an effort to improve one's community and the larger world beyond. In contrast to Christian principles of charity in which one's reward for good deeds exists in the afterlife, the concept of *gemilut* implies the reciprocity of service in which one receives an immediate reward or recognition for his or her kindness.[23] For Jews, whose historical experience of oppression and disfranchisement helped solidify their terms of mutual identification, *mitzvot* to the wider community often served as a crucial means of cementing their communal access to the benefits of cultural and juridical citizenship.[24] From their first encounters with the New World, Jews experienced citizenship of a limited kind, their recognition and acceptance contingent on their capacity to become self-sufficient and to ensure that poor coreligionists never became a burden to the larger community. Thus an implicit association of citizenship, in its multiple manifestations, as a reward for broad-reaching charity characterized the earliest instances of Jewish settlement in North America, where benevolent infrastructures emerged wherever Jews settled permanently.

The significance of Jewish legacies of service to their collective progress and belonging was captured in the words of Benjamin Franklin Jonas at the 1856 dedication of the New Orleans Jewish Orphans Home. The Kentucky-born attorney, who later served in the Confederate Army and in the U.S. Senate, told the assembled crowd of celebrants, "It has ever been the boast of the Jewish people, that they support their own poor . . . Their reasons are partly founded in religious necessity, and partly in that pride of race and character which has supported them through so many ages of trial and vicissitude."[25] Throughout the nation, "supporting their own poor" comprised the core of a uniquely Jewish charitable tradition and served as a shared value to which Jonas and others could gesture in ways meaningful to the Jewish public and its non-Jewish allies. Jonas's reference to Jewish "pride of race and character"—in the service of Jewish access to the benefits of universal citizenship—would recur among southern benevolent leaders, although explicit allusions to race would fade gradually to more subtle invocations of Jewish uniqueness.

"A Monument More Precious Than Marble": Hebrew Benevolence, Collective Memory, and the Lost Cause

In the minds of those who claimed the post-Reconstruction South as home, and in the words of Wilbur J. Cash, "the South [was] another land," one that vigilantly policed the boundaries between insider and outsider, and Jews struggled to remain in the former category.[26] The *Jewish South*, a newspaper first established in Atlanta in 1877 under the tagline "Independent and Fearless," exhibited the kind of regional influences that shaped ideals of southern Jewish citizenship. One of the paper's first issues invoked the glory of a shared Confederate past to generate support for Atlanta's Hebrew Benevolent Society: "Though the days of chivalry be past, its spirit yet remains; and in the audience before me many a heart beats wildly when woman weeps, and many a muscle stiffens to battle for the wronged." Conjuring the idealized (white) woman in distress, the anonymous author urged, "Gallant men of Atlanta, respond to the appeal which lovely woman makes for the aid of suffering woman; and if you may not avenge her with your sword, relieve her distress with your purse."[27]

In the plea for "gallant men's" financial support, postwar southern Jewish benevolence staked its legitimacy on a collectively produced sense of history that rested on the established logic of regional distinction and chivalric gender ideals. While "gallant men" of the past used force to "avenge" the "suffering woman," men of this new era would channel their passions into the fortification of a benevolent empire. The author concluded by summoning the "memory of the lost cause, and the dead who died for that cause." He urged, "Your dead heroes with one voice, could they speak, would exclaim, 'build up the Benevolent Home for our bereaved and poverty stricken women—that will be a monument more precious than marble, more enduring than granite.'"[28]

Jewish orphan homes in particular became these "enduring" and "precious" sites of authenticity and acculturation, and their procedures for aiding unfortunate brethren evince the complexities of transforming poor immigrants into respectable Americans, unambiguous citizens who would reflect a favorable image of Jewishness to the gentile world. The region's widespread embrace of Lost Cause nostalgia—the belief that the Union victory represented the bitter defeat of a noble and chivalrous way of life—provided an often unspoken but omnipresent backdrop for discussions of how best to protect orphaned Jewish children from the dual specters of pauperhood and conversion. If, in historian Gunja SenGupta's words, "pauperism marked a person as not quite white," then Jewish benevolence stood as a bulwark against the racialization of coreligionists whose poverty and cultural backwardness threatened communal Jewish access to full citizenship.[29] With a watchful eye trained on prevailing expectations for southern citizenship, benevolent leaders sought to inculcate their young charges with values of economic self-reliance and respectability while balancing Jewish cultural preservation with careful observation of the prevailing racial and gender etiquette. Taking care of those perceived as "their own" also enabled privileged Jews to showcase both their leadership in modern ideals of benevolence as well as their own success in class escalation. In the wake of the Civil War, the exemplary care provided by the southern orphan homes helped verify Jewish adherence to modern, capitalist ideals of progress in a war-ravaged region struggling to self-represent as civilized and cultured.[30]

Critical to the southern Jewish orphan homes' efforts to support poor coreligionists was an emphasis on Jewish distance from blackness and the social degradation it conferred within a violently mandated system of racial segregation. Superintendent Sonn recognized the necessity of aggressive intervention into the lives of poor Jews, a vigilantly reiterative process of "painting and repainting" to ensure that white posts remained white, for to "leave things alone" would open these vulnerable Jewish orphans up to the stigma of blackness. In defiance of anti-Semitic depictions of the Jew-as-outsider, the white posts of Sonn's report stood impervious to the dangers of the color line, their upright uniformity evidence of their indisputable belonging on the middle-class white southern landscape. In Sonn's reckoning, white posts maintained through meticulously applied layers of fresh paint reproduced the ideals of elevated cultural capital—what French sociologist Pierre Bourdieu termed the system of class-privileged knowledge by which one learned to navigate one's particular social terrain—in the city's finest neighborhoods.[31] Yet their neglect would surely render them "black," sullied by grime and emptied of aesthetic promise. Such contaminated posts could not stand sentry to the class-aspirant Jewish homes of Atlanta, nor could they guard the collective legitimacy and belonging of their community. Sonn's appeal to benevolent leaders to continue their efforts in "painting and repainting" suggests his awareness that race itself was a malleable construct, one that Jews could not leave to chance.

Race Uplift and the Ruling Ideologies That Produced Loving Kindness

Through their meticulous efforts to ensure that the fates of impoverished and unacculturated coreligionists were not left to chance, southern Jews demonstrated the significance of benevolence to the process of southern race-making. As historian Matthew Frye Jacobson has argued, "Caucasians are not born . . . they are somehow made. It's just a question of who does the making."[32] Indeed, the process of "making" race, and whether the tenuous category of whiteness would include Jews at a given moment, is a complicated story.[33] Jews were white in the eyes of the law, as demonstrated in their designation as "W" in the U.S. and state Census; their categorization as white in antimiscegenation laws, which forbade intermarriage between whites and people considered not-white; their ability to occupy public spaces reserved for "whites only"; and in their access to naturalization. Despite their unequivocal legal classification and citizenship, Jews were sometimes characterized as racially suspect, and Sonn's "white post" analogy suggests that they were aware both of their occasional liminality and the stakes involved in being perceived as indisputably white. Five years prior to Leo Frank's death, North Carolina minister Arthur T. Abernethy published a book proclaiming *The Jew a Negro: Being A Study of the Jewish Ancestry from an Impartial Standpoint*.[34] Abernethy's invocation of scientific "impartiality" lent credence to his claims about the common ancestry of Jews and African Americans, and the title alone was cause for consternation among Jewish citizens. Shifting understandings of the boundaries delineating "white" from "not-white," anti-Semitic and nativist responses to immigration, and the growing visibility of a newly resurgent Ku Klux Klan weighed heavily on the minds of Jewish leaders, like Sonn, who struggled to ensure that unacculturated and impoverished coreligionists did not bring dishonor to their increasingly variegated community.

To understand how southern Jews internalized and responded to shifts in their region's racial norms requires a close look beyond one-dimensional ideas of individual agency and self-awareness to scrutinize the ways in which coercion and self-interest manifested themselves in the ostensibly pure and autonomous altruism of loving kindness. Literary scholar Susan M. Ryan's analysis of "the power relations that structure well-intentioned acts" provides a model for analyzing the nuanced politics of Jewish loving kindness.[35] As Ryan argues, "Self interest . . . is not the opposite of genuine benevolence but rather its complement," and benevolent discourses must be studied within the contemporaneous systems of race, gender, and class inequality that gave them meaning.[36] When relatively privileged, established Jewish citizens reached out to help their impoverished and immigrant brethren, they did so in the name of self-preservation as well as altruism, guiding their beneficiaries according to their own regionally specific visions of ideal citizenship and class escalation.

This book builds on scholarship on the complex politics of "race uplift" whereby historically minoritized people traversed "a relatively narrow set of tactics," in historian Lawrence Schenbeck's words, to win "civic rights and economic security."[37] In their examinations of African American race uplift and the accompanying politics of respectability, historians Evelyn Brooks Higginbotham and Kevin Gaines underscore the ambivalence with which historical actors on either side of the benevolent relationship navigated their precarious journeys to civic inclusion.[38] A collective as well as an individual enterprise, uplift demanded that relatively privileged members of a minoritized community—in this case the black elite or "Talented Tenth"—struggle for communal improvement, helping lift their "race" as they scaled the social ladder. In defiance of the larger world's racist exclusions, members of the "Talented Tenth" showcased their superior respectability and class status in their public performance of good works, in the process hoping to prove the collective entitlement of African Americans to full citizenship.[39]

Established Jews similarly recognized that their individual success and acceptance depended on the success and acceptance of Jews collectively. In a 1914 letter to Simon Wolf, the first president of the Atlanta Hebrew Orphans Home, Mary Antin, immigrant advocate and author of *The Promised Land* (1912), voiced her belief in benevolent outreach as vital to communal Jewish success:

> There is not a Jew in this country . . . who is not affected in some degree by the triumphs or failures of Jewish public enterprises. The world is accustomed to judge us Jews in the lump. The sins of the least of us cover us all with shame; the merit of the greatest of us reflects credit on all of us . . . You and your colleagues in the good work have added another span to the bridge by which I, a Jewish woman, shall cross the chasm between my highest ambitions and the world's interpretation of my life.[40]

Writing in the midst of Leo Frank's trial, Antin saw to the heart of the command performance of Jewish charity. Imagined collectively by the non-Jewish world, regardless of their cultural heterogeneity, Jews would be judged "in the lump." Despite individual strivings and public triumphs, Jewish legitimacy rested on the success of their lowest common denominator, the impoverished and unacculturated masses whose perceived backwardness threatened the social standing of all who identified as Jews. Loving kindness was therefore not solely a means by which to take care of their own, as Jewish law commanded; it was also a carefully choreographed response to the unstable, often hostile social terrain in which Jews sought full membership.

Loving kindness also involved coercion, where recipients of charity were expected to comply with the mandates of their benefactors as a precondition for receiving aid. In Jewish tradition, the most revered form of *tzedakah*—justice to the poor—valorizes "double blind" charity given anonymously to an anonymous recipient. Yet, during the period under study, national shifts in understandings of poverty increasingly demanded expert supervision of the poor to ensure that only the "worthy" received material assistance. By the late nineteenth century, social uplift leaders nationwide frowned on "handouts" as an ineffectual and antiquated mode of charity while the emergence of the social work profession provided an army of trained experts to supervise poor clients and oversee the distribution of financial support.[41] Thus *tzedakah* could not be truly "blind" without violating the nation's scientific standards of charity. Individuals might still donate anonymously to the many benevolent institutions that served the Jewish poor, but the recipients of charitable aid were increasingly subject to the scrutiny and control of "professional altruists." For the duration of the benevolent exchange—where orphans were fed, clothed, and educated and where widowed and abandoned mothers received financial support along with home visits from trained social workers—the recipient of charity navigated a complex web of surveillance.

As the sources reveal, recipients of charity were far from docile bodies on which uplift strategies for middle-class success could be inscribed. They often rebelled—sometimes subtly—against the directives of their benefactors, and in these moments of conflict we witness the intricate ways in which southern Jewish identities took shape. Immigrant clients of Jewish benevolent institutions often chafed under the mandates of their social workers, sometimes resisting institutional budgeting by (mis)allocating funds to "luxury" purchases like piano lessons or domestic "help." These moments of resistance testify to the existence among impoverished, foreign-born southern Jews of distinct ideas about securing cultural citizenship and asserting their entitlement to belonging in a space hostile to foreignness and racial liminality.

Jewish efforts to find collective inclusion in the United States shared similarities on a national scale, but region proved a significant influence on the shifting meanings ascribed to citizenship in space and time. One's pursuit of social legitimacy in the post-Reconstruction South required close adherence to a system of what Louis Althusser called "ruling ideologies," the unwritten codes by which one negotiated one's legitimacy as a citizen.[42] The subjects of this study—the trained social workers, benevolent leaders, and the people whose hardship and poverty led them to the doors of charitable institutions—did not publicly announce their experiences as raced and gendered individuals, nor did they openly express the ways in which regional politics inflected their choices and behaviors. Yet traces of these historical actors' entrenchment in larger systems of normative values are evident in a close reading of the sources they left behind. As in Ralph Sonn's appeal for vigilant application and reapplication of white paint to so many vulnerable "posts," the sources testify to the centrality of internalized racial knowledge to the performance of loving kindness.

The negotiations that took place between clients, social workers, and benevolent leaders were part and parcel of the process through which minoritized people tried to self-define as normative citizens, entitled to the full benefits and protections of citizenship. This book attends to what literary scholar Helen Heran Jun calls "the constraining terms of citizenship" that often placed minoritized people at odds in their "coercively structured struggles and aspirations for national inclusion."[43] At this particularly volatile moment and location, the risks of challenging the ruling racial ideologies were high, and many complied with them as a matter of course and of survival. This book's approach to southern Jewish struggles to obtain legibility—the capacity to be recognized by others as full members of the polity, rather than as outsiders—owes much to religious studies scholar Laura Levitt's work on the "impossible assimilations" that compelled Jews to reinvent Jewishness to suit the dominant culture, in the process generating an "excess that always mark[ed them] as other."[44] The stories in benevolent institutional records lend insight into minoritized subjects' participation in the process of reinforcing, rather than challenging, the governing ideologies of their region and culture, even when these very ideologies underwrote their continued subjugation.

The process of making and reinforcing southern Jewish citizenship was marked by ambivalence and incongruity in the private spaces of the Jewish South. The social, economic, and cultural gulf that separated benevolent Jews from their less privileged, immigrant coreligionists was a source of significant tension. As they worked to improve the living conditions of their less fortunate brethren, benevolent leaders often simultaneously emphasized the social, educational, and cultural differences between themselves and these very beneficiaries.[45] And even as southern Jews benefited from what W. E. B. DuBois called the "psychological wage" of race privilege, collective Jewish identity formation was subject to the tensions and pressures of the color line, especially as more immigrant coreligionists made the South their home in the tumultuous years after Reconstruction.[46]

Given the volatility of what it meant to belong in the post–Civil War South, this book explores how Jewish ideals of benevolence and charity served as a means to help negotiate the color line for southern Jews. Often, this process of forging their claims to citizenship involved demonstrating their superiority over other racially marked groups, especially African Americans. For example, commonsense understandings about putatively natural human differences guided social workers' judgments of their clients' living conditions. Although they rarely used explicitly racial terms in their official documentation, a "good" neighborhood was by necessity a white one, and clients described as "fair" or "light-skinned" carried more promise than those with "ruddy" or "dusky" complexions. Jewish charitable institutions also helped introduce immigrant coreligionists to the norms of their new homeland, and understanding prevailing racial politics comprised a critical part of the acculturation process. Benevolent leaders, institutional affiliates, and professional social workers took great pains to ensure that poor Jewish families did not live close to or socialize with African Americans, although they often allowed their clients to hire black maids or laundresses. Hiring black "help" and distancing oneself from racially suspect neighborhoods were some of the myriad ways in which southern Jews, regardless of class status or national origin, demonstrated elite cultural capital and signaled to others their class mobility.[47] Such mastery of privileged class knowledge and its accompanying performances of respectability in turn reinforced Jewish claims to citizenship in a time and place marked by often violent racial struggle.

This book investigates the complex process of solidifying one's claims to citizenship at a time of significant change, social instability, and political violence by illuminating the elusive systems of power and meaning through which Jewish identities were constructed. Jews' attitudes toward their most vulnerable coreligionists—new immigrants, the indigent, orphaned children, and widowed or deserted women—reveal some of the composite attitudes around cultural citizenship that helped frame and contain southern Jewishness just as the category of "Jew" was shifting in response to a massive wave of migration. The point is *not* to show whether or not Jews were white in a given moment; the book asks instead how Jews in the Jim Crow South used benevolence as a vehicle to navigate the troubling waters of cultural citizenship in a region where gendered Confederate nostalgias and white supremacy defined the very contours of belonging.

In essence, this book argues that an exemplary performance of loving kindness was critical to the production of ideal Jewish citizenship in the post-Reconstruction South. While privileged Jews both north and south of the Mason–Dixon line threw themselves into the task of aiding the less fortunate, location in the South—by the 1880s a space of rigid racial prohibitions and an especially violent, extralegal system for upholding segregation—indelibly marked the boundaries of benevolence and belonging. Southern citizenship ideals during the time of Jim Crow ordered the social and political terrain on which people framed themselves as members of the polity, demanding that benevolent leaders and immigrants alike conform to prevailing racial norms or else place themselves and their coreligionists beyond the pale of social legitimacy. It is in the context of appeals to white racial domination that becoming American took on a particularly problematic tenor for Jews as a community with considerable internal variation.

The Sex of Race

Gender and sex were fundamental to the process of reiterative race-making. The dialectic of benevolence—where established, relatively wealthy and educated Jews and their impoverished, often foreign-born clients grappled over the meanings of belonging—provides a lens on the centrality of gendered "racial formation" to Jewish identity and identification in the Jim Crow South.[48] During the period under study, nationwide anxieties about the extension of formal citizenship rights to African Americans and immigrants gained expression through debates around gender, sex, and the reproduction of the citizenry. The popular science of eugenics, which purported to improve the nation through selective breeding, made a special appeal to native-born, middle-class white women to place motherhood above all other pursuits, in the service of the nation's health.[49] Mothers were the conveyors of culture to their children, and Jewish women in particular felt the burden of inculcating their children with the authenticity and quiet religiosity that would ensure the survival of Jewishness itself.

A simultaneous valorization and suspicion of motherhood was especially prevalent in the post–Civil War South, where white mothers served as the primary custodians and conveyors of the unwritten codes of racial etiquette.[50] "Ladyhood" and its attendant entitlements to chivalric protection applied only to white women, on whose sexual purity rested the endurance of the white race. Racial segregation and vigilante violence emerged as methods of protecting white women and children from the risks of sexual danger and contagion that were presumed to arise from social proximity to African Americans. At its root a means of policing sex, the color line was designed to protect white women from sexual violation by reputedly rapacious black men.[51] Even as black women's labor in the private space of the white home remained essential to the maintenance of white privilege, prohibitions against racial mixing were framed as gendered appeals to the security of individual and public welfare, and the protection of white women's and children's bodies was crucial to these projects of engineering the ideal citizenry.[52]

A close reading of previously under-researched sources, including confidential case files and institutional records from southern Jewish benevolent organizations, provides insight into the ways in which southern Jews navigated this complex, paradox-ridden path to southern belonging. In Superintendent Ralph Sonn's metaphor, a "black post" suggested not only racial degradation, but also a threat of interracial mixing that signaled a broader incapacity to blend into the southern, middle-class landscape. Such neglected "posts" were a threat to the others around them, as proximity to blackness and the contagion it signified compromised the respectability of all Jews. In Sonn's mind, successful orphan protection demanded the cultivation of elevated cultural capital—including a performance of race privilege and its attendant gender and class ideals—among the children of impoverished Jews. The color line and its accompanying gender prescriptions loomed large in the process of accessing the benefits and protections of full citizenship. Rules of race, sex, and gender comportment scripted the boundaries of belonging while shaping the conventional wisdom by which southerners came to see themselves and those around them as full, partial, or nonmembers of their community. For southern Jews, exhaustive knowledge of and adherence to these norms proved vital to communal efforts to flourish as southerners on the white side of the color line.

While some of these sources, such as public speeches, news clippings, scrapbooks, and other public institutional records, are open to the public, the vast majority of my research is based on the confidential social work files of southern Jewish benevolent organizations. I owe a particular debt of gratitude to the organization that grew out of the Hebrew Orphans Home of Atlanta, the Jewish Educational Loan Fund (JELF), which has provided interest-free loans to Jewish college students since 1991. The JELF Board of Directors generously allowed me access to the case files on the condition that I not use the real names of their institutional clients. In my efforts to honor the wishes of JELF and other charitable institutions that have made their confidential files available to me, I have by default assigned pseudonyms to all institutional clients as well as to any non-clients whose stories may be embarrassing to their descendants.

Organization of the Book

Building on and challenging a predominantly North-focused history of Jewish migration, acculturation, and institution building, the book begins with the establishment of the first southern Jewish charitable and mutual aid organizations. The first Jews who arrived in the American colonies were allowed to remain only if they took care of their own poor, and this mandate became a central part of Jewish claims to exemplary citizenship going forward. Narratives of unique self-sufficiency and loving kindness fortified Jewish claims to belonging and shaped the character and form of Jewish benevolence nationwide. However, in the wake of the Civil War, early southern Jewish appeals to universal, national citizenship shifted to accommodate a regional model of belonging based on chivalric ideals of honor and collective memory of the "Lost Cause." The concurrence of the violent "nadir" of southern race relations with economic crisis and the second wave of Jewish migration shaped the terrain on which collective Jewish claims to citizenship were made. As racialized gender ideals valorized white men's obligation to protect white women and children from cultural degradation and racial contagion, southern Jewish benevolent leaders increasingly appealed to the familiar language of chivalry and the redemption of the South's distinctly civilized way of life.

Chapter 2 addresses the historical context in which *gemilut hasadim* helped legitimize collective Jewish claims to honor and citizenship at the turn of the twentieth century. As eastern and southern European immigration came under attack and emerging scientific theories of degeneration characterized these groups as racially suspect, established Jews struggled to provide solutions to their immigrant coreligionists' poverty and cultural alienation. Jewish professionals, many of them women, joined the burgeoning social work movement, contributing their scientific methods and expertise to help systematize loving kindness for the poor. In the South, *gemilut hasadim* became inextricably tied to efforts to prevent coreligionists from falling into poverty and transgressing the color line. The public visibility of poor children— particularly girls—in spaces of interracial mixing challenged prevailing codes of gender etiquette, which placed white wives and daughters safely in private spaces, supported and protected by white fathers and husbands. Further, as shifting child-care standards brought orphanages into question, southern Jewish leaders and social workers toiled to transform their institutions into exemplars of modernization and respectable home life.

Ensuing chapters draw from institutional case histories to explore benevolent tensions among some of the critical constituencies for whom charitable institutions were designed: orphaned children, abandoned women, widows, and indigent families. Orphans and other dependent children take center stage in chapter 3's analysis of southern Jewish orphan homes as exemplary spaces for developing cultural citizenship and transforming the children of the poor into paragons of white respectability. Established in 1856 and 1889, respectively, the New Orleans Jewish Orphans Home (later renamed the Association for Hebrew Widows and Orphans, and then the Jewish Children's Home) and the Atlanta Hebrew Orphans Asylum (later renamed the Hebrew Orphans Home) provided shelter as well as superior care to the Jewish orphans of the South. Despite roiling debates over the viability of institutionalization, these homes served as vehicles not just for the relief of the poor but also for optimizing and showcasing communal Jewish success and belonging. For many Jewish leaders, the orphan proved a symbol of unsettling liminality, a harbinger of hope but also of danger, for her success promised communal pride and legitimacy, yet her failure to conform to the prevailing codes of gender and race respectability threatened the foundation on which Jewish civic entitlements were based. In direct challenge to larger systemic and epistemological threats to Jewish belonging, the two southern Jewish orphan homes worked to produce respectable men and women who would represent their people as outstanding citizens in the eyes of the larger world.

Gendered notions of respectability and "worthiness" are key to chapter 4's consideration of the ways in which Jewish benevolent institutions addressed the plight of the *agunah*—Hebrew for abandoned woman— and the development of policies for determining whether such women should receive mothers' subsidies. A mother's power to create an ideal home in which her children could carry on the traditions of their past was vital to Jewish continuity; so was her ability to inculcate her male children with the values of independence and self-sufficiency that were necessary to the attainment of full citizenship while modeling for her female children the principles of proper womanhood.[53] Eastern European immigrants exuded the gender expectations of their former homes, which often clashed with the New South's chivalric placement of white mothers and daughters in private spaces under the protection of white men. Mothers who did not follow benevolent workers' prescriptions for social escalation and child-rearing, and those who allowed their children to stray into spaces of mixed-race sociability, were often subject to coercive measures ranging from gentle prodding to the loss of institutional funding and even the loss of custody of their children. Case files from various communities throughout the South reveal how attitudes towards *agunot* reflected the region's anxieties about whether women whose husbands were unable or unwilling to protect them could qualify as true "ladies" and worthy Jewish mothers.

Chapters 5 and 6 investigate the case files of individual families who fell on hard times during the Depression, and the way Atlanta's Jewish benevolent network addressed their needs during this economically and politically turbulent time. Chapter 5 explores the case of an Orthodox, widowed immigrant mother of two daughters in Fort Pierce, Florida, at the time a small community with a modest Jewish infrastructure. The subsidized mother's six-year correspondence with her Atlanta orphan home social worker provides a window onto the intricate give-and-take of the benevolent exchange, and problematizes the process of acculturation by approaching it from the viewpoint of the recipient of charitable aid. The immigrant mother's insistence on hiring a black maid; her resistance to certain kinds of work; and her efforts to ensure her daughters' access to the trappings of middle-class respectability illuminate the gender and racial politics that shaped her efforts to forge a life of refinement and culture.

In an effort to explore the politics of racial differentiation that often characterized the relationship between Ashkenazim and Sephardim, chapter 6 traces the story of a Sephardic family who immigrated to Atlanta from Turkey and whose inability to subsist on the father's scant and unpredictable income drove them to request aid from Atlanta's Montefiore Relief Association (MRA). As in many cases, the financial support was intended to be temporary, yet the family's economic difficulties continued for almost a decade, during which time MRA social workers maintained a detailed file of their interactions with the family. While the case file provides only the Ashkenazic social workers' perspective, it offers useful insight into the means by which immigrant clients adapted the benevolent institution's interventions in ways they considered valuable, sometimes in direct defiance of their social workers' instructions. Such exchanges reveal the multifaceted gender and racial politics that informed Ashkenazic social workers' analyses of their Sephardic clients, and highlights the processes through which immigrant southern Jews worked to optimize their civic entitlements during a time of significant economic and political strain.

As these individual case histories reveal, loving kindness constituted a fundamental part of the Jewish response to the uncertainty of their cultural citizenship in the post-Reconstruction South. By the early twentieth century, the southern Jewish orphan homes were among the very best in the nation, providing their inmates with recreation, education, and cultural training far superior to most institutions serving the nation's poor children. Yet the story of these exemplars of benevolence is not purely heroic, for charity and uplift often worked in the service of white supremacy. This book therefore provides a simultaneous focus on the most celebrated alongside the most shameful aspects of the southern Jewish past. A critical interrogation of the politics of benevolence provides new insights into the ways southern Jews sometimes reinforced, sometimes contested, their region's shifting ideals of belonging and exclusion. Southern Jews saw themselves as active participants in the construction and reproduction of southern citizenship, and to demonstrate their "pride of race and character" represented a complicated tangle of pragmatism and social yearning, sometimes with calculated results, sometimes with unintended consequences. In Ralph Sonn's words, they signaled their communal claims to the benefits that racial and class supremacy conferred, painting and repainting white posts in an effort to fortify their authenticity as citizens of the South.

1

"To the Hebrews the World Is Indebted"

The Southern Roots of American Jewish Benevolence

Tsadakah Tatzil Mi-Mavet [Charity Delivereth from Death].
—Seal of the Charleston Hebrew Benevolent Society, 1784

The young nation's first Hebrew Benevolent Society was established in Charleston, South Carolina, on the heels of the Revolutionary War, and the first Jewish orphan society followed shortly thereafter.[1] The benevolent organizations that eventually provided institutional homes for all of the South's Jewish orphans emerged in 1856 and 1889 in New Orleans and Atlanta, respectively. From the establishment of the first benevolent society in Charleston to the opening of the Atlanta home, the cultural composition and size of the southern Jewish population changed significantly. In 1820, nearly half of the nation's Jewish population lived in the South, but by 1900 that percentage had fallen to less than 10 percent.[2] Yet southern Jewish contributions both to "supporting their own poor" and to wider social uplift efforts would help set the tone for national Jewish traditions of benevolence.

A study of benevolence sheds significant light on the role of history-telling in the formation of communal identities, and unearths the process by which Jewish Americans "wove themselves into the narratives of the nation," in the words of historian Beth Wenger.[3] From its earliest origins, the practice of American Jewish benevolence involved oft-repeated narrations of shared Jewish histories, or "special sorrows" as Matthew Frye Jacobson has termed the mobilization of collective memory in the service of a larger project of communal acculturation.[4] Narratives of Jewish persecution and triumph over adversity helped authenticate Jewish citizenship in a land of "freedom and equal rights," and

Jewish leaders publicly extolled the manifold Jewish contributions to the trajectory of American civilization.[5] These stories retained an essential national uniformity over the course of the eighteenth and much of the nineteenth century, as benevolent leaders nationwide related familiar, formulaic narratives of Jewish escape from persecution to enter the "favored land" of America.[6]

Yet nineteenth-century sectionalism fractured Jewish narratives of race and citizenship, and postwar devastation and the ossification of the color line indelibly marked ideas of what it meant to be a Jewish citizen of the "genial South."[7] After the Civil War, at the same time that Jewish immigrants from places as diverse as the Russian Pale of Settlement, the Isle of Rhodes, Greece, and Turkey arrived in the United States, southern citizenship increasingly relied on collective memories of Old South glory, and these stories and their accompanying gender and race ideologies permeated the performance of Jewish benevolence. Regionally specific anxieties and nostalgias haunted southern Jewish efforts to self-define as uniquely benevolent and self-supporting citizens whose adherence to racialized gender ideals was beyond question. Benevolent invocations of Jewishness as race difference would persist beyond the nineteenth century, serving at once to define Jews' particularity as exemplars of charity while justifying their universality as citizens, but postwar southern Jewish benevolence distanced itself from explicit race talk in favor of more ecumenical ideals of cultural preservation and authenticity. Celebrations of the Jewish woman as "ministering angel" gradually gave way to beliefs in Jewish women's need for chivalric protection in public dramatizations of southern loving kindness.[8] Benevolent Jewish discourses in the post-Reconstruction South evince the complexities of delivering charitable support to a growing number of impoverished and unacculturated immigrant brethren whose dependency placed them in precarious proximity to the line separating citizens from noncitizens, southern neighbors from racially suspect strangers.

"Charity Delivereth from Death": The Southern Roots of American Jewish Benevolence

Most Jews who arrived in North America prior to the nineteenth century were moderately privileged Sephardim, whose ancestors' expulsion from Iberia in the late fifteenth century led them to migrate west in search of religious freedom and economic opportunity.[9] The comparatively accepting political and religious climate of southern colonies like South Carolina and Georgia attracted Jewish immigrants as early as the late seventeenth century, shaping the ways in which benevolent leaders would articulate their claims to citizenship.[10] Despite nineteenth-century geographer and judge Charles P. Daly's characterization of the first Jewish migrants' "industry, energy, intelligence and probity" in comparison to many other colonist communities, their acceptance in the New World would be contingent on their ability to avoid burdening the public purse.[11]

The earliest Jewish settlers would have to prove themselves capable of complete self-sufficiency before they could find a permanent home in the American colonies. Landing in the Dutch-owned territory that would eventually become New York, a group of Portuguese Jewish settlers met with resistance from colonial leaders whose fears of a multilingual and multicultural society were intensified by anti-Semitic beliefs in Jewish "usury" and potential dependency.[12] In 1654, Peter Stuyvesant, the colonial governor of New Amsterdam, requested permission to expel the twenty-three Sephardim, explaining that their "deceitful" presence would corrupt the colony by opening it up to other undesirable groups such as Roman Catholics.[13] Members of the Dutch West India Company responded that "these people may travel and trade to and in New Netherland and live and remain there, provided the poor among them shall not become a burden to the company or to the community, but be supported by their own nation."[14] In 1733, forty-two British Jews were authorized to settle in Savannah, Georgia, provided that they remain fully supported by their well-to-do coreligionists in Europe.[15] These early Jewish settlers fulfilled their promises of self-reliance, contributing substantially to the growth and mercantile health of their colonies.

The colonies with significant Jewish populations—South Carolina, New York, Rhode Island, Georgia, and Pennsylvania—witnessed the formation of Jewish congregations to establish space for worship, to obtain burial grounds, and to support coreligionists who fell on hard times.[16] Two of the nation's first five congregations were established in the South: Kahal Kadosh (Holy Congregation) Mikve Israel in Savannah, Georgia, in 1733, and Kahal Kadosh Beth Elohim, in 1749 in Charleston, South Carolina. While both served as centers for charity and mutual aid for their cities' growing Jewish populations, the latter was the first to incorporate a separate institutional structure for benevolent aid.[17] In 1784, when there were fewer than two thousand Jews living in the young nation at large, Beth Elohim incorporated Charleston's Hebrew Benevolent Society—Hebra Gemilut Hassadim—the first society of its kind.[18] The founders wrote, "The object of this Society is Benevolence. In that one emphatic, grateful word, are comprehended all the tender offices of Charity."[19] Motivated in part by the destructive effects of the Revolutionary War, the community's "original motive . . . was the relief of the invalid emigrant who landed on our shores, and who might fall a victim to a climate less hospitable than ourselves."[20] Founding members took note of newcomers' heightened susceptibility to recurrent outbreaks of yellow fever, which was dubbed "stranger's disease."[21] The Society's seal—a skeletal angel of death holding in one hand an hourglass and, in the other, a scythe—reflected members' perception that benevolence would mitigate the deadly risks associated with poverty and alienation. Hebrew letters surrounding the image proclaimed *Tsadakah Tatzil Mi-Mavet* (Charity Delivereth from Death).[22]

The Society and other benevolent organizations that emerged nationwide originally depended on a dues-paying membership that pooled its resources for the purpose of alleviating the burden of sickness, death, and widowhood on individuals. Based on European traditions of mutual aid, such organizations distributed the weight of individual tragedy onto the shoulders of the community, basing collective responsibility on a group's social and cultural affinity.[23] Beyond the provision of financial aid to dues-paying members, Jewish societies also offered direct support to less fortunate coreligionists who lacked the means to become members, setting the tone for future Jewish efforts to "take care of their own."

By 1800, Charleston was home to between five and six hundred Jewish citizens, the largest and most prosperous Jewish population in a nation that held approximately 2,500 to 3,000 Jews.[24] Noting that the Benevolent Society alone proved inadequate to address the needs of the growing community, and following the establishment of the nation's first municipal orphanage in downtown Charleston, a group of twenty-three

Reproduction of Hebrew Benevolent Society seal, by Faith Murray, Charleston, South Carolina, 1967. Kahal Kadosh Beth Elohim. Photo courtesy of Special Collections, College of Charleston.

distinguished citizens founded the Hebrew Orphan Society, Abi Yetomim Ubne Ebyonim (Father of Orphans), in 1801.[25] The founders designated the Society "for the purpose of relieving widows, educating, clothing and maintaining orphans and children of indigent parents; making in a particular care to inculcate strict principles of piety, morality and industry."[26] Instead of providing housing, the group collected dues from its membership, comprised of the city's well-off Jewish citizens, and provided Hebrew instruction, clothing, food, and occasional direct funding to the area's impoverished and orphaned children, some of whom were placed in the city's municipal orphan home.[27]

In 1834, the Hebrew Orphan Society celebrated its thirty-third anniversary with a public ceremony to mark the laying of their new building's cornerstone. President Jacob Clavius Levy, a prominent Charleston merchant born in Poland, remarked on the historical significance of the occasion. Highlighting the organization's pioneer status, Levy declared before the assembled audience of Jewish and gentile Charlestonians, "We are the first, and the only Benevolent Society of Hebrews, on this Continent, that have succeeded in raising an Edifice to Charity, and it is with great satisfaction I state, that the pattern we have set has been followed by the Hebrews of New York, who have recently formed a Society, adopting the name of Abi Yetomim."[28] Southern Jews, he insisted with pride, had taken the lead in answering the cries of the "unprotected orphan" and the "bereaved widow."[29]

"Equal Station in This Favored Land": Jewish Benevolence in the Land of the Free

Early proclamations of Jewish benevolence celebrated the nation as a space uniquely suited to the good works proffered by benevolent Jewish citizens. Public proclamations of distinctive American freedoms served to unite Jews as citizens worthy of such liberty and to broadcast to the larger world their engagement in good works. Charleston's Abi Yetomim's Constitution paid tribute to the young nation's religious tolerance and its exceptional opportunities for all who demonstrated ability and ambition. The Society promised in 1801:

> to cultivate any indications of genius [orphans] may evince for any of the arts or sciences, that they may thereby become qualified for the enjoyment of those blessings and advantages to which they are entitled—kind Heaven having cast their lot in the United States of America where freedom and equal rights, religious, civil and political, are liberally extended to them, in common with every other class of citizens . . . they can and may freely assume an equal station in this favored land with the cheering conviction that their virtues and acquirements may lead them to every honor and advantage their fellow citizens can attain.[30]

The language of the Society's Constitution reveals a close association of cultural capital—implicated in the orphan's demonstration of aptitude in "the arts or sciences"—with the "blessings and advantages" of full citizenship. Such high praise of the nation's environment of religious toleration, political equality, and freedom of opportunity echoed among other Jewish leaders throughout the United States and served two generally didactic functions. First, non-Jewish allies who attended Jewish benevolent fund-raisers and anniversaries were reminded time and time again of the depth of Judeo-Christian mutual dedication to the "freedom and equal rights" at the heart of the American liberal state and their shared belief in a munificent "Almighty God." Well-to-do gentile citizens were reminded of the Jewish ability to rise above their persecution and to "assume equal station in this favored land."

Perhaps more crucially, such language educated Jewish audiences on the specificities of "Old World oppression" in contrast to "New World opportunity."[31] Jewish leaders characterized their good works, particularly their efforts to inculcate orphans with the trappings of elite cultural capital, as mutually constitutive with the liberal principles of "natural rights" that endowed individuals with an equal capacity to pursue success and independence. The public orations delivered in honor of benevolent organizations' anniversaries helped to unite Jewish people as participants in a vital effort to prove Jewish entitlement to the benefits of U.S. citizenship. Jews who attended such events were reminded of their obligation to repay "this favored land" for the privileges bestowed on their people. Such compensation would take the form of active engagement in benevolent uplift, whether in the form of financial contributions, volunteer energies, or both.

Jews involved in the slave trade were active participants in generating narratives of generosity that framed cultural capital and rights as the domain of white, propertied men. Myer Moses, commissioner of Charleston's schools and a well-known slave dealer, delivered the oration at Abi Yetomim's 1806 anniversary celebration. He asserted that "no country can boast more of an adoption of virtuous principles, than can this blessed land, in which it has pleased the Almighty to place us in."[32] Prominent in Charleston society, Moses would serve in the state legislature in 1810 and as a major in the War of 1812. His involvement in the slave trade likely bolstered his social and political standing, in no way undermining his public celebration of "the mild and liberal constitution of our country [which] knows no distinction in its citizens." He urged coreligionists to cherish the nation's tradition of liberalism: "To us, my brethren, should particularly belong a sacred love to this our country; for, when we look back to the oppressed days of our forefathers, we cannot but feel a self-importance arising from our happy lot, and duly appreciate the source from whence the cause arises."[33] Jews would prove their entitlement to the nation's unique freedoms by serving as models of citizenship through their contributions to benevolence and economic development in the growing nation. Moses described "the peculiar, though highly to be appreciated, situation of the Hebrews, in this country," as that which would generate a commitment to the public welfare, "that good, which ought to spring from the liberal footing they stand on in these, the United States of America!!"[34] His pronouncement of Jewish universality, their commonality with non-Jewish citizens, thus rested on the Jews' "peculiar" identity as a diasporic community, one indebted to the nation for its liberal treatment and generous dispensation of rights. Moses ended his oration with a grateful invocation: "O God of my forefathers, while I pronounce it so, receive my thanks, that I can boast in being born a citizen of these United States."[35]

Values of nonsectarian equality and the unifying power of benevolence echoed twenty-two years later in Jacob Clavius Levy's speech at the Hebrew Orphan Society's thirty-third anniversary celebration. Emphasizing the universality of Jewish benevolence and its exceptional ecumenical reach, he described how "all who apply [for Society membership], whose character is known and decent, are alike free to admission, without exception, and no sect or denomination is debarred from the right or bounty of the institution." Levy continued, "The Society does not alone tolerate, but it holds equal, men of every faith."[36] As he celebrated the Society's expansive reach and universalism, Levy extolled the distinctive virtues of the nation: "Such feelings [for the widow and orphan] . . . have guided us: they spring as they should do, from the American soil—from that soil, on which every weed of prejudice is destined to perish, under the genial influence of cultivation—that soil which has already yielded so much valuable fruit for man."[37]

In Levy's narration, like many other public invocations of Jewish benevolence prior to the Civil War, American soil provided Jews the opportunity to succeed, and to prove their worth as outstanding "cultivators" of the nation's strength and unity. The agricultural metaphor for equality—ironic given the role of slave labor in cultivating the soil at the time—evoked the principles of cultural elevation at the heart of Jewish benevolence, the effort to ensure that the Jewish poor were trained to serve as useful and patriotic citizens. In pursuit of benevolence, "the offspring of all that is refined in feeling and lofty in mind," privileged, patriotic Jews would elevate poor brethren through their own "refined" and "lofty" example.

That the Society was referring to free, *white* "men of any faith" was implicit in a time and place where blackness signified enslavement and its accompanying social degradation. Eric Goldstein argues that the early Jewish Americans, who constituted "a small and inconspicuous group that acculturated quickly to American standards," were "overwhelmingly seen as white" by their non-Jewish neighbors.[38] Jews of the pre–Civil War South were active participants in the region's slave-centered economy and the culture on which it depended. South Carolina's economic reliance on slave labor to produce rice and indigo helped generate a black majority beginning in the early eighteenth century, and African Americans would remain in the majority until the early twentieth century.[39] Despite their numerical majority, African Americans were excluded from Jewish proclamations of nonsectarian equality and comprehensive charity. So widely accepted was the practice of slavery in the state that Jewish benevolent leaders rarely questioned it as an affront to cherished ideals of liberty.[40] Those enslaved were not "men of every faith," nor were African American orphans of concern to the Society's leaders. The Society would serve the needs of *free* orphans, widows, and indigent children, regardless of faith.

The enslavement of a significant portion of the population did little to inhibit Jewish benevolent leaders' idealization of an American freedom that, to them, stood in stark contrast to European subjugation. Public narrations centered on the temporal placement of American opportunity and democracy in juxtaposition to earlier times and faraway places, wherein Jews were subject to persecution and hardship, barred from the benefits and protections of citizenship. Myer Moses decried in 1806 the "religious fanaticism" and "cruel persecution, resulting from the then ignorant state of mankind . . . None felt more the persecution of those days than did the Hebrews."[41] Levy similarly urged his 1834 audience, "Let us hope we are approximating—a point elevated and resplendent, contrasted to the darkness of the past, when the human intellect appears eclipsed, and the human passions, like a Volcano, overwhelmed all that was valuable to humanity."[42] In contrast to earlier times where the "darkness" of prejudice "eclipsed" the moral imperatives of toleration and kindness, American Jews were free to participate in the "elevation" of mankind.

This temporally distancing gesture was ubiquitous among public Jewish narratives of charity. Leaders framed their "here" and "now" against a remote, violent, and degrading past of persecution in an unenlightened, premodern elsewhere. These public orations, with elite Jews and gentiles in attendance, were authoritative instances of collective memory-making where Jewish cultural citizenship was established on essential principles of religious freedom and liberal rights, uniting Jewish and gentile men of means in the effort to protect the poor and helpless. Yet Jews would emerge distinct in the narratives as "a people, keenly alive to the softer feelings of our nature [who] in Benevolence . . . are all the same."[43] From the earliest public pronunciations of Jewish benevolence, leaders insisted on their universality as citizens by distinguishing their unique concern for humanity and their contributions to the vitality and strength of the Republic.

Founded in 1843, the Independent Order of B'nai B'rith (IOBB), Hebrew for "Children of the Covenant," demonstrates the close alliance of *gemilut hasadim* with Jewish struggles for cultural citizenship. In an effort to ameliorate what they perceived as the disgraceful living conditions of their city-dwelling coreligionists, the organization's New York City founders purported to "promote the moral character of the people of our faith."[44] Initially, the brotherhood provided financial assistance for members' burial and support to bereaved family members, and their mission soon expanded to supply disaster relief and more general aid to poor and suffering people. The popularity of this enterprise was such that, by 1861, B'nai B'rith lodges had been established in almost every city containing significant Jewish populations.[45] Noting the high incidence of orphanhood and poverty among Jews both North and South after the Civil War, the brotherhood established the Cleveland Jewish Orphan Asylum in 1868. As Jewish immigration accelerated at the end of the century, shifting from central to eastern Europe, the IOBB would become involved in the financial and administrative support of the Jewish orphan homes in New Orleans and Atlanta. Protecting poor children and ensuring their future self-sufficiency would comprise a vital part of the Order's performance of benevolent outreach.

A capacious vision of loving kindness marked southern Jewish benevolence from its very beginnings, framing the mission to protect the poor as a vital component of Jewish patriotism. Alongside efforts to "take care of their own," Jewish southerners took an active part in more general uplift efforts in their home communities. The earliest southern Jews, who were disproportionately well-off and quickly integrated into their larger communities, participated actively in non-Jewish philanthropic organizations. Southern Jewish benevolence was remarkable for its extensive reach, as Jews helped establish hospitals, schools, and even churches in their home communities. The Jews of Savannah were especially adept at joining forces with their non-Jewish neighbors to shape the city's benevolent infrastructure. One of the city's first Jewish settlers, Benjamin Sheftall, joined with four other prominent citizens in 1750 to establish the state's first benevolent organization.[46] Created "to support and educate orphan and indigent Boys," the Union Society would continue through the centuries to celebrate its Jewish cofounder and ecumenical leadership.[47] And while Jews comprised a small percentage of Savannah citizenry, only 2.5 percent on the eve of the Civil War, they played a prominent role in the city's state and local government.[48] The Jews of Montgomery, Alabama, likewise assumed visible positions as leaders and citizens. In 1875, the city elected a Sephardic Jewish mayor, Mordecai Moses, who would serve two terms.[49] Jewish elected officials were likewise plentiful in Memphis, Tennessee, where prominent Jewish businessman Joseph Andrews served as alderman in the 1840s and also helped institute the city's Hebrew Benevolent Society in 1850. Jewish Memphians also served as wharfmaster and on the Board of Education.[50]

Early southern Jewish Benevolent Societies were well integrated into their home communities and received significant support and recognition from their non-Jewish neighbors. Charleston's Hebrew Benevolent Society's 1847 charity ball was attended by over two hundred people, most of them non-Jews.[51] Representatives from both the Benevolent and Orphan Societies took part in the funeral procession for secessionist hero John C. Calhoun in 1850.[52] During the city's catastrophic 1858 yellow fever epidemic, the Societies worked with non-Jewish charities to aid the suffering, setting aside rooms in the Orphan Society's building to hold forty-six afflicted Charlestonians.[53] Jewish leaders in

Houston were similarly well regarded by their non-Jewish neighbors: the local paper described the founders of the local Hebrew Benevolent Society in 1855 as "among the most kind-hearted, humane, and high-minded businessmen of our city."[54]

While men assumed a public role in the charge against poverty, dependency, and ignorance, women often took on crucial, behind-the-scenes roles as fund-raisers for burial and mutual aid societies and for synagogue construction. In the nineteenth century, the nation's prevailing ideals of femininity, which celebrated women's "natural" capacity for charity and nurturance, provided middle-class women with justification for their forays into public spaces in service to their communities.[55] Some privileged and educated Jewish women served as leaders in benevolence, such as Rebecca Gratz of Philadelphia, who in 1801 established the Female Association for the Relief of Women and Children in Reduced Circumstances.[56] She helped found the city's nonsectarian Orphan Asylum in 1815 as well as a Female Hebrew Benevolent Society in 1819.[57] Most organizations headed by women, such as Ladies Hebrew Benevolent Societies, Sewing Circles, and Temple Sisterhoods, emerged after mid-century, often alongside and providing crucial financial support for men's benevolent efforts.

Ideals of virtuous womanhood were central to the process of making Jewishness synonymous with the values of charity, liberal freedom, and equality. While Jewish women participated actively in efforts to build a benevolent empire, their male counterparts valorized them in public orations and anniversary speeches as symbols of charity, celebrating their uniquely self-sacrificing feminine characteristics. The Jewish woman stood as the exemplar of charity for all Jews as well as the self-abnegating heroine whose quiet charity and behind-the-scenes labor made all Jewish benevolence possible. Invoked extensively in public orations and writings of benevolent leaders, the idealized figure of Jewish womanhood stood as the model of self-denial and piety, increasingly juxtaposed to the rational, rugged individualism of man.

In 1827, Charleston's Hebrew Orphan Society began appropriating funds to "widows and mothers of deceased members."[58] Despite the Society's outreach, explained President Levy seven years later, no women were availing themselves of this financial support, their hesitance a result of "a lofty feeling and refined delicacy." As he urged "these respectable ladies" to accept the financial support that was their due, he nevertheless expressed his admiration for "such self denial."[59] In Levy's reckoning, the Society's financial contribution to the wives and mothers of deceased members constituted part of their rightful inheritance since their own husbands and sons had faithfully served the Society. Yet their refusal to accept the Association's support provided Levy a poignant example of feminine self-sacrifice. Jewish femininity was at once powerful in its altruism and vulnerable in its natural dependence on male protection: "When female helplessness comes forth, thus shielded by independence, it speaks a language that finds a response in every soul vibrating to feelings of the purest tone. It speaks to the honor of matrons, whose motives of conduct place them as exercising virtues of the most exalted class. We claim them as our own."[60] These exemplary women, simultaneously proud and self-effacing in their refusal to accept the Society's charity, bolstered communal claims to belonging in a nation that cherished feminine modesty and self-denial.

Southern Jewish women experienced shifts in gender expectations, and the expansion of what was considered a woman's proper realm when the exigencies of war forced many of them to take on tasks reserved previously for men.[61] During the Civil War, southern Jews identified foremost as southerners and secondarily as Jews. When Memphis Jews incorporated a social club during the war, they named it the "Southern Club" until the Union's occupation drove them to rename it temporarily the "Memphis Club."[62] Southern Jewish women likewise placed their loyalty in the service of the South, pushing the limits of narrowly prescribed gender ideals as they threw themselves into the Confederate cause. Phoebe Yates Pember of Charleston helped administer a Confederate hospital outside of Richmond, Virginia, working tirelessly on behalf of fallen southern soldiers and publicly expressing her unbridled hatred for the Union.[63] Teenaged diarist Clara Solomon of New Orleans demonstrated her unflagging identification with the culture and politics of her region.[64] When her older sister, Alice, brought home a Confederate flag in the summer of 1861, Clara used it to express her devotion to southern sovereignty:

> Alice had a little confederate (of course) flag, which . . . I neatly arranged as a pendant to the gas fixtures—It is but a *very* miniature one, and yet

I love it. I placed it there with my own hands, and in the invasion of the city, dare any Federalist lay his polluted hand upon it . . . Yes, with my own hands, will I slay him.[65]

Their declarations of southern loyalty would intensify in the wake of the war, cementing their identification as a population subjected to gross injustice. Southerners' collective memory as citizens of a tragically ruined Old South fostered in native-born Jewish southerners a fierce devotion to their region.

The Jewish woman's self-abnegating role as "ministering angel" and her characterization as an authority in *gemilut hasadim* helped legitimize Jewish claims to citizenship, a concept that became increasingly tied to racialized notions of privilege and cultural capital after the war. Women's organizations reflected an emphasis on nonsectarian southern affiliation, like the Columbus, Georgia, Daughters of Israel, founded in 1874 to uphold universal principles of "True Charity" and benevolent universalism. This group, later renamed the Jewish Ladies Aid Society, promised to "extend its labor upon the broad field of charity and benevolence, but particularly in material assistance."[66] Over the years, their activities ranged from assisting poor families and providing milk to the community's disadvantaged children, to Red Cross work during the First World War. Their meeting minutes detail the women's zeal for general social reform and their collaborative bonds with non-Jewish women's organizations. As they helped build schools and hospitals and provided material support to poor women and children, they served as cultural ambassadors of upstanding Jewish citizenship in their larger community.[67]

"A Race, More Extraordinary Than Any Other": Universal Brotherhood and Jewish Particularity

A gendered language of race provided a strategic means of fortifying Jewish collective identification through much of the nineteenth century. Eric Goldstein has analyzed the ways in which late nineteenth-century Jewish leaders mobilized race discourse in order to consolidate Jewish identity amid escalating cultural, national, and religious variation. Finding it increasingly difficult to self-identify as a recognizable group, argues Goldstein, American Jews expressed their collective particularity in terms of essential biological difference.[68] Sources from the South suggest an earlier periodization for Jewish invocations of race, particularly as cultural, religious, and historical difference, but also the continued invocation of Jewish difference into the twentieth century. Race discourse worked in tandem with collective memories of triumph over adversity both to showcase Jewish benevolence and to strengthen their claims to exemplary citizenship in the New South.

Explicit invocations of Jewish racial difference characterized mid to late nineteenth-century southern benevolent discourse, and then transitioned into a still-racialized but often more subtly coded language of Jewish difference. References to Jewish race particularity appeared in benevolent public articulations throughout the nineteenth century, enduring through the sectionalism of the Civil War. At the Charleston Hebrew Orphan Society's 1834 anniversary celebration, Levy claimed, "In spite of the prejudices of the world, and the abject state which ages of wrong have forced upon the Hebrew character, still we are descended from a race, more extraordinary than any other, in the annals of man."[69] For Levy, all Jews were descended from a common origin, one distinguished by an admirable capacity to rise above multiple oppressions and to serve humanity as envoys of faith and charity.

While Charleston Jews established the first charitable organization for the support of Jewish widows and orphans, the Jews of New Orleans built the first southern institution to house these most vulnerable co-religionists.[70] Established in 1856 in response to the city's catastrophic yellow fever epidemics, the New Orleans Jewish Orphans Home would shelter thirty-three individuals, including seven widows and twenty-six orphans, two years later. Benjamin Franklin Jonas's speech at the dedication of the Orphans Home evinces the fears of Christian conversion and the subsequent erosion of Jewish authenticity that also helped motivate the institution's construction. The Kentucky-born attorney, who later served in the U.S. Senate and as an officer in the Confederate Army, asked the assembled crowd:

> Are we to permit our children of tender age, deprived of the fostering care of parents . . . to go forth starving and ragged . . . to sink their innocence in sloth, ignorance, and crime, or, if protected and taken by the

hand by some good Samaritan of another faith, to be educated in ignorance of their religion, and of the mighty destiny in store, for the ancient race from which they sprang? Never![71]

Considered in the context of broader epistemologies of human difference in popular circulation in the nineteenth century, Levy's and Jonas's words evoked common peoplehood, culture, and shared memory rather than immutable, physiologically located essence. Their words provide a contrast to the physiological notions of race that Goldstein traces in his study of late nineteenth-century Jewish efforts to unite their increasingly variegated community. The dispersion of Jews throughout the growing nation, their origins in many different regions around the globe, their emulation of different religious practices, and their swift acculturation to the norms of their adoptive homeland made it increasingly difficult to characterize the uniting features of a Jewish collectivity. The result of such diversity and dispersal, according to Goldstein, was the mobilization of race discourses to help unite the group around their shared bloodlines.[72]

While Goldstein's research reveals invocations of shared blood and ancestry to differentiate Jews as a particular people, southern Jews more frequently deployed race as a metaphor for culture and shared history. Jonas's speech confirms the framing of race as culture, an essential part of which was the Jewish capacity to protect "their own" poor. He celebrated Jewish values of self-reliance as well as ecumenical charity: "It has ever been the boast of the Jewish people, that they support their own poor, and relieve the necessities of their own unfortunate." Jonas explained that "religious necessity" was of primary importance, that Jewish law ordered them to "take care of their own." Further, he emphasized a special "pride of race and character which has supported [Jews] through so many ages of trial and vicissitude." It was, according to Jonas, an acquired characteristic—gained through a distinctively trying history—that moved Jews to take care of themselves without becoming "a burden" to others.[73] Wary of offending the keepers of public charity who might interpret Jewish self-reliance as a clannish aversion to public institutions, he justified Jewish self-reliance as a noble characteristic born of years of oppression. He reassured his audience that Jews "neither depreciate or scorn the noble charities of other denominations, or those erected and maintained at public expense, to the support of which they contribute with other citizens." Jews were prepared to contribute to public institutions in an effort to eradicate poverty among fellow citizens, but they were destined and obligated to see that their indigent brethren did not become public charges.

Insisting that "the Jewish people [are] no longer a nation forming a distinct body politic," Jonas argued that years of exposure to the nation's civil freedoms had enabled them to blend into society as full citizens who could not be categorized as a political monolith. However, while any trace of Jewish political distinctiveness had worn away, Jonas insisted that they still "possessed . . . a proud nationality" and were "bound together by the indissoluble ties of a common religion, by the certain knowledge of a common origin, and by the observance of the same ancient rites and customs."[74] United by shared histories and religious customs, Jews had managed to "maintain the same individuality of race, the same distinctive marks — the same religious rites, which they have preserved and transmitted from father to son, for centuries and thousands of years." Jewish "individuality of race" did not preclude their full participation as citizens, nor their capacity to "liv[e] among a different people, whom they respect and love as their fellow countrymen."[75] In fact, Jewish "racial" distinction, found in their "extraordinary" ability to rise above past oppressions, enabled Jews to express their gratitude to their adoptive homeland in the form of unequalled altruism.

Expected to emulate the values of charity and piety, middle-class Jewish women served as vital emissaries of their people, showcasing the strengths of the Jewish community while highlighting its unique contributions to the world at large.[76] In presenting herself to non-Jewish society, the benevolent Jewish woman borrowed and then elaborated on the familiar image of the Christian Lady Bountiful. She was morally formidable, respectable, pious, and nurturing.[77] But at the root of her virtue and altruism lay her specifically Jewish heritage and religiosity. In 1874 the Columbus, Georgia, Daughters of Israel prefaced their By-Laws and Constitution with the following: "Societies if ever so small in their infancy, or ever so humble in their origin, properly organized, can nevertheless more effectually carry out those noble and sublime principles of 'True Charity' which adorn most conspicuously the daughters of our race."[78] Designed to justify the creation of a new women's club and to record that event for future generations, this document served also as a call for Jewish women to unite and demonstrate publicly their exceptional capacity for "True Charity." The authors further declared that such principles "should . . . be fostered and inculcated" by "frequent gatherings of its advocates," in order to "devise proper methods, means and ways to do the most good." Finally, the Preamble defined the group's ultimate goal to "strengthen the bonds of fraternizations for the promotion of noble and generous deeds," and to "instill mutual love and respect." While the author referred to the importance of "love and respect" among the group's members, she also envisioned the importance of the group's activities to "[strengthen] the bonds" of friendship between themselves and the non-Jewish world.[79]

The Albany, Georgia, Hebrew Ladies Benevolent Society, founded in 1878, similarly expressed their universality as champions of charity whose good deeds reached beyond "their own." While their earliest activities included helping fund a new synagogue and the construction of B'nai B'rith District Grand Lodge Seven's Hebrew Orphans Home of Atlanta, they also cooperated with "gentile young ladies" to raise money for those suffering from yellow fever. While on some occasions they chose to minimize their difference by referring to themselves as benevolent southern ladies, they also often proudly and publicly declared themselves "daughters (or mothers) in Israel." Such public self-characterization broadcast their acts of benevolence while strengthening the associations between Jewishness, respectable womanhood, and exemplary citizenship.

Gender ideals conspired with prevailing assumptions of respectability to dictate that some forms of Jewish uniqueness, such as religious observance, remain hidden from the public eye. While they framed their public works of charity in terms of the Lady Bountiful, which celebrated women as uniquely endowed with the power to protect the suffering masses, they did so in a way that helped prove the direct correlation of Jewishness with general principles of benevolence. In so doing, they avoided representing themselves as culturally different from other privileged whites. In these characterizations of a Jewish Lady Bountiful, Jewish femininity was at once universal in its performance of ecumenical charity, but particular in its intensity and devotion. Benevolent southern Jewish ladies defined themselves as those who publicly led their communities in uplift but whose religious or ethnic particularity remained veiled.

Support from non-Jewish neighbors was a source of significant pride to southern Jewish benevolent leaders. In 1879, the president of the New Orleans Jewish Orphans Home acknowledged the "deep-felt gratitude of our Association for the noble charity bestowed upon it, not only by philanthropic co-religionists, but also by liberal-minded fellow-citizens of other persuasions."[80] The institution reserved special appreciation for "the late Mr. Charles Schmidt," a "non-Israelite" who bequeathed $4,000 to the institution. The president requested that a memorial tablet be placed "in a conspicuous part of our Home" in his honor.[81] Mr. Schmidt's generosity stood as a testament to the prominence and legitimacy of Jewish benevolence among non-Jewish New Orleans society.

Jewish women's financial support also became increasingly vital to the operation of the New Orleans home in times of economic hardship. In the years following Reconstruction, many of the home's members— in 1879, 85 out of 345—fell into arrears on their dues.[82] During the same year, the home listed among its donors numerous women's organizations, some representing small, distant towns. The Ladies Hebrew Benevolent Associations of Shreveport, Mobile, and Vicksburg donated $50, $150, and $15, respectively; and the Ladies Hebrew Benevolent Society of Victoria, Texas, donated $15.[83] Even the Ladies Hebrew Benevolent Association in the small town of Bastrop, in northern Louisiana, raised an impressive $74 from members and neighbors combined.[84] Since its founding in 1876, the Ladies Aid and Sewing Circle of New Orleans was a consistent source of hand-sewn clothing for the institutional inmates. Each of these organizations made the home's upkeep a central part of their mission to promote loving kindness in their home communities and to protect impoverished Jewish women and children. Their generosity bound them together in a shared identification with the project of social uplift.

The terms of Jewish collective identity and their invocations of essential Jewish difference were subject to subtle change over time. Despite Goldstein's observation of Jewish leaders' use of explicit race discourse in the late nineteenth century to help unite themselves in collective "blood" and lineage, southern records tell a slightly different story. Rather than use an explicit language of race difference, like Jacob Clavius Levy or Benjamin Franklin Jonas, Rabbi Jacob Voorsanger framed the exceptional Jewish contribution to charity in religious and cultural terms while addressing the 1886 New Orleans home's anniversary celebration. Rabbi of San Francisco's Temple Emanu-El after having formerly served Houston's Congregation Beth Israel, Voorsanger celebrated the "practice of loving kindness," yet he attributed such superior benevolence solely to religious difference. He explained, "[*Gemilut hasadim*] is the outpouring of every Jewish heart . . . educated and fostered by wise maxims and continued injunctions, which became so deeply rooted in the being of Israel, that benevolence became a part of their religion . . . [and] continued to remain a distinctive feature of the Jews."[85] Like his colleague, Benjamin Franklin Jonas approximately thirty years earlier, Voorsanger emphasized the Jewish influence on modern civilization and subsequent entitlement to acceptance in mainstream society. However, the different ways in which these leaders went about these tasks evince the impact of changes in race thinking that occurred between the two anniversary celebrations. While Jonas, addressing supporters of the New Orleans home in 1856, characterized Jewish difference by invoking a language of race and nationality, Voorsanger emphasized the religious and cultural roots of Jewish benevolence, carefully avoiding the increasingly divisive language of race.

While Voorsanger and others avoided explicit mention of race as a defining characteristic of Jews, presumptions about collectively shared, intrinsic qualities mediating Jewish claims to civic entitlement did not disappear from the self-defining rhetoric of Jewish loving kindness. In fact, as the nation entered the post-Reconstruction era, race became increasingly central to the ways in which civic entitlements were pursued and justified. In the South, the risk of Jewish poverty, cultural backwardness, and public dependency posed an especially pernicious threat to collective Jewish access to the rationality and autonomy that authenticated the modern American individual. Among southern Jewish leaders, race symbolism shape-shifted to reflect the region's principal ideologies, adapting to prevailing logics of gendered and classed ideals of citizenship.

"Our Genial South Where Jewish Hearts Do Beat": Gendered Benevolence and the Call to Chivalry

The Civil War obliged American Jews to take sides, and those affiliated with the Confederacy learned to frame their claims to citizenship in ways that would appear legible to fellow citizens of the South. Between the establishment of the New Orleans Jewish Orphans Home in 1856 and the Hebrew Orphans Asylum of Atlanta in 1889, Jewish benevolent institutions proliferated to support needy coreligionists and to prevent their reliance on the public purse or on Christian institutions.[86] Throughout the United States, Jewish benevolence emerged as both a response to the sacred imperative to give loving kindness and to develop self-sufficiency within a community that had encountered centuries of persecution, struggle, and disfranchisement. The southern benevolent impulse took on the region's prevailing logic of cultural citizenship, and gender ideals were key to Jewish efforts to self-define in a space of increasingly rigid racial proscriptions.

In the wake of the Civil War, the boundaries of manliness constricted to exclude the associations of tenderness and sympathy with masculine ideals of civilization. Elite white men increasingly rejected emotional vulnerability as an exclusively womanly characteristic, or as a trait befitting only men of lesser races.[87] Calm stoicism, rather than passion, became a trait associated with white masculine honor.[88] Male Jewish leaders participated in the construction of white masculinity as that which performed its works of loving kindness with the detached professionalism of emergent modern social work ideals.

While the home's masculine leadership was associated with cool detachment, the institutional spaces were imbued with the feminized characteristics of caregiving and sympathy. Attorney George Stern delivered the oration at the 1883 anniversary celebration of the New Orleans Society for the Relief of Hebrew Widows and Orphans. He opened the speech with an attack on anti-Semitic stereotypes, opining that no one having witnessed the outpouring of support for the association's work could accuse Jews of placing "material interest" above their "benevolent impulse." In tribute to his region's generosity, Stern described the "offerings of benevolence" that arrived "from every place amid the varied beauty of our genial South where Jewish hearts do beat."[89] While Jewish compassion in general was worthy of admiration, Stern reserved his highest praise for "angelic woman":

> Oh woman! the incarnation of every spiritual attribute! Her mission is ever holy... exercised like a heavenly blessing. Man can feel for the unfortunate; man can give relief when want doth cry for it, but woman... has that about her which gives a double charm to all the good she does. She moves as if sympathy and tenderness combined to make a living thing which wears her shape. Grief is hushed by the music in her voice, and pain forgotten 'neath her gentle touch. Like a heavenly messenger has she visited this place; like a ministering angel has she acted here.[90]

Here, as in multiple other orations, woman stood as the archetype of generosity and self-sacrifice. Her "spiritual attribute," her ethereal embodiment of the holy mission of charity, enabled her to become the emblem of Jewish largesse and benevolence. The synecdochal gesture of framing the Jewish woman as a symbol of the higher natures of her people was not new. Indeed, popular serialized literature in the English section of Jewish newspapers offered up stories of the virtuous and uniquely self-sacrificing Jewess as the paragon of citizenship.[91] The Jewish woman's unique capacity to feel and to assuage the suffering of others provided evidence of her people's worthiness of the benefits and privileges of American citizenship. While women continued to serve as key players in the administration of Jewish charity and as figures embodying the uniqueness of Jewish benevolence, the gender ideals that separated them from their male counterparts became more distinct in the post–Civil War era. In contrast to Jacob Clavius Levy's 1834 celebration of all Jews' capacity to demonstrate "the tenderness of women," George Stern characterized men's benevolent capacities as distinct from women's. A man could be "practical in the administration of charity" yet lack woman's "sympathy" and exceptional capacity to ease suffering. Even as more women joined the ranks of the benevolent infrastructure, founding and leading their own charitable organizations and joining with non-Jewish women to enrich their communities, the idealized Jewish woman increasingly became she who must be protected.

The sectional politics of the Civil War fragmented appeals to Jewish universality as servants of the nation, as citizenship itself was recast in terms of warring regional commitments. Southern Jewish benevolent undertakings differed from their northern counterparts in their approximation of southern notions of honor and sacrifice and in their vigilant adherence to codes of respectability centered on gendered and racialized conceptions of citizenship. The South's collective memory of courageous sacrifice and bitter defeat became the standard by which cultural citizenship was defined, adjudicated, and cultivated. Discourses of Jewish diaspora and transcendence worked in tandem with prevailing post-Reconstruction southern citizenship, where memories of past suffering and nostalgia for a lost way of life fueled the patriotic call to chivalry as well as gendered discourses of protection. However, while stories of bygone Jewish suffering were framed in a distant, unbearable past, white southerners identified with a romanticized Old South, where African Americans "knew their place" and enjoyed the protection of benevolent white masters in a mutually beneficial, racially integrated plantation economy. Retrospective celebration of the Old South fortified the supremacy of white southern identity and culture, and southern Jewish benevolence would bear the traces of that nostalgic longing.

Public invocations of a shared Jewish past and the nation's superior liberties continued to permeate Jewish institutional language throughout the nineteenth century. As illustrated in early calls for united Jewish benevolence, declarations of universal brotherhood often appeared alongside assertions of Jewish uniqueness. This paradoxical association of universalism with essentialism suggests the ambivalence with which southern Jews struggled to define themselves as a distinct community with a shared legacy. At the 1882 anniversary celebration of the New Orleans home, Henry L. Lazarus, a prominent New Orleans attorney, addressed the crowd with a brief narrative of Jewish history, describing the familiar story of Jewish survival and success despite enduring persecution. As Lazarus related the history of struggle, he equated persecutions past with primitiveness, and described the current oppression of Russian Jews as the antithesis of "enlightenment and civilization."[92] He explained, "The allowance of liberty of religious opinion, to those who differ from us . . . a feeling of charity towards the ignorant, the helpless and the dependent. Both spring from an advanced civilization. Both are the result of culture and refinement."[93] In the same breath, Lazarus applauded Jews for their benevolence and praised the non-Jewish citizenry for its acceptance of Jewish religious differences. Jews, according to Lazarus, were not a "race" but rather a group defined by its espousal of a particular religious doctrine. By extolling qualities of tolerance, he denounced as uncivilized, unrefined, and ultimately unmanly those who remained prejudiced against Jews. Echoing the earlier narrations of Levy and Moses, he gave his words additional impact by juxtaposing the civilized tolerance of the United States with the barbarous intolerance of Russia, at that point a place of increasing violence and persecution for Jewish citizens.

In the context of an evolving New South ethos of progress, Lazarus's language also offered a subtle denunciation of the growing xenophobia that surfaced at the intersection of southern Redemption and the rapid expansion of the immigrant population. By 1880, New Orleans was the tenth-largest city in the nation, whose population of 216,090 was 19 percent foreign-born.[94] Lazarus and other New Orleans leaders had become well integrated into the city's mainstream community, and he invoked "charity towards the ignorant, the helpless, and the dependent" as critical to "advanced civilization."[95] As historian Gail Bederman has shown, late nineteenth- and early twentieth-century standards of civilization were increasingly tethered to idealized white masculinity, which defined the "civilized" nation as independent and rational.[96] White masculinity stood increasingly in contrast to the feminine and/or feminized "ignorant, helpless, and dependent" masses, which included needy white women and children as well as the nonwhite, subjugated people living within the nation's boundaries. Further, in Lazarus's reckoning, Jewish men stood as paragons of "culture and refinement" in a nation working to justify its pursuit of hemispheric power and in a region struggling to prove its cultural transcendence and economic stability in the wake of a catastrophic war. Jews had risen, and would continue to rise up, from their past of subjugation and dependency, to exemplify independence and civilization. Vital to their cultural and political escalation was their capacity to model the gender and racial ideals of their region.

Explicit race talk did not disappear from the southern voices of Jewish exceptionalism. In "The Scattered Nation," a speech he delivered repeatedly during the twenty years before his death in 1894, non-Jewish

Confederate war hero and U.S. senator Zebulon Vance praised the "people of the Semitic race" for their unique faith, benevolence, and democratic principles of government.[97] Delivered chiefly to non-Jewish audiences throughout the South beginning in the late sixties or early 1870s, the speech recounted in detail the familiar narrative of Jewish persecution over the centuries.[98] Having praised their role in the "preservation of pure monotheism," Vance extolled "the beauty of that band of God's people, the charm of their songs, the comeliness of their maidens, the celestial peace of their homes, the romance of their national history, and the sublimity of their faith."[99] For Vance, Jews were models of southern civilization and piety, for they had "endured all the evils of an infernal wrath for eighteen centuries . . . endured with an inexpressible manhood that which no other portion of the human family ever has . . . *for the sake of God.*"[100] Jews' exceptional capacity to endure centuries of struggle and their retention of the basic principles of their religion—especially the admirable ideal of "pure monotheism"—were central to Vance's assertions of Jewish people's distinction from the rest of humanity. His romantic narration of Jewish triumph evinced a close parallel to concurrent accounts of the postwar endurance of Confederate values and honor.

Attorney J. Barrett Cohen, president of the Charleston Hebrew Orphan Society, similarly characterized Jewish particularity in gendered terms of exemplary piety, benevolence, chivalry, and citizenship. Delivered before Charleston's Beth Elohim congregation in 1884, Cohen's address in honor of the hundredth anniversary of the philanthropist Moses Montefiore's birth was titled "Judaism and the Typical Jew." However, in Cohen's reckoning, Jews were anything but typical. Perhaps given license because his audience was Jewish, Cohen explicitly invoked race to characterize the unique contributions of Jewish citizens. "Pride of race is one of the highest incentives to human action," declared Cohen to his audience of Charleston's Reform Jews, "and the man who feels such pride will strive to emulate his ancestors, will endeavor to cultivate the virtues which they practiced, and will seek to avoid every act and thought which will not do honor to those from whom he sprang."[101] He echoed Vance's celebration of Jewish uniqueness, especially the benevolence of their "united family, in which," asserted Cohen, "the men are industrious, the women pure, the children obedient . . . all ready at all times to extend a helping hand to the poor and to the distressed."[102] Celebrating a Jewish heritage that had survived centuries of persecution, Vance and Cohen similarly linked the masculine trait of durability with a divine capacity for benevolence, for according to Cohen, "no effete people preserve their individuality."[103] Indeed, the speeches of Vance and Cohen were only two among many late nineteenth- and early twentieth-century efforts to recover the contributions of the Jewish people from the dustbin of history. In the South, this effort took shape alongside the construction of the region's proud legacy as a bastion of civilization and chivalry.

"To the Hebrews the World Is Indebted": The Atlanta Home as Sanctuary for Southern Jewish Orphans

Atlanta's Jewish community would experience its zenith following the Civil War and would contribute to the city's reinvention as a model of New South success. The population grew substantially during the war as Jews moved from the hinterlands into the relative safety of the larger cities, from a mere fifty in 1860 to almost four hundred, ten years later.[104] Atlanta's Hebrew Benevolent Society was established in 1860, yet the work of orphan protection began in earnest only after the war. In 1867, Jewish Atlantans incorporated the Hebrew Benevolent Congregation, later known as the Temple. Prompted by the Civil War's alarming loss of life and the resulting upsurge of orphans and half-orphans, B'nai B'rith District Grand Lodge Five discussed building an orphanage in 1870, deciding that the city to raise the most money would become the institution's building site. Three cities, Washington, Richmond, and Atlanta, competed for the honor, and Atlanta triumphed after raising over $31,000. The processes of raising the necessary funds and constructing the building were impeded by postwar devastation and the catastrophic depression of 1873, which lasted the better part of a decade and had a disproportionate effect on the war-torn southern states. Serving the orphaned children of Georgia, Virginia, the District of Columbia, the Carolinas, and Florida, Atlanta's Hebrew Orphans Asylum was established in 1889, when the city's Jewish population reached almost two thousand—2.2 percent of the total population— before doubling by 1910.[105] Perhaps in response to escalating critiques of institutionalization, the "Asylum" was renamed the Hebrew Orphans Home in 1901. Between 1891 and 1901 its inmate population grew from forty-seven to sixty-eight. By 1915, over four hundred children had passed through its doors, most of them the children of immigrants.[106]

Employing gendered rhetoric similar to that used in praise of the New Orleans home, Atlanta's benevolent leaders held up the Jewish woman as an exemplary caregiver and conveyor of cultural citizenship. In an 1894 issue of *The Magnet*, a newsletter published to raise funds for the Atlanta home, Rabbi Leo Reich penned an essay titled "Position of Women: A Comparative Study." The leader of Atlanta's Hebrew Benevolent Congregation, which by 1890 boasted the membership of Atlanta's most privileged and acculturated Jews, Reich opined, "The degree of civilization of all nations is marked by the treatment woman receives at the hand of man."[107] Positioning its gender roles as emblematic of the nation's superior civilization, he juxtaposed "primitive" societies, like Austria and Germany, in which he claimed women were treated as "chattel" and deprived of choice when it came to marriage and child-bearing, with the modern gender sensibilities of the United States. Reich's characterization of other nations as "primitive" resonated in a culture heavily invested in shoring up its power over people pronounced racially incapable of self-rule. Further, to accuse other nations of misusing their women as "chattel" in the 1890s was to borrow familiar rhetoric in celebration of the recently *re*-United States as a superior civilization based on values of self-determination, independence, and individual freedom. Although American women lacked the political rights of men, they were explicitly *not* chattel, but rather protected and valued conduits of virtue for the nation's future citizens.

Ostensibly couched in a nationalist idiom, Reich's essay drew from regional gender ideologies to applaud Jewish contributions to modern, civilized standards of chivalry. In his reckoning, "the world owes a gratitude to this ancient and God-chosen people for striving to preserve the chastity and purity of woman."[108] Framing civilization as a gendered project based on the sexually coded language of "chastity and purity," feminine traits also celebrated in Cohen's and Vance's speeches, in turn implicated a regional ideal to which Jewish contributions were pivotal. Penned in a time and place where significant stock was invested in the maintenance of strict racial boundaries designed to protect white womanhood, Reich's celebration of the preservation of feminine virtue would have resonated among his southern readership, Jew and gentile alike. For Jews were not simply models of civilization in the modern United States; they were the exemplars of southern chivalry: "To the Hebrews the world is indebted for the powerful impulses they gave to the moral elevation of the sex, by raising woman to equality with man, and . . . allow[ing] her to stand out pre-eminently as a type of piety and patriotism."[109]

At the heart of Reich's argument lay a uniquely Jewish contribution to women's "moral elevation" and the significance of female "chastity" and "piety" to modern ideals of civilization. The language of this passage echoes the region's celebration of white woman's purity and her protection from the threat of sexual and racial defilement. Southern codes of chivalry idealized the unsullied "lady" as entitled to white male protection, and Reich emphasized that Jewish women were southern *white* women whose "piety and patriotism" were crucial to the project of regionally specific nation-building.[110] While race difference remained unspoken in Reich's passage, it was critical to the standards by which a society could be judged as civilized, as well as to the specific *type* of women deemed worthy of "elevation" and "preservation." By showcasing a uniquely Jewish commitment to protecting such women, Reich bolstered Jewish claims to exemplary citizenship.

Rabbi Reich represented the growing and upwardly mobile population of Atlanta Jewry in a city ambitiously rebuilding its war-torn infrastructure. The efforts of Jewish business owners and industrialists were vital to Atlanta's transformation as a model New South city, and the community took pride in its increasing visibility among a cast of elite participants in the recovery of the economically resilient "Gate City."[111] By the time Reich published "Position of Woman," Atlanta's Jewish population was experiencing growing pains as the arrival of newcomers from the Jewish Pale of Settlement coincided with seismic shifts in ideals of southern citizenship. The Jewish population increased from 562 in 1880 to 1,440 in 1896.[112] By 1910, Jews comprised one-third of Atlanta's foreign-born population.[113] The growth in Atlanta's Jewish population through the migration of eastern European immigrants coincided with a time of severe social and economic instability, including a series of depressions that disproportionately affected the South and the region's increasingly violent negotiations of the color line. The response of native-born southern Jews to these converging social changes and the racial volatility that accompanied them demonstrate their heightened anxieties around issues of acculturation and authenticity.

With the South's "redemption" from the mandates of Reconstruction came new legal and social codes, alongside new modes of racialized representation and identification that increasingly tethered one's citizenship to one's emulation of a naturalized (and naturalizing) script of white supremacy. Reich's essay revealed shifting ideals of Jewish particularity, in which earlier invocations of a unique Jewish "race" had largely given way to a more universalized discourse of religiously distinct peoplehood. For Reich and many others engaged in late nineteenth-century benevolence, Jewish particularity was expressed through their extraordinary, patriotic contributions to the nation's status as the archetype of civilization and a specifically Jewish capacity for ideal citizenship. As will be addressed in further detail in chapter 2, such contributions lay at the heart of southern cultural citizenship and were often framed in the language of chivalric rescue and honor.

Reich's invocation of patriotism likely carried dual meanings that underscored a Jewish commitment to regional gender values while emphasizing Jewish women's particular contributions to the nation's success. Paired alongside "piety," "patriotism" reflected the Victorian ideal of women's civic engagement rooted in her religiosity and devotion to fostering a domestic haven wherein true (male) citizens were cultivated. By 1894, Victorian ideals of domesticity were gradually eroding under women's escalating access to education, demands for political rights, and increased visibility and leadership in the Progressive movement. Thousands of middle-class Jewish women had joined the women's club movement that was rapidly sweeping the United States. Having first entered the world of charitable work as members of a religious community, helping raise money for synagogue construction and upkeep, female activists found their motivation in the wave of immigrant Jews who began arriving in significant numbers in the 1880s. By the late nineteenth century, the task of "Americanizing" Jewish newcomers became the major impetus behind Jewish women's public benevolence, boosting their visibility as leaders in efforts to educate and support their immigrant coreligionists.[114] When the first Jewish

Women's Congress opened in September 1893 in Chicago, half of the papers presented to the overflowing crowd were on the subject of social work and efforts to improve the lives of the less privileged and unassimilated.[115] This meeting of Jewish women from across the nation resulted in the creation of the National Council of Jewish Women, an organization whose membership would climb to almost five thousand by the turn of the twentieth century.[116]

While the creation of southern Jewish women's clubs often lagged behind the North due to the region's comparatively smaller Jewish population, the societies and benevolent organizations that emerged there were broad-based and far-reaching in scope. Beth Wenger notes that, more so than their northern counterparts, southern Jewish clubwomen demonstrated an eagerness to collaborate with their non-Jewish fellow citizens.[117] Like their early benevolent precursors, these Progressive southern Jewish clubwomen collaborated with non-Jewish women's groups and dedicated significant time, money, and energy to acts of charity for the general community. This was due in part to differences in population, since cities in the South generally held smaller Jewish communities, therefore prompting southern Jewish clubwomen to federate with non-Jewish women for reasons of expediency. Yet cooperation with non-Jews also afforded southern Jews a public opportunity to prove their commitment to universal ideals of communal uplift. They were not simply out to support "their own"; they were committed to the momentous task of improving the lives of all poor southerners.

As they assumed more public roles as crusaders for the communal improvement of their unassimilated brethren, southern Jewish women both challenged and reinforced post-Reconstruction southern codes of white purity and honor. Reich's passage celebrated women's centrality to the reproduction of a virtuous citizenry, highlighting their fundamental contribution to the endurance of Jewish authenticity. Validated in part through their distinctive claims to piety, women's growing public presence was in tension with residual Victorian ideals of women's position as moral guardians of the home. Certainly such tensions were prevalent nationwide, but in the New South, they were intensified by the region's fierce commitment to the color line and the socioeconomic, cultural, and political powers it served. As journalist Harry Golden has asserted, "The South cherishes its womanhood."[118] Prevailing codes of gender propriety confined white women to a protected domestic space, and the southern home assumed primary importance as a source of cultural authenticity as well as protection from the treacherous public world, posing unique challenges to the implementation of *gemilut hasadim*. The institutional home provided a citadel of safety, but it was above all a space of socialization to the ruling ideologies of the region, and the success of these institutional spaces was essential to Jewish claims to southern honor and citizenship.

After the Civil War, regionally specific values of patriotism, honor, and Lost Cause nostalgia gradually suffused southern ideals of *gemilut hasadim* with the cultural and political currency of the vanquished South. As the boundaries of citizenship shifted to deprive African Americans of their constitutional rights, and as emerging discourses of biologically based race difference challenged the legitimacy of eastern European immigrants, it was increasingly on cultural—rather than juridical—terrain that Jewish citizens were called to perform their civic entitlements. Established southern Jews extolled the virtues of benevolent enterprise as they sought to prove their unequivocal loyalty to the region as well as their racial legibility as citizens. Their efforts to support their most vulnerable brethren, and the ways in which these less fortunate coreligionists responded to such efforts, offer a view onto the evolution of prevailing southern ideologies and their impact on Jewish identity formation.

A paradoxical juxtaposition of universalism with race essentialism suggests the ambivalence with which southern Jews struggled to define themselves as citizens. Carefully invoking a putatively collective Jewish memory of persecution and exile, Jewish leaders reminded their coreligionists of their duties to their host nation. Many lauded U.S. toleration but simultaneously referenced its instability, its contingency on Jews' capacity to remain quietly responsible for their own needs. It was their duty as leaders in the Jewish community to ensure that their poorest coreligionists did not become a burden, but rather a benefit, to the larger society. Behind each celebratory portrayal of Jewish people as welcome guests in the country loomed the warning that they could wear out their welcome should a wave of poor and culturally backward coreligionists strain the public purse, jeopardizing their tenuous claims to honor and acceptance.

2

"For the Honor of the Jewish People"

Gender, Race, and Immigration

The Jew betrays an inherent dislike for violent manual or outdoor labor, as for physical exercise or exertion of any kind.
—William Z. Ripley, *The Races of Europe:
A Sociological Study*, 1899

History is replete with facts that the Jew, wherever he has resided, has demonstrated a loyalty, a patriotism, a willingness to share the modest honors of citizenship even at the sacrifice of life.
—*History of the Jews of Louisiana: Their Religious, Civic, Charitable and Patriotic Life*, 1903

The Jew of to-day, as well as his ancestors in other times, is the kinsman and descendent of the Negro, holding the Negro's features and characteristics through the long years of racial transmutations, and . . . in spite of the Jewish intermarriages into other races which fact is so thoroughly established by history.
—Arthur Talmage Abernethy, *The Jew a Negro:
Being a Study of the Jewish Ancestry from an
Impartial Standpoint*, 1910

When Simon Wolf, the Bavarian-born founder and president of Atlanta's Hebrew Orphans Asylum, published *The American Jew as Patriot, Soldier and Citizen* in 1895, the six-year-old institution was home to sixty-three children, the majority of them daughters and sons of immigrants.[1] Trained as an attorney and devoting much of his career to public service in the interest of immigration, Wolf wrote his book in response to recent denunciations of Jews as unpatriotic and opportunistic, and he broadcast to the wider world the long and storied history of American Jewish military service, from the Revolution to the Civil War.[2] In addition to his exhaustive treatment of military service, Wolf also provided examples of Jewish philanthropy, and he dedicated all proceeds from book sales to the Atlanta home. Published at a time when efforts to exclude southern and eastern European immigrants were intensifying and scientists were inventing a dizzying array of new categories to contain the "races of Europe," Wolf's work evinced the intimate connection between benevolence on behalf of impoverished and dependent Jews and the project of illuminating Jewish patriotism to the larger world.[3] The book's final chapters confirmed the author's proselytizing mission by addressing Russia's persecution of its Jewish citizens and the tragic plight of the Jewish refugee.[4] Wolf hoped this public revelation, this bold retelling of American Jewish history, would generate a more sympathetic attitude toward Jewish citizens, in turn putting anti-Semitic and nativist sentiments to rest.

Wolf's book was one of many Jewish responses to mounting nativism, and the project of benevolence took on new urgency as approximately six hundred thousand eastern European newcomers entered the country by the mid-1890s.[5] The number had risen to over 1.5 million by 1910, at which point American Jews were spending $10 million annually on benevolent efforts to care for "their own."[6] Benevolent leaders noticed that the distribution of new immigrants was sharply unbalanced, with a significant majority settling in northern urban centers, and many worked to correct that imbalance by sending newcomers to the comparatively less populous South and West. When the Civil War began, approximately twenty to twenty-five thousand Jews lived in the eleven states of the Confederacy, comprising between 13 and 17 percent of the nation's Jewish population.[7] While the population of Jews in the South increased dramatically over the century, their percentage of the national whole dropped from approximately 14 percent in 1878 to 5 percent in 1907.[8] No more than forty thousand of the approximately 2.5 million eastern European newcomers who arrived between 1880 and 1924 chose to move South, yet by the time Leo Frank met his death in 1915, Jews represented the largest foreign-born group in the state of Georgia.[9]

It was in part the conspicuousness of this considerable wave of immigrants, whose arrival coincided with an especially turbulent time for the nation and for the southern states in particular, that would challenge collective Jewish citizenship and fracture ideals of a unified Jewish community. Although they derived from distinct causes, the effects of southern Redemption and eastern European immigration were nevertheless simultaneous and overlapping, and they shaped the racial terrain on which Jewish claims to citizenship took shape. The arrival of new Jewish immigrants in the states of the former Confederacy coincided with the process of color line fortification, complicating an already turbulent racial terrain by adding a new population of people unfamiliar with prevailing racial etiquette and contributing to the status anxieties of their established and acculturated brethren. The South's bifurcation into strict categories of black and white coincided with the arrival of thousands of poor, non-English-speaking coreligionists, presenting native-born Jews with a uniquely troublesome problem: how could they retain their status as exemplary citizens and maintain control over the meanings of Jewishness when they were suddenly outnumbered by foreign, unassimilated "strangers"? Further, the economic depression of the 1890s disproportionately battered the economically vulnerable southern states, resulting in the closing of many textile mills and escalating rates of unemployment, and immigrants often became convenient scapegoats for increasing frustrations over a rapidly changing social and cultural landscape. Benevolent efforts to support and educate the poor provided one answer to these pressing concerns about Jewish belonging in the Jim Crow South.

Given the rising tide of immigration, and perceptions of new Jewish immigrants as unassimilable, the protection and training of poor, often foreign-born children proved critical.[10] *Gemilut hasadim*, benevolence at its most comprehensive, with its attendant claims of Jewish citizenship and respectability, was a resounding answer to what Wolf decried as the "inculcated prejudice" of anti-Semitism.[11] Yet the unique political and cultural terrain of the New South added complexity and risk to this effort. The racial politics that generated the color line and simultaneously emerging racial sciences invested Jewishness with a shifting, unpredictable set of meanings, as illustrated in the 1910 publication of Arthur Abernethy's *The Jew a Negro* and the racially charged rhetoric surrounding the 1913–1915 murder trial of Leo Frank.[12] Gendered notions of purity and racial contagion, specifically white women's and girls' vulnerability to a mythical black rapist, demanded a white masculine performance of rescue. Southern Jews, poised anxiously at the intersection of anti-immigration panic, evolving notions of race difference, the ossification of the color line, and the post-Reconstruction embrace of Lost Cause nostalgia, developed their benevolent infrastructures with an eye to the region's ideals of cultural citizenship. Their efforts to protect the needy thus reflected their investment in defending Jewish honor in the "blessed land" of the South.[13]

The Racial Politics of Immigration

The late nineteenth century witnessed significant shifts in the nation's understanding of race, which in turn influenced efforts to reduce the flow of "undesirable" immigrants into the nation. Having restricted the immigration of Asian contract workers in 1875 and all but the most professionalized and wealthiest classes of Chinese in 1882, U.S. policy makers drew from emerging scientific theories to justify additional exclusions targeting other populations of poor, oppressed, and/or displaced immigrants. Newer waves of immigration might hail from Europe, but turn-of-the-century racial science discovered multiple European "races" that were not all cut from the same cloth.[14] Perceiving the significant growth in immigration from eastern and southern Europe, policy makers and scientists devised complex new subcategories, suggesting that not all Europeans were equally assimilable to the ideals of U.S. citizenship.

In 1899, economist-turned-anthropologist William Z. Ripley published *The Races of Europe*, where, argues historian Nell Irvin Painter, he "spoke to a race-obsessed nation by delivering the right opinions dressed up as science."[15] Ripley's division of Europe into three races based on skull and body shape would influence U.S. racial knowledge for the first quarter of the twentieth century, setting the scene for additional efforts to stem the tide of European immigration. In 1907, Congress assembled a commission, chaired by Senator William P. Dillingham, to investigate the impact of immigration on U.S. culture and economy. Published in 1911, the resulting report included a "Dictionary of Races or Peoples," prepared by Elnora C. Folkmar, a physician, and her husband, Daniel, a Census statistician. Compiled to achieve "a better understanding of the many different racial elements that are being added to the population of the United States through immigration," the study provided scientific documentation of the pernicious consequences of unlimited immigration of racially inferior people.[16] The Folkmars' study, and the other data compiled in the forty-one-volume Dillingham Report, proposed that eastern and southern Europeans were outbreeding native-born whites, congregating in spaces plagued by poverty, and straining the nation's resources while contributing little to economic growth. Studies like Ripley's and the Folkmars' mobilized widespread beliefs in scientific objectivity to generate support for restrictive immigration policies that targeted immigrants from southern and eastern Europe.[17]

The invention of new categories of racial inferiority accompanied reformers' efforts to seek ways of improving the population by encouraging reproduction among native-born whites and discouraging the increase of "unfit" races.[18] Endorsed by President Theodore Roosevelt, a burgeoning eugenics movement railed against the "race suicide" of the nation's "original stock."[19] Popular texts of the early twentieth century, such as Lydia Kingsmill Commander's *The American Idea*, reflected the view that the current wave of "imported mobs" were a drain on the nation's resources and a threat to its status as an international beacon of civilization and democracy.[20] As their numbers reached one million, and as new scientific discoveries highlighted the "prolific" fecundity of "Semitic swarms," the new wave of Jewish immigrants were quickly becoming one of the suspect categories of "inferior races."[21]

Some Jewish leaders responded to growing suspicion of eastern European immigrants by celebrating a uniquely Jewish capacity to assimilate to the nation's democratic tradition and culture and by positioning Jewishness in contrast to other racially suspect categories of people. Some invoked the Chinese as a category of undisputed Otherness and unassimilability, beside whom new Jewish immigrants appeared politically and culturally compatible with U.S. citizenship. In an 1894 article titled "Human Brotherhood" in *The Magnet*, the Atlanta orphan home's newsletter, Rabbi David Philipson, member of the American Jewish Historical Society, condemned the "Chinese wall" of intolerance and prejudice, thereby labeling as "Oriental" and primitive those who excluded or discriminated against Jews.[22] He called for human universalism and brotherhood, ascribing values of civilization and moral superiority to those who disregarded "race or creed."[23] For Philipson, Jewish benevolence stood as evidence of Jewish "brotherhood" and commonality with mainstream society, in contrast to the Chinese, by then an excluded category of noncitizen.

As he sought greater acceptance for the "Russian refugee" immigrating to the United States, Simon Wolf similarly invoked the Chinese as an unassimilable race against whom to define eastern European Jews as racially and "politically" compatible with the conditions of U.S. democracy. Conceding that "political reasons may justify a restriction . . . of certain defined classes of immigrants," Wolf argued that Chinese "assimilation with the rest of the population is practically impossible." Since Chinese were considered to be of the "Mongolian races," asserted Wolf, they were not fit to be "merged with the general population."[24] The first category to be targeted by U.S. immigration laws, the Chinese had been characterized as racially *not*-white, and "Asian" or "Mongolian" had begun appearing in the antimiscegenation laws of most western states as groups excluded from marriage with whites.[25] Given the shifting racial terrain in which the legibility of eastern Europeans was increasingly placed in question, Wolf worked to ensure that the two immigrant groups remained distinct in the public imagination, with Jews designated safely in the "Caucasian" category.

"Congenial Occupations" and Jewish Immigrant (Re)Settlement

Amid the growing condemnation of immigrant coreligionists, and the emergence of new scientific categories of racially suspect peoples, established Jews developed benevolent strategies to challenge anti-Semitic claims of Jewish inferiority and economic non-productivity and to mitigate the impact of immigration on northern urban centers. Leaders were especially concerned that concentration in cities would feed negative stereotypes of Jews as ghetto-dwellers and the equally pernicious assumption that Jews were incapable of rigorous, "manly" forms of labor, like farming and construction.[26] As the population of new immigrants grew, Jewish leaders looked for ways to distribute their coreligionists away from northern cities and into less-populated areas. Convinced that anti-Semitism would abate as more Jews became farmers, Bavarian philanthropist Baron Maurice de Hirsch invested millions of his fortune to channel Russian immigrants into the rural spaces of the Americas. In 1891, he created the Baron de Hirsch Fund, which remains one of the oldest charities still in operation, and the Jewish Colonization Association (JCA), to provide land for Jewish settlement.[27] Several years after the baron passed away, his fund helped establish the Industrial Removal Office (IRO), which relocated Jews from northeastern cities to under-populated regions in the West and South.

While the IRO succeeded in resettling over seventy-five thousand people between 1901 and 1922, helping develop Jewish populations in cities west of the Mississippi River, such as Fort Smith, Arkansas, and Lawrence, Kansas, other reformers sought to divert Jewish immigrants away from northeastern cities before they even had a chance to set foot on American soil.[28] The Galveston Plan, the brainchild of northern financier and philanthropist Jacob H. Schiff, brought ships carrying immigrant Jews to the port of Galveston, Texas, instead of through Ellis Island. Once in Galveston, immigrants were greeted by trained social workers, religious leaders, and benevolent volunteers, who worked to place them in appropriate towns throughout the West and Southwest. Ideally, leaders sought communities wherein the immigrants' skills would be most welcome, and they provided transportation and housing until the families could become self-supporting. Between 1907 and 1914, ten thousand Jews landed at the Galveston port, but despite these innovative efforts to re-concentrate the volume of eastern European immigrants, the vast majority continued to settle in the Northeast.[29]

Other Jewish resettlement efforts focused on creating farming colonies where immigrants might prove their worth as rugged producers and independent citizens. The nation's earliest recorded effort was launched by Moroccan-born Moses Elias Levy in Florida in the 1820s. A study in contradictions, Levy was a slave-owner as well as an ardent abolitionist who in 1828 anonymously authored "A Plan for the Abolition of Slavery, Consistently with the Interests of All Parties Concerned."[30] Levy purchased land in central Florida, on which he planned to establish a Jewish farming colony complete with a school for Jewish children, but very few settlers joined the undertaking.³¹ More permanent settlements would emerge later in the nineteenth century, largely in response to migratory shifts resulting from intensifying anti-Semitism in eastern Europe. Am Olam—Hebrew for "The Eternal People"—originated in 1881 in Odessa and was based on an effort to create collectivist, self-sustaining agricultural Jewish communities in the United States.³² By 1900, several thousand immigrant families had participated in such settlements, with decidedly mixed results. Although the most successful and lasting of these efforts were located in northern rural areas, such as Woodbine, New Jersey, and Colchester, Connecticut, some looked to the South as a place of opportunity where resourceful immigrant coreligionists could distinguish themselves as industrious workers and citizens.

The South's agricultural economy appealed to those seeking to sculpt the new immigrants into producers—farmers and tradesmen—whose labor would bolster the region's struggling economy while rescuing Jews from characterization as a parasitical consumer class.³³ Idealized as the locus of rugged masculinity and patriotic, independent productivity, farming carried a special appeal for Jewish leaders hoping to find "congenial occupations" for their immigrant brethren.³⁴ Further, narratives of the Jewish past highlighted the effect of prior persecution on the Jew's "natural" ties to agriculture. For example, North Carolina senator Zebulon Vance argued that "their law made [Jews] agriculturalists for fifteen centuries; their exile transformed them into a mercantile people."³⁵ The Jews of Vance's romanticized "Scattered Nation" were not to blame for concentrating in business and finance because centuries of oppression had disinherited them from "their agricultural simplicity."³⁶ Many Jewish leaders similarly believed that returning the new Jewish immigrants to the land from which their ancestors had been displaced provided the best hope for their swift absorption into their new homeland, and the post-Reconstruction South provided the fertile soil on which to establish their authenticity as American producers.

In the wake of Reconstruction, the South often demonstrated warring attitudes toward immigration: on one hand, a "general dislike of outsiders," and on the other, a hope that European immigrants might supply essential manual labor to the economically beleaguered region.³⁷ Assumptions about African American workers' intrinsic recalcitrance fueled the latter impulse, inspiring southern leaders' active calls for European immigrants to come south.[38] Starting in the 1870s, southern states recruited immigrants to fill the postwar labor shortage, their appeals grounded in racialized notions of productivity and the belief that "the negro cannot furnish either in quality or in quantity the labor necessary to develop the South."[39] For many southerners, African Americans' intrinsic "laziness" and "worthlessness" stood in stark contrast to the productivity and independence of European immigrants. As one early twentieth-century political scientist put it, "The most fertile soil of the South is still in the hands of the negroes, who do not equal in production the white farmers on the poorest land."[40] Reformers' beliefs in the South as a genial space to cultivate Jewish belonging often hinged on similar understandings of labor, where even the most impoverished Russian refugee could outperform an African American worker.

The nation's first agricultural community of Russian Jewish immigrants settled in 1881 in Sicily Island, on the site of an abandoned plantation two hundred miles northwest of New Orleans. The colony drew its financial support from the New York–based Hebrew Immigrant Aid Society and the French Alliance Israelite Universelle.[41] Approximately sixty immigrant families participated in the experiment, which sent men up the Mississippi River by steamboat while wives and children remained behind in the city.[42] The colonists set to work building homes and farming the land in hopes of forming a permanent settlement where they could eventually bring their families. Despite enthusiastic support from established Louisiana Jews, who were eager to see their immigrant coreligionists rehabilitate the war-ravaged land, the colony was short-lived. In the spring of 1882, the Mississippi River flooded, destroying much of the settlement and dampening the colonists' hopes of continuing their efforts.[43]

South Carolina, with its historic black majority, became another site of experimentation in the recruitment of eastern European immigrants to the rugged life of farming.[44] Ebbie Julian Watson, the state's commissioner of agriculture, commerce, and immigration, led the effort to begin recruiting Jewish immigrants to the state in 1905.[45] That winter, supported by Jews and gentiles from both the North and the South, some ten Russian families settled in the Montmorenci community they renamed "Happyville," to live off the land.[46] From its nascent stages, the settlement was as much a racial project to bolster the state's white population as it was an effort to enhance the state's struggling economy.[47] Those supporting the effort, including Columbia journalist and banker August Kohn, reasoned that the infusion of immigrant Jews into the state's hinterland would serve multiple purposes: it would alleviate the burden of immigration on the northeastern cities; provide Jewish immigrants an opportunity to become established and self-sustaining citizens; and serve the state's economic development. Kohn believed that the collective would "do much to get rid of the twaddle that the Jews as people are not producers but that they are parasites and live off of others."[48] According to Kohn and other supporters of the movement, the unique industriousness of Jewish immigrants would help rescue the region from its economic doldrums, in the process solidifying Jewish racial legibility in juxtaposition to the putative incompetence of African Americans.[49]

Despite the financial support of their benefactors and the settlers' strenuous efforts to farm what turned out to be less-than-ideal soil, the colony only lasted two years. Like many similar experiments in southern Jewish agricultural settlement, "Happyville" was thwarted by a combination of factors, including immigrants' inexperience in farming, harsh weather conditions, sickness, and relative isolation.[50] The last of these limitations was absent in the comparatively successful Jewish farming settlements established in the 1880s in rural New Jersey, New York, Connecticut, and Pennsylvania. Historian Ellen Eisenberg describes how the northern settlements' proximity to the big cities of New York and Philadelphia enabled a steady flow of new settlers as well as consistent support from the colonies' sponsors.[51] The relatively transitory nature of most southern experiments in Jewish agricultural settlement also reflects the difficulties of settling Jewish immigrants in spaces isolated from sources of cultural and religious continuity.

"To the Honor of Our Southern Land": A Southern Politics of Benevolence

Despite earlier calls for immigrant workers, by the early 1900s much of the South's anti-immigration sentiment took shape around concerns that the southern economy was vulnerable to the infusion of unskilled workers, whose poverty and willingness to work for low wages would undermine the value of native-born, white labor. In 1908, the Immigration Restriction League, established in 1894 to curtail the flow of immigration, issued a press release titled "The Attitude of the South toward Immigration," denouncing public assertions that "the South wants more labor."[52] The League argued that excessive immigration was harming southern workers and business interests, and it laid the responsibility at the feet of "the railroads and steamships and others interested in securing the introduction of cheap labor, irrespective of quality."[53] While they encouraged the migration of "a careful selection of the best immigrants," they asked that unskilled workers, "the kind of immigration which has been coming to us recently in the largest numbers," be excluded. The League did not specify Jewish immigrants as their target, and certainly the growing population of Italian immigrants at the time would have attracted notice, but southern Jewish leaders took seriously the task of ensuring that their immigrant coreligionists were prepared to contribute to the southern economy.

The arrival of the new wave of Jewish immigrants coincided with a period of intense racial repression whose effects were more concentrated and visible in the states of the former Confederacy.[54] After Reconstruction ended, African Americans lost through state voting restrictions and white supremacist violence most of the rights and protections promised in the wake of the Civil War, and lynching increased as a strategy for securing white masculine supremacy. The new immigrants were also experientially foreign to the collective memories that exemplified "true southernness."[55] In her study of South Carolina's efforts to attract immigrant Jewish settlers to "Happyville," historian Jenna Weissman Joselit illustrates how the state's infusion of new immigrants, which more than doubled the Jewish population between 1907 and 1920, generated fractures in southern Jewish identity. "Newcomer and old-timer did not have a common history," argues Joselit, and the Civil War reminiscences that constituted the affective boundaries of the South were initially elusive to those in the former category.[56] Given their many differences from the newcomers, acculturated Jews struggled with their feelings of suspicion that their immigrant coreligionists might jeopardize their hard-won social stability and status. The presence in the South of potentially dependent newcomers brought into question the ability of Jews to blend into the social landscape of a rapidly changing, politically and economically turbulent region.

Many of the late nineteenth-century Jewish immigrants were poor and desperate war refugees, in many ways alien to their acculturated brethren. Some adhered to Orthodox modes of worship, and prevailing Reform practices were foreign to them, as were many southern Jewish cultural and ritual adaptations, such as the creation of Sunday schools for children and creative revisions to the dietary laws of *kashrut*.[57] Having escaped the extreme violence and religious persecution of their homelands, they did not immediately possess the resources to join the middle class. Many were unskilled or semiskilled craftsmen whose training had few immediate applications on a largely agricultural southern economic landscape.

The Jewish orphan home provided a response to new immigrants' struggles to acculturate and a safety net for families plagued by poverty, sickness, and death. As the region faced the pressures of immigration and postwar economic turmoil, the composition of the Atlanta and New Orleans orphan homes' inmate populations changed to reflect shifts in immigration. By 1900, the inmates of both institutions represented a mix of Russian and German lineage, with children of Russian-born parents becoming the majority by the 1920s. According to the 1900 Census, fifteen of the one hundred thirty-six children living in the New Orleans home were foreign-born (with all but two from Russia), the rest born in the South to Russian or German parents.[58] During the same year, the sixty-three Atlanta home inmates included six children born in Russia, but the vast majority were of German lineage. Of one hundred twenty-eight children living in the New Orleans home in 1910, almost all had been born in the South, with the largest group—forty-three—from Texas.[59] While the 1910 Census takers failed to list parents' nations of origin, Atlanta home case files suggest that most of the parents of the seventy-nine inmates were Russian. The 1920 Census listed fifty Atlanta home inmates, eleven of whom were foreign-born. The Census taker wrote "unknown" for all parents' national origin, but then crossed it out and wrote "U.S." for most parents' place of birth, except for those with foreign-born children. Five children were from Russia; three from Turkey; one from Canada; and one born in England. In 1920, the New Orleans home held one hundred nineteen inmates, all uniformly listed as having been born in the "U.S.A.," likely the Census taker's strategy to expedite the process of accounting for so many children. Most parents were listed as "Russian," and about one quarter were said to have originated in the "U.S.A."⁶⁰

Since most of the inmates at the two southern Jewish orphan homes were born to immigrant parents, their cultural liminality became a source of both anxiety and opportunity for benevolent leaders seeking to fortify Jewish cultural citizenship. The dependent child symbolized the twin vulnerabilities of American Jewish identity, with under-assimilation and foreignness on one side and cultural erosion on the other. If neglected, the orphan might fall prey to conversion in a Christian institution, but more menacing than conversion was the threat of the orphan's public pauperhood and dependency, which would stigmatize the Jewish community by exposing their failure to "take care of their own."

The work of orphan rescue was at once an answer to the call of *gemilut hasadim* and a command performance of Jewish legitimacy as honorable citizens of the South. Chapter 1 illustrates how a shared history of diasporic trauma served as a rallying cry for those seeking to bolster the visibility of Jewish loving kindness. A sense of communal loss and alienation, what Diana Pazicky has termed "cultural orphanhood," characterized these struggles for legitimacy, providing additional urgency for leaders' activism on behalf of actual orphans.⁶¹ In telling and retelling narratives of Jewish dispossession alongside stories of their contributions to their adoptive homeland, leaders dramatized the transformation of Jewish people from a persecuted minority to a community characterized by ingenuity and success. Regional loyalty—an unequivocal affiliation with "Southernness"—proved critical to Jewish efforts to reinforce their identity as patriots and citizens. For elite southern Jews, whose ethnic or religious particularity took a backseat to their affiliation with the trappings of New South cultural citizenship, the plight of the orphan represented a communal condition of loss and the possibility of redemption.⁶² Rescued from poverty, the dependent child signified both the proof of Jewish altruism and self-sacrifice and the hope that poor Jewish children would become exemplars of southern citizenship.

Having long celebrated their role as protectors of poor women and children and as chivalrous bastions of higher civilization, benevolent Jewish leaders took for granted their authenticity as southerners as well as their entitlement to full social and political inclusion. Their benevolent efforts would assume the additional weight of the post-Reconstruction racial order and bear witness to the classificatory power of southern white supremacy. The mission to protect the weak, particularly widows and orphans, would prove central to southern Jewish emulations of honor. Framed in familiar narratives of collective trauma, the stories of Jewish persecution and transcendence followed a gendered unifying trope similar to the rhetoric of the Lost Cause.

White southern codes of postwar honor rested on the South's triumph over adversity, providing a justificatory frame for the violent political realignment and Redemption that followed a decade of government-mandated Reconstruction.[63] The Columbia, South Carolina, journal *The State* published "The Voice of the Fair Southland" on Memorial Day of 1898 as a tribute both to fallen Confederate soldiers and to "Southern women . . . the guardians of our dead."[64] The anonymous author celebrated the heroism of soldiers alongside the complementary virtue of "Southern women," whose devotion would guarantee the resilience of the region. Having struggled for years "to dissociate themselves from American citizenship," asserts historian Paul Gaston, southerners after the Civil War looked for ways to assert their role in the economic, social, political, and cultural success of the reunited country.[65] In the wake of the war's devastation and Reconstruction's bitter assault on their sovereignty and way of life, southerners set out to show the larger world that they had something unique and essential to contribute to the nation. A space of incomparable mourning—"the blessed ministry of woman"—with its transcendent memory born of grief, the South stood united in collective memory and patriotism: "The South has not forgotten; the South cannot forget."[66] In the endurance of its proud legacy of patriotism, rooted in gendered codes of honor and shared mourning, the South would rediscover its unique place in the nation, and Jewish southerners would participate actively in the effort to raise the region up from its ashes.

Originally published in Atlanta just after Reconstruction's end, the *Jewish South* proclaimed its devotion to "the interests of Southern Judaism and dignity of the South."[67] As the "only Jewish journal this side of 'Mason and Dixon's line,'" the paper offered essays on literature and religion while emphasizing the divergent "morals of the two sections."[68] Analyses of Civil War battles, details of the first convention of the Council of American Hebrew Congregations, and efforts to develop an authentic southern literary voice accompanied news of Jewish social and benevolent activities in various southern communities.[69] For reasons unknown, the newspaper ceased publication in 1879 and was later sold to Herman Jacobs of New Orleans, where it temporarily resumed publication until the early 1880s.[70]

When the *Jewish South* rose again, this time in Richmond, Virginia, in 1893, Editor Herbert Tobias Ezekiel invoked a need for a newspaper to represent "the intelligent Jews of the South."[71] As the purveyor of most of the city's printing, Ezekiel used his position to produce a new journal to answer "a profound need . . . to defend Judaism against silly, even dangerous charges." He further promised that the journal would "never be silent when the honor of its faith is assailed" and would "endeavor to raise Judaism and the Jews unto such lofty planes of life."[72] Ezekiel's response to inquiries about the necessity of a new southern Jewish journal provides insight into perceptions of affinity between Jewish and southern ideals of honor:

> Judaism and the South (in its broadest sense) are closely allied in many ways. It was in a southern country that our religion sprang into being and reached its zenith. It was in a southern country that it stood the torture of the inquisition. And it was to the South that most of the first Jewish emigrants who landed in America wended their way.[73]

Judaism's origins in a "southern country" corresponded to those of early Jewish settlements in the colonial American South, but the parallels did not end there. According to the Ezekiel:

> Both [Judaism and the South] have been charged with being sentimental. But when stern war beckoned, three decades ago, the armies of the South were not a sentiment, but obstinate facts. Like Jews have often been, they were crushed by irresistible odds, but the cause is still alive. Time and again Judaism has lain dormant, but when occasion required, men able and willing to defend it have always responded promptly.[74]

Ezekiel's assertion of a historical and affective kinship between "Judaism and the South" gave voice to Jewish efforts to defend their legitimacy as citizens in a place of political and racial turbulence. The "men willing and able to defend" Judaism were the same men who would continue to defend the interests of the postwar South. A foundational fantasy of honor bound together the parallel tropes of Jewish diaspora and Old South nostalgia, providing legitimacy for public expressions of white masculine power in the name of protecting the feminized helpless.

"The Institution Comes to the Rescue": Protecting Dependent Southern Children

Benevolence would provide a vital key to Jewish claims to southern authenticity. Julie Newman, an inmate at the New Orleans home, delivered the blessing of thanks at the institution's fortieth anniversary in 1895. Praising the institution as a "'Temple of Charity'—to the glory of Thy name and to the honor of our Southern land," Newman described how the home stood as "a shrine of benevolence and humanity for our brethren throughout the Southern land."[75] By the late nineteenth century, the prevailing narrative of Jewish citizenship, which framed the nation as a homeland with uniquely fertile soil for benevolence, had fractured to reveal a southern story in which nostalgia for a racially pure, socially ossified, chivalrous home echoed Jewish tales of diaspora and deliverance, effecting a shift in the way southern modes of benevolence fulfilled their mission to protect and elevate impoverished coreligionists. Regional identity inflected the gendered organization of power, shaping benevolent Jewish discourses of patriotism, citizenship, and honor.

White patriarchal anxieties about miscegenation and socioeconomic displacement grew during this period of rapid social change, naturalizing violence as a system of social control. Those living in the post-Reconstruction South were subject to a barrage of imagery and language that helped validate a social order based on rigid boundaries between races, ostensibly in the name of preserving white feminine purity.[76] So went the familiar narrative: if white men did not lynch black men, the latter would rape white women, placing in jeopardy the region's honor and racial integrity.⁷⁷ The story—framed and legitimated by the nation's general acceptance of emerging racial sciences and related theories of deviant sexuality—was used to sanctify the Lost Cause as a catastrophic battle in defense of a social order that protected white women from sexual violation. In the region's postwar collective memory, the war had represented the Confederacy's valiant effort to defend white femininity and the future of a racially pure citizenry. Perceptions of a crumbling social order reinforced nostalgia-infused longings for a mythologized era of white racial purity and fueled violent efforts to police the boundaries separating white and black.

By the early twentieth century, the care of dependent children was a prominent topic of debate among policy makers, progressive activists, educators, and social work professionals. As racial sciences took hold of the public imagination, guiding efforts to limit immigration and to curb reproduction among "unfit" populations, the white child increasingly came to signify the imperiled future citizenry of a nation overrun by "imbeciles," "foreigners," and otherwise tainted progeny.⁷⁸ The orphan signified innocence and hope on the one hand, but also the potential for degeneration if not properly protected from corrupting influences. Policy makers and reformers debated the optimal way to ensure that such children developed into self-sufficient and upstanding adults. Living in the South deepened the Jewish orphan's vulnerability, and to the dangers of conversion and pauperism was added the threat of exposure to spaces of racial and sexual contamination.

Southern Jewish attitudes toward orphan care departed from national trends, which by the late nineteenth century questioned the validity of institutionalization. As the number of the nation's orphan asylums tripled between the Civil War and 1890, and the population of these institutions continued to climb through the 1920s, social workers, policy makers, and laypeople condemned institutions as a threat to children's social development.⁷⁹ At the 1909 annual meeting of the Atlanta home's board, President Wolf discussed his attendance at the first White House Conference on the Care of Dependent Children. Convened by President Theodore Roosevelt, the conference brought together over two hundred attendees, among them the nation's foremost experts in child care, with the central aim of developing alternatives to institutionalization for orphans and neglected children.⁸⁰ Wolf explained, "There was a great deal of argument . . . that children when found with mothers should not be taken from the mother but kept with the parent, and that whatever amount of money the child should cost per capita should be given to the mother in aid of not only educating and caring for the child, but also in caring for herself." Wolf praised the Atlanta home for having already adopted this policy "some years ago" but expressed concern that more "practical" measures be taken to place children "either with the mother or other competent woman whose interest might be enlisted in caring for the child."⁸¹ Yet widespread faith in mothers' natural capacity to raise their children were tempered by suspicions about culture and class. Wolf continued:

> No one can question the sanctity and importance of the Home; the affection and love which emanates from the mother to the child, and that all things being even, the child that needs care and protection has more natural affinities in the home circle than anywhere else. But unfortunately these conditions do not always exist. Indeed, to a large extent they are absent in the home of those whom misfortune, death, or poverty has overtaken, and thus the institution comes to the rescue and stands in the relation of parent or parents to the extent of bettering the condition of the unfortunate child.⁸²

While northern Jewish institutions generally followed national trends, turning to foster care and mothers' subsidies in an effort to place orphans in private homes, the orphan home remained central to southern Jewish orphan rescue efforts.⁸³ The New Orleans home rejected mother's subsidies in favor of institutionalization for impoverished Jewish children. And while the Atlanta home provided subsidies for "worthy" mothers who possessed no other means of support and eventually instituted highly selective foster care in the late 1920s, both southern homes held tight to the notion that—given the absence of an ideal private home and a "worthy" mother—theirs were the foremost spaces in which children of the poor could receive vital training in the trappings of southern citizenship. A significant part of this mission involved protecting Jewish children from the influences of racial contagion and exposure to spaces of poverty and potential degradation.

"Away from Her People": Rescuing Jewish Girls from Their Own Families

In the summer of 1910, Atlanta home superintendent Ralph A. Sonn received a letter requesting admission for the "orphaned" children of a "shiftless and n'er-do-well" father in Greensboro, North Carolina. The author of the letter, likely a member of Greensboro's local B'nai B'rith chapter, described in heartrending detail how the four Schulman children, ranging in age from four to ten, had lost their mother and lived "in a state of squalor" and "under the most unfavorable surroundings possible." Concerned that the children would degenerate into "public charges" if left with their father, the letter's author urged Sonn to admit them all to the Atlanta home as soon as possible.[84] While these early letters did not specify what made the children's surroundings "unfavorable," later correspondence suggests that the Schulman home's proximity to African Americans was of great concern to the members of the Greensboro Jewish community.

Once the home's Board of Control had approved their admission and the four children had passed the necessary medical examinations, they were admitted to the home, only to be released in 1914 when their father remarried. However, in the eyes of Greensboro's Jewish community, the addition of a new stepmother and two stepbrothers did little to improve the original conditions of the Schulman home. In August 1914, Sonn received another letter, this time from Emanuel Sternberger, a prominent and well-respected member of the city's elite, as evidenced by his membership in the Carolina Motor Club as well as the Greensboro Rotary.[85] The German-born president of Greensboro's Revolution Cotton Mills pleaded with Sonn to readmit the children, as they had been "seen in company with negro children." He explained his fears of "hav[ing] all the good you did undone" by exposure to an environment of poverty and interracial mixing.[86]

Sternberger's urgent petition that Sonn "see the necessity of keeping these children away from such surroundings" should be considered in the context of the racial turbulence and Jewish anxiety that resulted when Leo Frank was found guilty of murdering thirteen-year-old Mary Phagan only a few months earlier.[87] Fallout from the trial included widely distributed anti-Semitic assertions of Frank's sexual perversion by well-known populist leader Thomas E. Watson, who placed Jewishness and blackness side-by-side and judged the former to be more alien and threatening to the values of southern honor than the latter.[88] Sonn and the home's board members would have been well aware of the racial precariousness of Jewish identity as they considered Sternberger's concerns. His letter appears to have had some effect, for the two oldest Schulman children were allowed to remain residents of the home. While it is unclear why the home's leaders decided to keep only the older children, they may have reasoned that children with two parents, however desperate their circumstances, did not qualify for institutional assistance. Therefore eight-year-old Becky, her brother, and her stepbrother were sent back in September 1914 to live in North Carolina with their parents.

Subsequent correspondence between other members of the Greensboro community and Superintendent Sonn sheds additional light on the decision not to retain all the Schulman children, despite reports of the parents' deficiencies. In reply to one letter, Sonn wrote that "inadequate financial assistance" from constituent communities was a significant source of difficulty. "Take Greensboro, for instance" reasoned Sonn. "She has sent us four children, but has at no time supported even one."[89] To Sonn and the members of the home's board, Greensboro appeared to be a prosperous community, which by 1915 numbered approximately 150 Jews, among whom were eminent business people like Sternberger and his colleagues in industrial development, Moses and Cesar Cone.[90] Yet none among them had contributed to the upkeep of their "little dependents," as Sonn called the home's North Carolinian inmates.[91] Sternberger wrote again shortly thereafter, describing the Schulman children as "badly neglected and thrown on the streets without any care or attention," and assuring Sonn that the Greensboro community would help support them if the home would rescue these "pitifully neglected" children.[92]

Yet it was not until the Shulmans' separation that the home would consider readmitting Becky and her brothers. Sternberger wrote once again, this time to appeal only for Becky's readmission. Offering to contribute $200 per year toward her support, he begged Sonn to "give her the right protection so she may grow up to be a good and useful woman."[93] According to Sternberger, Becky's poor upbringing would have a pernicious effect on her development as a "good woman," echoing beliefs that girls and women were especially vulnerable to the ill effects of poverty, social alienation, and association with nonwhites. Several weeks later, he wrote again, declaring that "we would like for her to be protected and where she could be under Jewish influence."[94] Although this letter did not immediately have the desired effect, several months later the correspondence of Sarah Weil, a prominent Greensboro leader who would later found the North Carolina Association of Jewish Women, succeeded in convincing Sonn that the case merited great consideration, perhaps even a reconsideration of the home's rules of admission.

Since the southern orphan homes served vast geographical regions — New Orleans covered seven states and Atlanta, five — leaders relied on a system of nonprofessional, benevolent community members who worked as informants. Usually affiliated with a benevolent organization, such as B'nai B'rith, a synagogue, or a Ladies Aid Society, these volunteers monitored their communities for impoverished or neglected children for whom the institution might provide relief. Often, these volunteers worked to persuade the homes to rescue particular children even when institutional rules dictated against the acceptance of non-orphans. Some overlooked professionalized understandings of "need" and "worthiness" when impoverished coreligionists' public spectacles of poverty threatened collective Jewish propriety and independence. In the fall of 1917, Sarah Weil had received a letter from the superintendent of the North Carolina Children's Home Society, requesting that an appropriate Jewish family or institution be found for eleven-year-old Becky Schulman. Describing her as "a bright, attractive Jewess," the superintendent of the children's home warned that "if you want to save the girl morally and religiously try to get her in the Atlanta Home or any Jewish home away from her people."[95] Sharing a copy of the letter, Weil implored Sonn to consider accepting Becky back into the home's care: "There are too many Jewish ones falling away — too many who hold out hands for help."[96] Despite Becky's non-orphan status, Weil believed that the institution could not ignore her plight. For, if left to rely on a non-Jewish charity, Becky might "fall away" from her faith like so many others. Furthermore, allowing a Jewish child to become the charge of a non-Jewish institution threatened the foundations of self-sufficiency on which a collective Jewish reputation was based. Weil made it clear that the home had no choice; readmitting Becky was the only way to save her from degeneracy and pauperism on one hand, and Christian conversion on the other.

Becky was promptly readmitted to the home after Sonn received Weil's letter, and she remained there until her graduation in September 1925. With a no-interest loan from the home, she attended the North Carolina College for Women, after which she became a teacher in Washington DC. It was often the policy of the home to maintain their files on children who had long since "graduated" from the institution as a means of ensuring their survival and keeping track of their whereabouts. Particularly with female inmates, the southern orphan homes took special care to ensure that their charges found appropriate employment or were channeled into proper homes, monitored by family members or benevolent institutional affiliates.

Although self-sustaining and independent, Becky continued her correspondence with "Aunt Sarah" Weil, and with the home's new superintendent, Feist M. Strauss. Becky's letters described her work as a teacher and her ongoing efforts to pay back the orphan home, the "wonderful feeling when you find yourself able to earn a livelihood, pay debts, and also have a bank account." She discussed "going to a summer school [to] take the latest course in Nutrition and Red Cross work," for she could not imagine "spending [her] money on anything better than higher education."[97] Weil apparently found in this letter the ideal justification for her earlier pleas on Becky's behalf and shared it with the superintendent. In addition to becoming self-sufficient as a college-educated teacher, this formerly neglected child demonstrated earnest appreciation for the institution and its affiliates. Future letters also described her hopes of obtaining a master's degree and her tendency to spend her free time either studying in the library or making her own clothes. Becky's self-sufficiency, frugality, and modesty stood as justification for the institution's intervention on her behalf. Her successful deliverance from the degradation of poverty proffered a shining example of the values that benevolent workers struggled to impart to their beneficiaries. Becky Schulman would remain among the Atlanta home's great success stories: rescued from her family's "state of squalor," she developed into a "good and useful woman," an example of the power of the southern

Jewish benevolent institution to convert even the lowliest pauper to the trappings of respectability.

Despite their exceptional vigilance and high-quality care, the two southern orphan homes could not rescue all of the region's poor Jewish children, and some went without the institutions' guidance and support. While the Atlanta home might intervene in a case—like Becky's—where a child's stepmother proved incapable of providing adequate care, they resisted intervening on behalf of children whose birth parents were living and married, unless there was evidence of abuse or abandonment. For example, beginning in the late 1910s, a disadvantaged and infirm immigrant couple with five children began receiving a small monthly subsidy from the Montefiore Relief Association, the family welfare division of Atlanta's Federation of Jewish Charities. When the couple's two daughters prompted the outrage of some anonymous Atlanta neighbors for their nighttime carousing on Decatur Street, there was little their social worker could do to correct their behavior.[98] As a location notorious for its speakeasies, dance halls, prostitution, and violence as well as its predominantly poor and mixed-race population, Decatur Street raised the specter of vice and interracial mixing.[99] Despite the efforts of MRA staff, it appears that the girls continued to flout the rules governing feminine respectability, and several years later the younger sister bore a child out of wedlock.[100] Just as Becky Schulman became an example of the good work's capacity to rescue Jewish womanhood from poverty and degradation, neglected immigrant daughters provided the cautionary tale of communal indignity and shame. The southern Jewish orphan homes made it their mission to ensure that the children they rescued modeled the prevailing codes of racialized gender etiquette and did not fall prey to such treacherous temptations.

"Conserving the Honor of the Jewish People": Immigrant Participation in Social Uplift

The communal investment in respectability was not deliberated only through elite, southern-born community members, as foreign-born, working-class Jews also participated actively in efforts to ensure that the children of the poor were well cared for and not allowed to burden the public purse. Despite their recent arrival, foreign-born Jewish southerners often demonstrated a profound understanding of the relationship between social uplift and honor, perceiving benevolence as a safeguard against the non-Jewish community's negative judgment. Their voices are elusive in the historical record, but benevolent institutional case records lend insight into the ways less-privileged actors worked within the channels of benevolence, asserting collective pressure to maintain regional expectations for respectability.

Small town Jewish communities also participated in efforts to ensure that the dependent children of poor coreligionists did not contribute to the larger society's unflattering assumptions about Jews. When the five Blaustein children in Waycross, Georgia lost their mother in childbirth in 1914, the predominantly foreign-born Jewish community appealed to the Atlanta home for help. Situated approximately 250 miles southeast of Atlanta, Waycross had welcomed its first Jewish family in 1902 and many soon followed, establishing themselves as small business owners and consolidating a congregation in 1920.[101] The threat of collective shame and the desire to preserve their "honor" weighed heavily on the minds of fifteen "Jews of Waycross" who wrote in Yiddish to Superintendent Sonn in August 1914, requesting the children's immediate admission. Among the authors was the children's uncle, who had recently emigrated from Lithuania. The letter described the bereaved father, "alone and broken in health and livelihood," who could not stand to separate his children from one another.[102] Promising that the children's father, Isidore Blaustein, would contribute regularly—five to eight dollars per month—to the children's upkeep, the letter's authors urged the home to take all five children into their care until their father could get back on his feet. It was not only the family's best interest the authors had in mind, for they alluded to possible "bad consequences [to] the moral and honor of the Jewish people" should the children remain in their father's impoverished, motherless home.[103] Their use of Yiddish suggests that all were fairly recent immigrants, yet they were keenly aware of the need for Jewish children to receive the proper upbringing and for their dependency to remain hidden from the larger public gaze.

Sonn praised the authors for being "imbued with the necessity of conserving the honor of the Jewish people," but insisted that they, too, provide material support for the children in the home's care and serve as guarantors of Mr. Blaustein's financial obligations.[104] "We are willing to believe that you impose this duty on yourselves first," wrote Sonn, "and that you are capable of making sacrifices to subserve the great cause." Without the community's material support, explained Sonn, "the sending of children to the 'Home' is no help."[105] As a privately funded institution that prided itself on self-sufficiency, the home depended upon regular financial support from the constituent communities in the five-state region, without which their mission to protect and raise indigent orphans would not be possible. The home especially sought financial support from its inmates' home communities, and Sonn reminded the citizens of Waycross of their duty to the children's ongoing care, a more expansive sense of obligation to "the great cause" of merit to all Jews. He challenged the Waycross citizens to "exemplify [their] good faith" by "subscribing and forwarding a liberal amount, per year, toward the upkeep of this institution."[106] Sonn believed that all Jewish citizens should take an active role in supporting their orphaned children.[107]

Southern Jews—native and foreign-born alike—were bound together in shared identification, and when eastern European immigrants were characterized as unassimilable, racially liminal, and "foreign," such assumptions threatened even the most acculturated Jewish Americans. The project of benevolence sought to generate a public performance of honor, one in keeping with prevailing southern principles of gendered respectability and chivalrous protection of the vulnerable. Rescuing poor Jewish children from starvation and ignorance was a significant part of the mission to prove Jewish entitlement to the full privileges of citizenship. Raising them to reflect the values of elite southern cultural capital issued a bold challenge to the stereotypes that plagued American Jewish identity in this turbulent time and place. While it is not clear whether the Waycross Jews, as a group, contributed regularly to the home, Sonn and other home leaders took seriously their urgent request for help, and four of the Blaustein children were sent by train to Atlanta, where they became part of a fortunate class of institutional inmates. The rescued children would find in the institution not only a surrogate parent but also a training ground for the privileged knowledge of class and a citadel of elevated cultural capital that would usher them out of their poverty and into a space of irrefutable honor and respectability.

The following chapter explores the ways in which the cultural capital of southern privilege was instilled in the children of the poor and foreign-born. Although the two southern Jewish orphan homes differed in their approach to orphan care—one enthusiastically adopting a mothers' subsidy plan and foster care while the other favored institutionalization—each offered their young charges in-depth training in "ideal family life" as well as the tools of success to maximize their chances of independence and self-support. As illustrated in Becky Schulman's case, orphans who excelled academically were also given the resources, usually in the form of generous, long-term, no-interest loans, to pursue higher education. Certainly not all orphans demonstrated such talent, and those who did not were encouraged to complete high school and receive practical training in an appropriate trade. Perhaps most important, the homes offered spaces of elevated cultural capital wherein poor Jewish children could learn to approximate their more privileged and acculturated coreligionists in the trappings of respectability.

3

"Virtue, Rectitude and Loyalty to Our Faith"

Jewish Orphans and the Politics of Southern Cultural Capital

What I've heard of orphanages, we lived at a country club.
—Jacob Blaustein, Atlanta home inmate from 1914 to 1922

In an interview conducted in 1991, Jacob Blaustein described how inmates of "the Home" were rotated through specific jobs, in addition to their daily chores. Jacob's job was "taking care of the pantry" in which food staples were kept, organized, and dispensed. At meal times he "would dish out the food to the cook," Fannie Young, whom he described as "an old ex–Civil War slave."[1] Born in 1854 in Georgia, "Aunt Fanny," as children and administrators called her, oversaw the preparation of meals for all of the home's young residents.[2] Jacob described how "she used to always tell me that I reminded her of her old master [also named Jacob]. And I don't know whether it's something I should be proud of or not (laugh). But those were the stories she used to tell me about the old slave days."[3] Jacob did not expand on the content of Ms. Young's stories but suggested that he "was closer to her than some of the others" because of their working relationship. His laughter at the memory of "Aunt Fanny's" comment suggests his recognition of the ways in which racial politics had changed over the seventy-year period. He likely experienced unease over his recollection of the elderly black woman's oblique criticism of his childhood supervisory power over her.

Jacob's close proximity to Ms. Young, and the fact that the two chatted amiably in the course of their work together, reflects the widespread presence of black women in southern white children's upbringing and the ambivalent intimacies, marked by a complex pairing of nurture with subjection, that characterized race relations in the Jim Crow South. As the laws prohibiting public interactions between whites and blacks grew more rigid, intimate interface between black women and their white employers flourished in private spaces, and children in particular were common recipients of black women's affective labor. This physically and emotionally demanding work was as necessary to maintaining respectably clean and orderly domestic spaces as it was to nurturing the young. And although they were prohibited from occupying public spaces designated for "whites only," black women stood as benign, even beloved figures essential to the process of reproducing a white citizenry.[4]

Such care, and the quotidian lessons in white, middle-class respectability that accompanied it, helped imbue orphan home inmates with a sense of themselves as racially privileged citizens of the South.[5] Even the poorest orphan or half-orphan learned to see herself as a consumer, rather than as a performer, of certain forms of menial labor, and children became accustomed to black women's presence as sources of affection and warmth as well as of particularly undesirable forms of work. In a departure from earlier chapters, which explored the larger context in which southern Jewish benevolence functioned, this and subsequent chapters investigate the more intimate and often less transparent spaces of the institution and the private home. While benevolent ideals of *gemilut hasadim* helped serve "the honor of the Jewish people" at a time when that honor was precariously in doubt, the interior of institutional and private spaces provided young, under-resourced future citizens with lessons in what historian Jennifer Ritterhouse calls the "'etiquette' of race relations in the Jim Crow South."[6] The Hebrew Orphans Home of Atlanta and the New Orleans Jewish Orphans Home—both situated in relatively well-to-do sections of town—provided the education and cultural capital the children required to find acceptance in the socially regimented world beyond the institution's walls.

In addition to protecting orphans from the twin threats of poverty and conversion, the Jewish orphan home was vital to the process of cultivating model citizens. While Jewish orphan homes were not an official arm of the state, they constituted a carefully institutionalized apparatus through which poor Jewish children learned to perform their social roles in relation to the larger community's values and priorities.[7] The orphan home served as a space wherein American Jewish identities could be fostered according to the values of its benevolent stewards, and the approximation of an authentic "home life" was crucial to this project. As Superintendent Ralph Sonn explained in his annual reports to the Atlanta home's Board of Directors, orphans required constant supervision and support to ensure their transition into upright, self-supporting adults who would reflect a positive image of Jewishness to the larger world. Alternatively, their poverty and dependency threatened to expose Jews as "black posts" collectively lacking the intrinsic qualities of southern cultural capital. Institutional spaces were therefore critical to the project of fortifying Jewish belonging, as they helped raise poor children, many of whom had immigrant parents or were themselves foreign-born, "to be loyal Jews and Jewesses, true American Citizens and the type of men and women of whom we can justly be proud."[8]

From the complex etiquette of fine dining and competitive sports to the conventions of "American-style" religious ritual and worship, the orphans learned to internalize the gender, race, and class ideals that comprised the essence of southern citizenship. This meant that orphan home leaders worked to produce manly, chivalric men who were capable of making a living and serving as future breadwinners for respectable, unassuming Jewish families living and socializing in "nice" (white) neighborhoods. Jewish girls were trained to become good housekeepers and mothers, respectable ladies whose religiosity was discreetly confined to private spaces. And, before children could be discharged, the institutions required proof that reputable relatives or friends, living in approved neighborhoods and in safe and refined surroundings, could ensure the former inmates' careful supervision. For many children, the institution remained a parental presence until long after discharge, providing housing, financial support, and vigilant mentorship as they prepared for, in the words of New Orleans inmate Julie Newman, "a life of virtue, rectitude and loyalty to our faith."[9]

The experiences of the children for whom the Atlanta and New Orleans orphan homes served as actual homes help uncover the process of orphan uplift as a means of cultivating idealized citizenship. The Atlanta home's case files contain detailed information about orphans and their relatives, and two former inmates, Joseph Green and Jacob Blaustein, contributed oral histories in the late twentieth century. The New Orleans home case records no longer exist, but annual reports, newsletters, a 1925 report from the Child Welfare League of America, and Marlene Trestman's forthcoming biography of Bessie Margolin, a New Orleans home inmate who became a leading champion of the Fair Labor Standards Act, provide insight into the strategies by which Jewish orphans learned the fine art of belonging in the segregated South.

Taken together, these materials offer an intricate portrait of the institutions' efforts to nurture orphaned and indigent children, and to teach them how to conform to regional norms so that their legibility as citizens—their capacity to be seen by non-Jews as upstanding, white men and women—would remain undisputed. Central to this effort was the work of instilling the children of the poor with the internalized logic of class and its symbolic social advantages that would distance them from their Old World roots and distinguish them as honorable members of society. I place the children's lives within the larger context of shifting standards for raising dependent children and the ways in which Jewish agencies modeled national ideals in orphan care and social work. Given the early twentieth century's increasing emphasis on "home life" as crucial to nurturing dependent children, institutions came under fire for their uniformity of care, regimentation, and absence of personal warmth.[10] In addition to providing impoverished Jewish children with valuable lessons in proper comportment that would lend legitimacy to their claims to belonging in a southern community, the homes offered a measure of virtually familial influence through a variety of motherly figures, including home "Matrons," "Big Sisters," and professional social workers. Further, black women hired as servants assumed a vital but retrospectively obscured role, one that would help instill in these children of the poor and foreign-born the values of respectable gender and race comportment.

"The Loss of a Wife and Mother": Sheltering Half-Orphans

Although theirs had not been a carefree existence, the Blaustein children's troubles began in earnest in June 1914, when their mother died in childbirth, leaving the five of them in the care of their father. Isidore Blaustein struggled to support his young family with his tailoring business, but he was unable to provide consistent supervision for the children, who ranged in age from two to twelve. Friends urged him to send them to live with various relatives scattered throughout the eastern seaboard, but Blaustein could not bear imposing the additional hardship of separation on his grieving children. Witnessing his difficulty, the Waycross Jewish community appealed to the Hebrew Orphans Home of Atlanta to accept the four younger children into its care until he could work his way out of debt. Sally, the youngest, was below the legal age of admission, so her three older siblings began new lives in the big city of Atlanta, and she followed several months later. Once admitted, Sally would remain in the home for fourteen years, where she and her siblings received vigilant supervision, education, sustenance, and, perhaps most crucially, socialization to the norms and expectations of their region as they transitioned to young adulthood. The Blaustein family's experience with the Atlanta home, told through the letters contained in their case files, as well as through the oral histories provided by Jacob in 1991 and his friend and fellow inmate, Joseph Green, in 1989, testify to the extent to which children of the institution came to see it as their home, its professional managers as surrogate parents, and how they learned the subtle messages of good citizenship in a region strictly regimented by race, gender, and class.

Given the lack of surviving case files from the New Orleans home, I've looked to legal scholar Marlene Trestman's detailed biography of Bessie Margolin for a glimpse of what institutional life offered. Margolin's story bears a striking resemblance to the Blausteins', as her parents also left the Jewish Pale of Settlement shortly before her birth in New York in 1909. Her mother died several years after the family relocated to Memphis, Tennessee, leaving Bessie, her younger brother Jacob, and her older sister Dora in the care of their father. The Margolins became institutional wards of the New Orleans home in June 1913, all three spending most of their childhoods in the institution's care and each receiving an exceptional education from the institution's signature private school, the Isidore Newman School.[11] Like the Blausteins and Greens, the Margolins were first-generation Americans, children of impoverished circumstances who nevertheless "made good." Their time in the southern Jewish orphan homes educated them far beyond their parents' humble means, instilling in each the capacity to earn a living and the knowledge necessary to navigate the complexities of the larger world beyond the institutional walls.

Since their respective founding, each southern home stood as a refuge for orphans and motherless children for the states comprising "the fair Southland." The Atlanta home served B'nai B'rith District Grand Lodge Five—Georgia, Florida, the District of Columbia, Virginia, and the Carolinas—while the New Orleans home served District Grand Lodge Seven—Louisiana, Arkansas, Texas, Alabama, Tennessee, Oklahoma, and Mississippi.[12] From its opening in 1856, the New Orleans home boasted a generous admissions policy, accepting into its care widows as well as poor and neglected Jewish children. Starting in 1880, the home relocated its elderly widows to the Touro Infirmary, providing younger widowed mothers with financial support so that they could remain in their own homes.[13] During the same year, the institution was renamed the Association for the Relief of Jewish Widows and Orphans, which was changed again in 1905 to the Association for the Relief of Jewish Widows and Orphans of New Orleans. Given the institution's increasing focus on dependent children, it was renamed the Jewish Children's Home in 1924.

By contrast to its New Orleans counterpart, the Atlanta home purported to limit admission to orphans and half-orphans, particularly motherless children, and never provided institutional housing to widows. As Sonn responded to the Waycross Jews' initial queries about the Blaustein children, "The loss of a wife and mother entitles the children to our care."[14] Although fathers were not expected to raise their children in the absence of a wife and mother, they were expected to provide financial support. By the 1910s, when the Blaustein and Margolin children fell into crisis after losing their mothers, leaders of both institutions had become increasingly concerned about fathers taking advantage of institutional generosity. While they suspected some mothers of being incapable of raising good citizens, benevolent leaders expressed concern about fathers shirking their breadwinning responsibilities.[15] Gendered anxieties about parental responsibility would plague Mr. Blaustein's relationship with the Atlanta home throughout the fifteen years of his children's residence. Further, during the time of their institutionalization, the children's class and cultural distance from their father would grow, widening the gulf separating an immigrant father from his upwardly mobile American children.

"The Precarious Nature of Private Charity": Paternal Responsibility and Material Support

Managing the considerable financial burden of orphan care was a complex matter. The founding members of both southern institutions echoed widespread concern that unfettered, thoughtless charity would result in a complacent, lazy poor rather than an independent citizenry, and they insisted that theirs would be organizations based in self-help rather than individual charity. The framers of the New Orleans home's Constitution warned, "The precarious nature of such private relief must be obvious to every reflecting mind."[16] Written three decades before a wave of eastern European immigration would significantly tax the institution's resources, founders expressed ambivalence regarding their foray into uplift work and reflected the larger society's suspicions about pauperism. While the home provided direct relief to needy children and widows, it also promoted what the medieval philosopher and rabbi Moses Maimonides extolled as one of the highest levels of *tzedakah* by providing the poor with the means to become self-supporting.[17] The home's emphasis on self-help was rooted in the guiding principle that *all* Jews had a stake in seeing that the poorest among them became independent, contributing members of society, calling to mind the associational and communal legacy of earlier Jewish benevolent efforts.

As demonstrated in prior chapters, the nation's first Jewish benevolent societies were associational, with members required to contribute to a pool of money, out of which they received support in times of need.[18] This organizational structure shifted in the nineteenth century as growing numbers of poor could not afford the cost of membership in many elite benevolent institutions but were nevertheless in need of aid when they fell on hard times. It was at the crossroads of increased immigration of impoverished Jewish populations and critical shifts in thinking about benevolence as handouts rather than entitlements that "private relief" came under mounting suspicion among social reformers nationwide.[19] As social Darwinist explanations for poverty took hold among late nineteenth-century reformers, fueled by nativist responses to eastern and southern European immigration, a more punitive vision of the poor emerged among Jewish benevolent leaders.

Anxieties over the spread of excessive dependency among coreligionists scripted the boundaries of loving kindness, creating categories distinguishing the "worthy poor" from the pathological "pauper."[20] While they celebrated the construction of a benevolent empire, leaders' words reflected prevailing suspicions of misguided charity. Austrian-born entrepreneur Jacob Furth wrote in an 1895 issue of *The Magnet*, "Those who have fallen into the pauper class should be made to understand that there is no room for them as Jews."[21] Not merely a temporary setback on one's path to success, pauperhood signified a pathological incapacity for independence and a basis for exclusion from community membership.[22] The concept also suggested failed masculinity, for those men who fell into the "pauper class" could not emulate the key characteristic of masculine citizenship, namely, the ability to support a family. Such men were threats to the public performance of Jewish self-reliance in a region that placed significant stock in masculine self-sufficiency and honor, scoundrels against whom true citizens must be protected. Failure to distinguish between these "shiftless" few and the "deserving poor" therefore threatened the institution's legitimacy in the eyes of the larger world.[23]

By the late nineteenth century, leaders' anxieties over the "precarious nature of private relief" had escalated, and many feared that aiding the wrong kind of people placed them in the risky position of appearing less discerning and competent than other, non-Jewish charities. Such concerns drove a sharp wedge between established Jewish citizens on one hand and their immigrant coreligionists. The former possessed the means to help the latter, but with that support came the former's judgment about how to be properly American. Such conflicting notions of acculturation were compounded by the South's intensifying racial politics, where the rules of belonging were rigidly scripted and inextricable from idealized notions of class.

Gender remained at the heart of debates around pauperism and worthiness as benevolent leaders sought to ensure that their efforts did not serve those considered to be "chiselers" and irredeemable "paupers." The founding documents of both institutions declared a commitment to supporting orphans and widows—but not impoverished fathers, who were expected to provide financial support for their children even if they could not serve as caregivers in the absence of wives and mothers. Thus institutional policy took shape around gendered understandings of paternal obligation, where a good father provided financial support toward his institutionalized children's upkeep. In response to initial queries about the Blaustein children's admissibility, Superintendent Sonn explained that the loss of the children's mother "entitles the children to our care, but it does not relieve the father materially from their support."[24] New Orleans home policy similarly presumed that bereaved and/or physically incapacitated fathers could apply for the home's help in raising their children, but they signed a contract promising to contribute a monthly amount toward their children's upkeep.[25] This amount, usually a few dollars per month, signified a vital component of both institutions' commitment to gendered ideals of paternal support, and it often proved a great hardship to struggling fathers.

Fathers who failed to support their children committed an unpardonable sin against breadwinning norms, and the Atlanta home's responses ranged from disapproving letters to occasional legal action. Underlying the home's policies was the widespread assumption that fathers alone could not be trusted with their children's supervision and upbringing, and temporary institutionalization—until the father remarried—was the optimal substitute for a mother's unique socialization and care. While the Atlanta home increasingly allowed widowed mothers considered "worthy" to keep their children and receive a monthly subsidy to support them, a man was not expected to keep his children without a female caregiver. Further, his material responsibility to his institutionalized children reflected his obligation to the larger community.[26] Sonn explained, "The general public cannot be expected to make monetary sacrifices unless the beneficiary—in this case the applicant—makes every reasonable sacrifice first," and he asked that Blaustein "agree to pay, monthly, an amount acceptable to us, and then give us his [promissory] notes for three years in advance."[27]

Blaustein's early letters to the home evince his sense of obligation to his children's upkeep, as he promised to contribute $100 per year, with "twenty dollars in advance."[28] Blaustein also assured Sonn that his children's institutionalization was a temporary measure, and that he didn't wish "for the children to stay there always because I am only 36 years old and I may be able to go back to house keeping some day."[29]

For many fathers who fell on hard times after the loss of a spouse, the orphan home seemed an ideal temporary solution to their straitened circumstances. But those very circumstances often made it difficult, indeed impossible, for fathers to shoulder the financial burden of their children's support. Before admitting the children to the home, Sonn secured Blaustein's promise, via legal contract, that he would send twelve dollars per month to the home in support of their upkeep. The three middle children, Oscar, Jacob, and Annie, were sent to the home in September 1914, soon to be followed by their sister Sally, who would remain there until the summer of 1929.

Blaustein's inability to contribute regularly to his children's support was a consistent source of strife. During the fifteen years of his children's institutionalization, his failure to keep up with his monthly payments resulted in tense relations with the institution's leadership, at one point resulting in legal action against him. Sonn insisted that Blaustein fulfill his financial obligations and urged him to "be a better father from now on."[30] Blaustein repeatedly begged forgiveness for his "neglected duty," explaining his failures as a result of ill health and difficulty securing regular work in a saturated market.[31] His letters to Sonn described in detail his efforts to fulfill his responsibility, at one point making his "own home in my back shop in order to able myself to pay some money to the home. I cannot make no harder struggle as I am."[32]

Despite his failure to meet the institution's expectations for financial support, Blaustein maintained a faithful correspondence with his children, who remained safely in the institution's care. When she was still very young, a local couple offered to adopt Sally. Due to Blaustein's failure to contribute regularly to his children's care, the home would have been within its legal rights to allow the adoption, but Sally's siblings protested, and the home capitulated to their desire to remain together.[33] While their father was unable to provide regular support, the institution never faltered in its provision of care, and from 1914 until 1929, the children received the home's untiring and vigilant supervision. Although there exist no records of his financial contributions, Bessie Margolin's father likewise found it difficult to support his children as they spent the remainder of their youth in the New Orleans home. For both families, what began as a temporary solution to a father's financial crisis became a way of life for the children.

"Through the Channels of Environment": Institutional Quarantines and Refined Spaces

The southern institutions prided themselves on their capacity to provide protective spaces in which the ideals of citizenship could be cultivated among their young and impressionable charges. They carefully policed their borders to ensure that outside contaminants—social as well as biological—did not infect their children, and perceived themselves as keepers of inmates' "physical, mental and moral well being."[34] Before the Margolins or Blausteins were allowed into their new institutional homes, they underwent thorough medical exams to ensure that they were "of sound mind, not Scrofulous, in good bodily health, and entirely free of Skin, Scalp or other disease," and that they measured up mentally to standards considered normal.[35] While the Blausteins were admitted to the Atlanta home after passing their medical inspections, the Margolins were subjected to a quarantine, "placed in isolation chambers for a period of two weeks" before integration into the home's population to allow "time for any infectious or contagious disease to develop."[36] The quarantine provided home staff "close observation as to habits, etc., [and] a complete physical examination" to ensure that new children did not infect the other inmates.[37] The Atlanta home's lack of a quarantine occasionally resulted in the admission of children with contagious medical conditions that were not initially detected by the institution's staff. In 1922, a recently admitted ten-year-old boy from Jacksonville, Florida, was discovered to be "in a deplorable syphilitic condition."[38] Deciding that the boy's presence constituted "a menace to the wellbeing of the other children," the home's leadership promptly returned him to his mother, providing a subsidy for his support.[39]

As they worked to protect inmates' health, institutional professionals also sought to keep them free of any "bad habits" that could assert an adverse or corrupting influence over others. A significant part of the institutional mission involved protecting the inmates from the outside world's pernicious influences. The homes' methods of addressing non-physiological "infection" suggest that scientific theories about the communicability of disease influenced notions of social corruption and the channels through which culture could be transmitted from individual to individual. Culture—whether harmful or salubrious—was influential in shaping human character, and the institutions worked to ensure that children were exposed only to what were perceived to be the most edifying influences. Children had to be protected from social contaminants at all costs, and, in the New South, such notions of corruption and degradation were inflected by the region's gendered and racialized ideals of cultural capital.

Equal in importance to their physical well-being was the children's moral purity, and both homes prized their reputations for respectability and virtue. Sexual innocence was of particular significance for girls. When considering the admission of new girls, especially those over the age of ten, superintendents at the Atlanta home inquired after their "manners" and "habits," terms coded with moral implications beyond simple good conduct. Girls who exhibited signs of "sophistication" or "corruption" were strictly prohibited from entering the home, where their behavior might pollute the minds of the institution's unsullied occupants. In 1899, Superintendent Sonn reported on the application for admission of the "Rosemann girls aged 9 and 12 years [who were] very wild and unclean, but also very corrupt." He urged the board not to admit them, insisting "that their language, their manners, and their everything else are bound to exercise a most deplorable influence on other children."[40] Perceived as a threat both to the personal and spiritual hygiene of the other inmates, the girls were duly refused admission even if their family's circumstances were dire. In this case, the institution's child-saving mission gave way to their need to preserve the home's internal purity. Even if the Rosemann girls were impoverished and lacking parental support, the home's leadership could not risk exposing the other children to such a "deplorable influence."

The protection of white feminine purity was a central theme informing hegemonic gender and race ideals throughout the nation, but such mandates found particular resonance in a region that prized white female virtue as a justification for a violently policed system of racial segregation. Many native-born whites perceived the South as a space of exceptional danger for white femininity. An editorial in the August 1897 issue of the *American Jewess*, a periodical published in Chicago, emphasized the necessity of lynching as an extralegal, but essential, effort to prevent black men's attacks on the "defenseless white women of the South."[41] Frank J. Cohen, editor of the *Jewish Sentiment* in Dallas, also expressed his support of lynching to curtail black men's commission of "the unmentionable crime" of rape against white women.[42] Southern white women's unique need for protection provided a bulwark for racialized ideals of gender and citizenship and informed the cultivation of these norms in the private spaces of the South.[43]

In the confines of the institution, corrupted femininity was irredeemable and constituted a menace to the purity of other institutional wards. In 1886 the New Orleans home faced scandal when Superintendent Simon L. Weil was accused of "revolting acts" with a female inmate.[44] The home president discharged Weil in February, and, in an effort to quell rampant rumors and to rescue the institution's reputation as a space of unblemished conduct, he reported at the March annual meeting on the "charges of immoral conduct on the part of the Superintendent towards an inmate of the Home."[45] Referring to "the secret crime committed by the late Superintendent," he explained that "but one inmate was involved, who is now discharged from the Home." Having removed the sources of moral contamination—both the adult staff member *and* the female inmate involved in the "secret crime"—the president reassured those in attendance "that all the remaining inmates are pure and innocent, and as regards morality and chastity, our Home is in as excellent a condition as can be desired."[46] In the minds of the institutional leaders, the girl's moral contamination could not be reversed, and her continued presence would only impose a corrupting influence on others.[47]

In addition to fearing the effects of destructive outside influences, the homes' leaders also acted on assumptions that individuals and spaces could serve as carriers of salubrious cultural influence. Just as children in possession of "bad habits" could not be allowed to infect the home's other inmates, regular exposure to people of higher class standing and cultural capital would help poor children move into higher social strata. Maintaining the institution's internal purity while also allowing inmates the opportunity to obtain experience navigating the external social world was a complex balancing act, where the staff worked to broker the children's relationships with friends, family, and one another. New Orleans home president Joseph W. Newman told the board in 1923, "A careful study of the child over a period of twenty years has brought me to the conviction that we must combat the hereditary tendencies, if not based on disease, through the channels of environment."[48] Beyond providing for the "care of the individual child's physical condition," the home promised its inmates a "higher if not the highest education, thereby raising them far above the social stratum from which they came, elevating them to the social stratum of intellectuality which after all is the only one that counts [and] putting them on an equal footing with those more fortunately situated."[49] For Newman and other leaders of early twentieth-century orphan institutions, exposure to the right "channels of environment" would counteract all but the most vicious "hereditary tendencies."

In a significant departure from what Reena Sigman Friedman describes as the "total institution" philosophy of most northern Jewish orphan homes, where leaders sought to limit inmates' contact with the outside world, the protective boundaries of the southern homes were selectively permeable.[50] Orphans at the Atlanta and New Orleans homes were encouraged to socialize with affluent individuals who

New Orleans Jewish Orphans Home. Photo courtesy of Jewish Children's Regional Service of New Orleans.

Atlanta Hebrew Orphans Home, 1910. Photo courtesy of Cuba Family Archives of the Breman Museum.

would provide valuable lessons in elite cultural capital but were limited in their interaction with culturally corrupting influences, like impoverished relatives and the poor, often racially mixed neighborhoods from which many of them came. The homes' physical location in middle- and upper-class neighborhoods would facilitate inmates' exposure to their relatively well-off, native-born Jewish neighbors. Originally constructed on Chippewah Street, the New Orleans home was relocated in 1887 to a new, larger building at 5342 St. Charles Avenue, in "one of the best residential sections of the city."[51] From their lofty position in this fine neighborhood, residents were geographically separated from their unacculturated kinsmen.[52]

The Atlanta home's similar social geography in a relatively prosperous part of town and its rules governing leisure and socializing exposed inmates to specific class and cultural values while shielding them from others. The founders constructed the institution in a space of elevated cultural capital, at 478 Washington Street, near Atlanta's German-descended Jewish neighborhood and within walking distance of the Reform Hebrew Benevolent Congregation (aka the Temple), where most of the city's native-born and elite Jews worshipped. In an effort

Hebrew Orphans Home of Atlanta Residents with Ralph A. Sonn, 1906. Photo courtesy of Cuba Family Archives of the Breman Museum.

to familiarize inmates with the world outside their institutional walls, both homes encouraged inmates' social interactions with the relatively privileged children in the surrounding neighborhoods.

Inmates in the New Orleans home were given important lessons in elite socialization through regular exposure to the home's "Honorary Matrons." Starting in 1880, the institution's board voted to enlist the help of local women, usually the wives of the institution's wealthy board members, to provide the children with guidance, friendship, and vital training in social graces. Honorary Matrons were elected each year to serve as "Big Sisters" to inmates, paying regular visits to the home and helping girls with their sewing and other domestic arts. On some occasions, local women's groups like the New Orleans chapter of the Council of Jewish Women joined the Honorary Matrons in efforts to sew clothing for the children.[53] Children's exposure to elite women served the dual role of providing motherly figures to orphans while also offering young girls valuable role models for proper, refined femininity. Bessie Margolin enjoyed the companionship and guidance of her prosperous Big Sister, Hannah Stern, wife of the president of a cotton brokerage firm.[54] Attending dinners at their Big Sisters' elegant homes gave inmates intensive exposure to an elite lifestyle to which they might aspire. In New Orleans, Big Sisters and Brothers' influence continued after children's demission, helping them secure respectable employment and ensuring that they became incorporated into the proper channels of society.

As in other orphan homes, the southern Jewish institutions valued strict regimentation and structure, carefully scheduling the children's time throughout each day, including specific times for leisure and play. They inculcated their charges with the importance of cleanliness and order, and their daily life was routinized around required showers, meals, inspections, schooling, and chores. The vigilance they demonstrated in their admissions policies was carried through to their inculcation of values of cleanliness of mind and social habits as well as body. At the Atlanta home, children awoke at 6:00 a.m. to take a required morning shower before dressing and going to breakfast. Careful inspections preceded each meal so that children's personal hygiene could be closely monitored, and they also took an evening shower before bed.[55] Children were responsible for straightening up their own beds and personal belongings, losing privileges if they failed to maintain the institution's high standards of cleanliness and order. Such vigilant emphasis on cleanliness appears to have been particular to the southern Jewish orphan homes, with their relatively smaller populations, which afforded more careful monitoring for each child. For example, Reena Sigman Friedman describes how the Cleveland Jewish Orphan Asylum, which served the states of B'nai B'rith Grand District Two, including Kentucky and the Midwest, allowed for communal baths only once a week.[56]

In addition to modeling ideals of social stratification for impoverished children, the institutions imparted a more Americanized version of Judaism than that embraced by many of the inmates' immigrant parents. Gary Polster's study of the Cleveland home describes institutional efforts to "reform the Orthodox" as a crucial strategy of converting the children of the poor into proper and respectable Americans.[57] Such efforts to expose orphans to Reform Judaism were amplified in the South, where the movement to transform and modernize American Judaism originally took root in the 1820s and 1830s.⁵⁸ The South's smaller Jewish population, combined with the prevalence of Protestantism, created additional motivation for Jewish ritual adaptations, including Sunday schools and Confirmation for children and the incorporation of instrumental music in services.⁵⁹ The goal of southern Reformers, to make Judaism more closely resemble the larger culture, dovetailed neatly with orphan homes' efforts to maintain inmates' religious observance while mainstreaming them culturally.

From its founding in 1856, the New Orleans home maintained its own on-site space of worship open to community members as well as orphans and staff. In 1926, in an effort to expand inmates' social world, the home divided them among the three local synagogues for Sunday school and Confirmation. The home continued holding its regular services, but children were channeled to one of the local Reform congregations: Touro Synagogue, Temple Sinai, or Congregation Gates of Prayer.⁶⁰ During the 1920s these three congregations experienced significant growth and prosperity, building new synagogues and playing increasingly visible roles in community outreach. Their inclusion as members of the Reform synagogues constituted an important part of the orphans' incorporation into the city's larger Jewish community.

As in New Orleans, the Atlanta home actively sought to integrate its inmates into the city's elite and acculturated Jewish community. From the institution's founding, inmates attended the Hebrew Benevolent Congregation, or Temple, where most of the city's middle-to-upper-class, German-descended Jews worshipped. When the congregation replaced the more traditionally inclined Rabbi Leo Reich with twenty-three-year-old David Marx in 1895, they signaled their commitment to a more modern and culturally adaptable form of worship. The son of German immigrants, Marx was raised in New Orleans and believed in a quiet and respectable Judaism confined within the private realms of home and temple.⁶¹ Marx served on the boards of many benevolent organizations, including the orphan home, and proved a leading figure of Jewish citizenship for the larger Atlanta community. His role as "ethnic broker" between Atlanta's gentile community and the rapidly growing Jewish population reflected his desire to mediate the possible ill effects of rapid eastern European immigration.⁶²

Jacob Blaustein and Joseph Green both described how all the children from the home walked together for Saturday services and to attend Sunday school among the Temple's upstanding congregation.[63] Hebrew instruction was limited to memorizing a few Torah portions that one needed to know for Confirmation. Jacob's close friend Jack Lichtenstein lived across the street from the home in a family that was significantly "more strict" about worship.[64] While the boys played together at Jack's house and walked to Technical High School together, on Saturday and Sunday they parted ways so that Jack could attend a more observant synagogue, likely the nearby Ahavath Achim, an Orthodox synagogue established in 1887.[65] Jacob's poverty and orphanhood precluded his participation in Jack's more religiously devout mode of worship, for the Reform religious practice emphasized respectability and assimilation to the region's prevailing norms of worship and comprised a vital part of orphans' education as citizens of the southern social landscape.[66]

Institutional life held a certain rigidity, but inmates were also encouraged to be children. Life in a house full of children meant that one never lacked for a playmate, and there were many opportunities for recreation and as well as for independent play.[67] Both institutions invested substantial resources in the construction of spaces for children's sports

New Orleans Jewish Orphans Home "Where the Girls Play," n.d. Photo courtesy of Jewish Children's Regional Service of New Orleans.

Children Roller Skating at the Atlanta Hebrew Orphans Home, n.d. Photo courtesy of Cuba Family Archives of the Breman Museum.

and leisure, including playgrounds, baseball diamonds, tennis courts, and a roller skating rink. Boys especially were encouraged to play sports in the fields adjacent to the homes, where children from the neighborhood frequently joined them.[68] Staff at the Atlanta home encouraged inmates to mingle with the children of the established, predominantly German-descended Jews who lived nearby. The child of a Russian and a Polish immigrant, Joseph Green spent his downtime playing sports and socializing with what he called "the finest people in Atlanta."[69] While the institution retained supervisory control over these relationships and reserved the right to discontinue friendships that threatened the home's disciplinary structure, the superintendent and other leaders understood the benefits of wards' interactions with non-orphaned, relatively privileged, local children. The New Orleans home also invested significant resources in providing salubrious recreational time and space for its inmates. Although one must consider the selective staging of photographs created for the benefit of elite members of the home's board and other valued sources of revenue, images from the *Golden*

City Messenger, the home's newsletter, feature children playing on well-appointed playgrounds and socializing on the home's expansive and manicured grounds.

By the 1910s, children at many Jewish orphan homes nationwide enjoyed summer vacations at camps located at a distance from their institutions.[70] Atlanta inmates, including many of the institution's subsidized children, attended summer camp at Camp Fendig in South Carolina. New Orleans inmates likewise enjoyed two weeks each summer at the "Federation Camp," in Bay St. Louis, Mississippi, a sixty-mile train ride from the home.[71] Excerpts from children's letters included in the "Children's Page" of the New Orleans *Golden City Messenger* confirm that camp was a radical departure from institutional life. Inmates described the beautiful scenery and time spent hiking, swimming in the Gulf of Mexico, canoeing, fishing, roasting marshmallows, and simply enjoying an unstructured, carefree departure from institutional life. The staff of both homes believed that such exposure to the outdoors and to less-regimented recreational and social time had a healthful influence on children's development. Superintendent Leon Volmer, of the New Orleans home, referenced "eminent authority" Stanley Hall's

New Orleans Jewish Orphans Home, n.d. Photo courtesy of Jewish Children's Regional Service of New Orleans.

Residents of the Hebrew Orphans Home at their Yearly Campout at Lakewood Park, 1920. Photo courtesy of Cuba Family Archives of the Breman Museum.

theories about the necessity of leisure and outdoor activity to healthful childhood development, explaining that "the boys and girls return from camp invigorated in mind and improved in health."[72]

While such beliefs were pervasive nationwide, the southern Jewish orphan homes excelled in the provision of outdoor recreation to their inmates. Even when they weren't attending summer camp, the children were encouraged to participate in outdoor play and scouting activities. While girls too took part in outdoor excursions and hiking trips, Hall and other child development experts heralded leisure, strenuous play, and exposure to the outdoors as critical to the cultivation of manly men.[73] Photos from both institutions depict boys preparing for camping trips and participating in outdoor activities like campfire-building and fishing. Boys at the Atlanta home embarked on camping club outings, hiking without adult supervision to Lakewood Park and camping overnight. Jacob Blaustein described with fondness the excursions taken with his older brother, Oscar, and other members of the camping club.[74] Such forays into the wilderness, albeit only a mile from the center of the bustling city, were thought to have a wholesome impact on young men, on whom an overabundance of "civilization" supposedly had a weakening effect.[75] The boys who participated in regular outdoor exploration and play would be more likely to evolve into the kinds of independent, vigorously manly young men whose comportment would reflect well on American Jewry.

"The Unit of All Civilization": Jews and Exceptional "Home Life"

Indoor spaces were also vital to shaping the southern home inmates into honorable men and virtuous women. The southern homes' cultivation of a homelike atmosphere evinced a commitment to developing children's sense of themselves as individuals and citizens of worth. As demonstrated in the prior chapter, the late nineteenth century saw a significant increase in children's institutionalization just as criticism of institutional life's effect on children's emotional and social well-being was gathering steam.[76] At his foundational White House Conference on the Care of Dependent Children, President Theodore Roosevelt described "home life" as "the highest and finest product of civilization [and] the great molding force of mind and of character," and emphasized the home's role in "the preservation of high standards of citizenship." Committed to the virtues of home life, Roosevelt declared that "children should not be deprived of it except for urgent and compelling reasons."[77]

Social workers nationwide increasingly agreed with this philosophy, and as institutional care came into question, Jewish benevolent leaders celebrated their capacity to create a "home life" within their institutional walls. Some envisioned familial affect as an essential element of Jewishness. At the fiftieth anniversary of the New Orleans home in 1905, Dr. Lee K. Frankel of New York invoked "the home [and] the family life . . . [as] the unit of all civilization" and insisted on the Jewish people's status as "exemplar[s] of the ideal family life."[78] According to Frankel, Jews epitomized superior "family life" in their development of exceptional domestic environments in which proper citizens could be raised. Such language stood in marked contrast to the assertions of popular Virginia author Thomas Nelson Page, who wrote one year prior that southern "Negroes . . . have scarcely any notion of the foundation principles of pure family life."⁷⁹ By the early twentieth century, Page's literary portraits of a glorious Old South were well-known and celebrated throughout the nation, providing the New South with a set of collective memories on which to base a white supremacist logic of cultural citizenship. In these literary representations, cultural degradation was essential to blackness, and popular depictions of black immorality helped justify the exclusion of African Americans from the civic rights and privileges of full citizenship. Given the South's close linkage of racialized culture to citizenship, Jewish benevolent leaders struggled to prove their people's worth by providing their orphans with a contrasting model of transcendent "pure family life."

In the early twentieth century, both southern Jewish orphan homes instituted changes to ensure children's development as individuals, each dispensing with uniforms in an effort to help the children blend into the larger community, rather than standing out as institutional inmates.⁸⁰ Blaustein and Green describe having worn coveralls as "play clothes" while on the home's premises and changing into "street clothes"—knickers and stockings for boys and dresses for girls—when going to school, temple, or on outings into town.⁸¹ The institutions provided regular forays into the outside world so that inmates could enjoy trips to the opera and cinema, baseball games, summer camp, and, in New Orleans, to the elegant homes of their Big Sisters. As institutional wards, southern Jewish orphans were given exposure to a range of social, recreational, and cultural experiences that would help shape them into citizens with higher class aspirations than most of their predominantly immigrant families could have imagined.

Efforts to duplicate an authentic "home life" were especially pronounced at the New Orleans home, where institutional regimentation was tempered by an appeal to the individual child's need for a sense of belonging in a smaller familial group.⁸² Beginning in 1911, the home initiated the "Golden City Plan" in which children were grouped into "families" headed by two older children, one boy and one girl, who would serve as the guides and mentors, as well as the disciplinary overseers, of their family's smaller children.⁸³ Family groups included eight to ten children, and they ate together at designated tables during every meal. Leaders of the New Orleans home expressed pride in their efforts to provide inmates a more family-modeled lifestyle and

New Orleans Jewish Orphans Home Band, 1903. Photo courtesy of Jewish Children's Regional Service of New Orleans.

emphasized how the home's structure inculcated inmates with the values of the middle-class nuclear family, headed by a man and a woman, giving each child much-needed practice in performing these normative gender roles. Indeed, participating in smaller family groups instilled in children the value of the very familial organizations they would be expected to emulate as adults. Each child would enjoy the companionship, protection, and mentoring of older children, and, as they grew, each assumed the role of guardian and protector of younger children. Each family group was assigned a Big Sister from among the Honorary Matrons, who visited their "families" for meals and celebrations, providing guidance as well as motherly affection to the children.

The homes diverged somewhat on the issue of discipline, with the New Orleans home implementing financial incentives so that children who observed the rules of comportment were rewarded with a higher amount of weekly allowance.[84] Atlanta home children received small payments for work they performed, such as sewing and darning for the girls and carpentry and gardening for the boys. Those who broke institutional rules might be subject to discipline ranging in intensity from Jacob Blaustein's semi-regular confinement to a corner of Superintendent Sonn's office to the surprisingly severe penalty Joseph Green received for conducting a secret correspondence with his sister, who was convalescing at another institution. Green and Blaustein both described in vivid detail the "harsh" sentence Superintendent Feist Strauss imposed on Green, forcing him to sleep outside for two weeks on one of the home's porches during the winter.[85] But while Jacob's "tough" sister Annie got into several scrapes with some of the boys, she seems not to have been punished for fighting.[86] There was significant range in the ways various home staff meted out punishment, but most agreed that corporal punishment, in the form of physical beatings, had no place in the Jewish institution.

Leaders of the New Orleans home took the material effects of cultural capital very seriously, constructing the home's interior to resemble, as closely as possible, the inside of a well-appointed private home. According to President Newman, prolonged exposure to appropriate "channels of environment" would place poor children "on an equal footing with those more fortunately situated."[87] Exposing inmates to refined surroundings, such as those depicted in the article's accompanying photo of the children at a well-appointed Seder dinner, would allow them to rise "far above the social stratum from which they came."[88] Other photographs published in the *Golden City Messenger* depict the style and refinement of the home's common and reception areas, and the emphasis placed on good taste and middle-class consumption. Dining tables featured white tablecloths and simple place settings. Floral arrangements graced each tabletop and the children were dressed in elegant but simple clothes. The photos suggest that the children regularly participated in fine dining in their "family" groups, often alongside their cultured Big Sisters. Such performances required the mastery of a complex system of social graces and manners by which one was characterized as genteel, and the children's regular participation in such ritualized dining experiences was fundamental to their socialization.

Certainly, the photographs selected for the newsletter, which circulated to the home's board members, constituent lodges in the B'nai B'rith District, as well as to other supporters in the region, were designed to depict the home in its best possible light, and we may assume that ordinary dining was less elegant. However, social worker Anna Berenson confirmed in her 1933 master's thesis that tablecloths and napkins were "changed regularly" and comprised the norm of the children's daily dining experience.[89] Berenson also described the home's "attractively furnished" social spaces and reception areas, which included "pianos, artistic pictures, paneled walls, attractive rugs and lamps, appropriate furniture, an imposing chandelier (donated by a friend) [which] give the entrance of the institution the appearance of a large, attractive private home."[90]

Such elegant accouterments may not have been the norm in Atlanta, but the home's records also confirm formal events held throughout the year, where inmates socialized with and performed pageants for their wealthy benefactors. Table manners and social graces were held at a premium, and Atlanta inmates also experienced a quality of life much elevated from their prior conditions. Jacob Blaustein and Joseph Green both described their ordinary meals as "plain" and unmemorable, but, like their peers in New Orleans, they were served regular, reliable meals that exceeded the health standards of the day.

The institutions encouraged inmates to socialize with the children—non-Jews as well as Jews—who lived in close proximity to the institutions' middle- to upper-class surrounding neighborhoods, but they maintained strict rules on correspondence with family members living outside the home. At the Atlanta home, letters were written and received every Sunday, and home staff inspected each one. Inmates often chafed under these restrictions on their privacy, particularly when it came to personal correspondence with family members. Just as Joseph Green was punished for breaking the rules of correspondence, Sally Blaustein also experienced the institution's stern reprimand when she tried to maintain a secret correspondence with her father, using a neighborhood friend as an intermediary. The confiscated letters suggest that others had transpired between the two during the fourteen years of Sally's residency. Given her father's continual state of financial arrears to the institution, his efforts to maintain contact with his youngest child and to send her small amounts of cash on the sly are not surprising. Yet the home saw such secret correspondence as a threat to inmates' development into responsible and honest adults, and they worked to filter the impact of relatives' potentially harmful influences on the children's development as morally upright citizens.

Institutional Intimacies: Domestic Labor and the Production of Middle-Class White Cultural Capital

The preservation of race and class boundaries was a vital component of southern Jewish orphan education, to the point where institutional sentiment against admitting children with two living parents could be swayed in order to ensure that children were not exposed to the poverty and potential racial degradation that, in many benevolent leaders' minds, characterized the immigrant poor. While orphans might mingle with the children of wealthy Jewish citizens and with their non-Jewish, white classmates, the institutions' location in relatively prosperous parts of town kept them separate from the cities' poorest Jews, among whom often lived their own family members. By World War I, Jews represented Atlanta's largest foreign-born population, and many of the poorest of these newcomers lived in or near southeast Atlanta, interspersed with the city's poor African American community.[91] Case files and board meeting records confirm that benevolent leaders perceived orphans' location in the institution as highly preferable to the homes of their kinsmen. As discussed in the prior chapter, the home agreed to admit the two non-orphaned Schulman children rather than leave them in the care of their father and stepmother who allowed them to keep "company with negro children."[92] Similarly, the institutions sought to limit inmates' exposure to impoverished friends and family residing in nonelite, racially mixed neighborhoods. From their meticulously regimented homes on Atlanta's Washington Street and New Orleans's St. Charles Street, Jewish orphans were protected from such precarious interactions as they witnessed and internalized the middle-class lifestyles of their white neighbors and classmates.

While orphan home inmates were strictly forbidden from socializing with black children, they experienced close interaction with black servants. Black domestic workers served the material needs of white staff and inmates while also providing children crucial lessons in the process of white individuation. Historian Grace Hale describes how, in the post-Reconstruction South, "the white home served as a major site in the production of racial identity precisely because there this racial interdependence [of whites and blacks] was both visible and denied."[93] Institutional records provide only a partial glimpse into this interdependency, as the names of the black women who served as maids, laundresses, and cooks were often left off the homes' official, publicly shared documentation. While members of the institutions' "servant staff" were not considered essential to the homes' mission to protect and educate orphans, their presence comes into focus in the backgrounds of photographs depicting domestic spaces and in stories, like Jacob Blaustein's, of institutional daily life.[94] Further, the centrality of black women's labor to the project of orphan care and uplift becomes visible in subtle but telling silences, such as in institutional debates about the kinds of labor female inmates could perform without compromising their future success as respectable ladies.

During his thirty-five-year tenure as superintendent of the Atlanta home, Ralph Sonn vehemently resisted wealthy Jews' appeals to hire home inmates as domestic servants, chastising them for being "not so much in favor of domesticity as they are in favor of domestics."[95] While northern institutions channeled their female "graduates" into private homes in which they could earn a living as domestic laborers, southern Jewish institutional leaders frowned on this practice.[96] Sonn's resistance reveals his understanding of the ways in which the region's racial order dictated a subtle yet significant divergence in institutional implementation of the policy to train girls in the domestic arts. Insisting that the home was "founded as a protest against the prevailing idea that the orphan is a bond-servant, or in any way inferior in needs or rights to anybody's child," Sonn supported orphans' elevated class aspirations and directed orphan girls into forms of work less closely associated with black femininity, as was domestic labor in that place and time.[97] Historical studies of black women's labor reveal that regional ideals of race and gender restricted all but the most elite black women to the most abject and toilsome forms of work.[98] Post-Reconstruction associations between blackness and servility further reinforced the power of such labor to "blacken" those who performed it, and Sonn recognized that poor Jewish girls had little hope of becoming proper white ladies if forced to perform the work associated with those at the bottom of the racial hierarchy.[99]

Employing African Americans to perform menial labor was a taken-for-granted part of institutional life in the South, and inmates in both southern homes would have grown accustomed to seeing black workers performing crucial but undervalued tasks like groundskeeping, laundry, cooking, and cleaning/maintaining the lavatories. This last task proved a vital component of Atlanta leaders' efforts to improve the home's hygiene in the late nineteenth century. Proposing that the children's "ill health" was a result of inadequately hygienic water closets, the home conducted an overhaul of the space and employed a "colored boy . . . to look after the cleanliness of the closets constantly which will entail another well-spent dollar per week."[100]

White homes continued to serve as sites of racial mixing long after the plantation system of slave labor ended, and it was in these intimate spaces where Hale suggests "white children learned racial difference, where the culture of segregation began."[101] The black women hired in southern Jewish institutions served as conveyors of racialized class values, as "broad signifiers of whiteness as well as nurturers, protectors, and teachers of manners to middle-class children," according to Hale.[102] Some workers, like Fannie Young and a "yardman" named George Kendrick, lived on-site in their employing institutions, but many worked as day laborers and commuted from their homes across town.[103] While the New Orleans home employed several Irish servants, who lived in the institution in the early twentieth century, they also budgeted funds to employ black women for laundry, general cleaning, and as caregivers for the youngest wards in the nursery.[104] The women's persistent but under-documented presence was vital to the children's socialization as consumers of black workers' menial and affective labor. The letters children sent from summer camp suggest their nascent sense of racial self-definition. From the Federation Camp in 1923 two New Orleans inmates wrote, "The water is fine. I have gotten so sunburnt that when I get home I will look like an Indian," and "Guess what! I am so brown I look like a negro."[105] Playful efforts to describe their suntanned bodies nevertheless evince children's internalization of the logics of racial differentiation through which they came to know themselves by what they were not.

A photo montage in the April 1923 *Golden City Messenger* featured the headline "Just a Big Family" with photos of girls "Preparing the Meal" in the New Orleans home's well-appointed kitchen and in the presence of an African American cook.[106] She stands inconspicuously in the back of the photo as several female inmates work in the foreground. Despite her unobtrusive presence in the photo, where the photographer's lens captured her as if by accident in an effort to depict the girls in the act of "Preparing the Meal," the unnamed black cook played a pivotal role in the girls' domestic arts training. For young white girls who would someday govern their own households, the quotidian presence of a black servant groomed them in the expectations of racialized labor.[107] The black cook helped guide the institution's young charges in proper methods of food preparation, but, above all, her presence confirmed their status as refined young ladies in training. For behind the newsletter's photographic staging of the elegant dining room with seven to eight well-dressed and neatly groomed children seated around each white linen–covered table was the nearly invisible labor of the black woman, she who made the white woman's performance of domestic tranquility and decorum possible.

Black women's close interaction with institutionalized children was uncontested as long as it was limited to what appeared to be menial labor like cleaning and cooking, but controversy arose when their roles as teachers or conveyors of culture became explicit. A 1925 report of the Child Welfare League of America noted the New Orleans home's practice of hiring black women to manage the children's nursery: "It is quite obvious that the colored maids who assist in the nursery are largely responsible for the activities of the children. The pre-kindergarten group are having almost nothing in the way of mental stimulation."[108] "Colored maids" might provide white children with supervision and basic care, but they were judged incapable of serving children's need for "mental stimulation." While black women were a constant and influential presence in private institutional spaces, serving as conduits of "the manners that signified class" and inevitably shaping the racial landscape on which white children's racial consciousness took root, their roles as conveyors of culture could not be made "obvious" to outside observers.[109] The invisibility of black women's influence over white children's development was critical to their role in southern race-making. As consistent but under-represented fixtures in private white spaces, their presumed insignificance veiled their enduring effect on the production of a privileged white citizenry.

"Let Us Make of Them Fine Mechanics": The Politics of Southern Labor and Education

Perhaps Jewish orphanages' greatest distinction from their non-Jewish counterparts involved the issue of secular education. While Jewish institutions as a whole expended varying levels of resources on children's religious education, most promoted secular, public education as a means to integrate orphans into the larger community.[110] Jewish benevolent leaders throughout the country placed great stock in the role of secular education as an acculturating force, but they often struggled over the means by which to accomplish this goal. Were these children to be raised as the benevolent leaders would rear their own children, or should they join a Jewish working class, engaged in manual trades instead of professional, high-status occupations? In 1894, New Orleans home superintendent Michael Heymann declared, "We do have a few bright children, who will become professional men or women, but the majority will have to do manual labor for a living. Let us make of them fine mechanics."[111] Some disagreed, urging institutions to provide each inmate an equal chance to excel and obtain professional success. Arguments over orphan education ultimately hinged on conflicting notions of the role of class in creating exemplary citizens and the optimal means of combatting anti-Semitic stereotypes while cultivating self-sufficiency among the children of the poor.[112]

Proponents of manual instruction perceived such training in "practical" and "manly" work as the ideal refutation of the avaricious, effete Shylock stereotype.[113] Efforts to combat this dangerous stereotype of failed Jewish masculinity had their roots in a centuries-old struggle to unseat claims of Jewish men's incapacity for manual labor. In his 1857 speech in New Orleans, David C. Labatt referred to the genesis of the Shylock stereotype through enemies who "[drove] this proud race to employments considered ignoble in those aristocratic days." Labatt argued that their channeling into "ignoble employments" and continuous "association with uncongenial occupations" was incompatible with prevailing masculine ideals.[114] Diverting poor Jewish boys and men into more "congenial occupations," like farming, carpentry, and other forms of manual labor, reasoned Labatt and his benevolent contemporaries, would undermine the racializing stigma of anti-Semitic stereotypes.

New Orleans Jewish Orphans Home School Room, circa 1890. Photo courtesy of Jewish Children's Regional Service of New Orleans.

Since the governing leaders and staff of the southern institutions believed that inmates would benefit by controlled exposure to the larger community, both promoted public education alongside non-Jewish, white children. Beginning in 1868, the New Orleans home began sending some of its charges to the local public school. Since they maintained their own internal school, which included Hebrew and religious education as well as secular subjects, this decision signaled the home's commitment to ensuring that its wards would be socialized in the world beyond. In 1883, out of one hundred twelve inmates, thirty-seven of the children aged ten and over attended the local public school while fifty-four received in-house instruction from the home's teacher, Hattie Conn.[115] By the turn of the century, ninety-one inmates attended the local grammar school, two attended the high school, and thirty-six were enrolled at the local kindergarten. Only the home's smallest children remained on-site for their secular education.[116]

When debates on the nature of orphans' secular education gained momentum shortly after the Atlanta home's founding, arguments often turned on divergent understandings of "manual" training. The term took on multiple meanings; for some, the term suggested low-status, toilsome occupations that might squelch orphans' aspirations for more prestigious work. For others, it implied the "practical" side of education, the endowment of children with skills that would ensure their capacity to become self-supporting. Joseph Magner, New Orleans home board member and author of a 1905 history of the institution, espoused an expansive vision of manual education that would "enable our children to adapt themselves for a higher range of occupation than common drudgery work, and which constituted a bar to their progress in life."[117] For Magner, and for many other proponents of manual education, the key to orphans' future success in "a higher range of occupation" was the accumulation of practical skills that would save them from "common drudgery."

Atlanta home leaders and staff also engaged in heated debates, including one that raged between Superintendent Ralph Sonn and President Simon Wolf. The Atlanta home's primary founder and foremost financial contributor, Wolf proposed that all inmates receive manual training so that they would not graduate from the institution "overeducated" and unable to make a living in a world already brimming with "theorists" and "professionals."[118] Yet Sonn believed that manual training would funnel the orphans into lower occupations, and he led a crusade to ensure that intellectually talented inmates received support to pursue higher education, sometimes against Wolf's wishes. Sonn adamantly refused to see class as a barrier to Jewish children's opportunities for an advanced education, vocally criticizing those who appeared to "trample the Golden Rule under foot" and promising that he "would 'move Heaven and Earth' before planning for my own son or daughter the career of the menial."[119]

Arguments for vocational or "practical" training turned on gendered understandings of labor, respectability, and class. In 1889, New Orleans home president Isaac L. Leucht expressed concern that female inmates were lacking "for the practical side of life; that too much attention was paid to school advancement and not sufficient scope allowed to home education." To train girls for "practical" life, Leucht suggested that "girls above the age of fourteen must be placed under the special supervision of the matron, for the purpose of performing housework, such as sewing, cooking and washing, etc., preparing our girls to step into any household as useful helps, earning a living 'by their own might.'"[120] By contrast, Superintendent Sonn expressed significant concern over the nature of orphaned girls' education, fearing that exclusive training in "domestic arts" might lead to their employment as servants in wealthy households.

The language of manual training held rigid assumptions about gender, race, and breadwinning, with emphasis on young men's preparation for their roles as heads-of-families and young women's domestic transformation into respectable wives and mothers. Institutions addressed concerns about female inmates' preparation for life beyond the institution by providing them with "scientific" home management training for domestic competence in their own private homes, rather than as servants for others. As with discussions of manual training for boys, debate over this issue revealed how dominant understandings of gender and class propriety intersected to inform elite Jews' decisions in educating needy children. Jewish benevolent leaders likewise asserted their institutions' superior value as spaces of refinement and elevated cultural capital. The necessity of teaching "our girls" how to be proper housewives and to raise families in clean, orderly, Jewish homes was of paramount importance to the benevolent mission.

At the New Orleans home, the voices in favor of manual training triumphed in the October 3, 1904, opening of the Isidore Newman Manual Training School several blocks away from the home. Isidore Newman, a German immigrant who made his fortune in investments and established a successful department store in New Orleans, donated the funds to build the school. The school's curriculum combined manual training with rigorous academics and was open to all white children, regardless of religious background. Rabbi Isidore Lewinthal, the German-born leader of Nashville's Reform congregation Ohavai Sholom and longtime orphan home supporter, pledged at the opening celebration that the Newman School "will do more to remove the prejudice which unhappily still exists against the Jew, than any other means." Assuring his audience that "the Jews' wits have been sharpened by long centuries of oppression," he urged leaders to turn their full focus to manual training. According to Lewinthal, "Familiarity with tools will not breed contempt, but love, and while our wards acquire skill, they will learn that there are other fields of profitable usefulness besides finance and commerce."[121] Echoing David Labatt's speech half a century earlier, Lewinthal promised that teaching Jewish orphans how to use their hands, thereby channeling them out of "finance and commerce," would offer non-Jewish society an alternative vision of Jewishness as rugged, independent, and manly. Leaders like Labatt, Lewinthal, and Wolf agreed that teaching Jewish boys to perform manual labor would challenge stereotypes of Jews as usurers, feminized by their lack of engagement in strenuous labor. As discussed in the prior chapter, the nineteenth-century glorification of the yeoman farmer enjoyed an extended life in the South, due in part to the survival of a largely agricultural economy even as many larger cities blossomed as bases of industrial growth. Gendered celebrations of "manual training" mirrored the South's embrace of strenuous, hands-on work as the key to a productive masculine citizenry, one that would rescue Jews from the pernicious stereotypes that plagued them.

The Newman School's emphasis on manual training in no way compromised its students' preparation for high-status occupations. In fact, within several years of its opening, Newman had earned a reputation as one of the South's most elite institutions of secondary education, a space wherein Jewish orphans developed practical and intellectual skills alongside the children of the wealthy.[122] By 1923, the *Golden City Messenger* extolled the Newman School as "one of the best preparatory schools in the South." Offering rigorous college preparation alongside training in "household arts," "industrial arts," and "the commercial subjects," the school inculcated its students with "the dignity of hard work."[123] The school's "atmosphere of refinement and culture" fostered "a keen sense of honor, a feeling of responsibility, an abiding enthusiasm, and a genuine loyalty" among its students.[124] Berenson described in her 1933 study how all the younger inmates and some of the older ones were enrolled at the Newman School, which "enable[ed] them to become good Americans, good Jews."[125] Those orphans who did not demonstrate the aptitude for the Newman School's rigorous combination of manual training and academic excellence attended nearby public schools. For the three intellectually gifted Margolin children, the school provided exceptional preparation for life beyond the home; in Bessie's case, Newman paved her way to college, graduate school, and a high-powered career in law.[126]

While the Atlanta home did not open its own manual training school, institutional records, oral histories, and case files confirm that a similar balance of "manual" or practical training with intellectual development prevailed. The institution maintained a "domestic science kitchen," complete with state-of-the art appliances and "delft blue and white" plates and curtains. As in the New Orleans home, female wards enjoyed "the able assistance of many interested ladies of our Jewish community" in their pursuit of domestic training.[127] The home also maintained a self-supporting "Industrial Guild," where boys learned basic carpentry and mechanical skills, selling much of their workmanship to help pay for materials and tools.[128] All or this existed in harmony with the Atlanta home's well-stocked library, curated by a vigilant Superintendent Feist Strauss, who was applauded for "not allowing [the children] to read trash."[129]

Of all the Blaustein children who occupied the Atlanta home, Jacob was the only one not to finish high school. Under Sonn's leadership, students were expected, at a minimum, to complete their education at one of the city's local high schools, and Jacob's decision in 1922 to leave the home just before his sixteenth birthday proved a source of considerable concern. Mr. Blaustein wrote to Sonn on Jacob's behalf, requesting his discharge, "as he has lost his interest for studying school any longer."[130] His older brother, Oscar, had recently graduated from high school and begun working in Waycross in his Uncle Nathan's tailoring business, and Jacob likely felt the pull of family responsibility as well as a desire to join his brother's wage-earning efforts. While he regretted Jacob's decision to quit school, his father recognized that his interests lay elsewhere, "so I decided to let him come to me and make his own struggle for life."[131] Sonn also regretted Jacob's decision, describing him as "above the average in education." While he was "unspeakably sad that Jacob will not be persuaded to continue his studies," Sonn "recognized that seeking to earn a living would be good for the family." "He is a fine young man, possessed of good principles," continued Sonn, "and he will make good in any pursuit he may enter. Perhaps it is providential that he shall seek to become a bread winner, as he may be instrumental to help you to reunite your family."[132] Throughout his post-institutional years, Jacob worked to develop his skills as a printer and entrepreneur, always maintaining contact with his sisters, and sending money for their upkeep. Despite his success as a breadwinner, however, Jacob would come to regret having ended his education early, and he made sure that his sisters did not make the same mistake.

While comparatively few young women of such humble backgrounds pursued their educations beyond high school, female wards at both southern orphan homes enjoyed opportunities usually afforded only to the well-off. Both Annie and Sally Blaustein graduated from the local high school, and Annie pursued additional training in stenography at Georgia State College for Women in Milledgeville, Georgia. Thanks in large part to Ralph Sonn's insistence on raising institutional expectations for orphan education, the Atlanta home provided generous loans and financial aid to cover the costs of higher education. After Annie graduated from Atlanta's Commercial High School, the home helped pay her $325 college tuition.[133]

The Margolin children similarly took full advantage of the substantial educational opportunities that the New Orleans home provided. Dora, the eldest, remained in the home until her 1923 graduation from the Newman School, later pursuing both a teaching and a nursing degree. She later returned to the home to serve as a nurse, where she met her future husband, who was one of the home's physicians.[134] Bessie enjoyed numerous academic opportunities that helped pave her way to becoming an attorney at the U.S. Department of Labor. Upon graduating in 1925 as the valedictorian of her Newman School class, Bessie matriculated at Tulane University's Newcomb Women's College, graduating four years later with a bachelor's as well as a law degree. Her academic achievement ultimately earned her a fellowship at Yale.[135] After his graduation from the Newman School, Bessie's younger brother, Jack, followed his older sister to pursue an undergraduate degree at Tulane. He also obtained a master's degree from Dartmouth before serving in the navy during World War II.[136]

"If They're Good Girls, They're Going to Stay Good": Policing Gender, Protecting Girls

Southern Jewish institutions took seriously the need to ensure that inmates did not leave the home until they were prepared to be self-supporting and until a responsible and respectable adult could supervise their integration into the larger world. Concerns about safety and preparation were particularly evident in the discharge policies for girls. Sally's graduation from high school in 1929 prompted heated discussions about the family members with whom she would make her new home. Having spent most of her life—almost fourteen years—in the institution, her release into the larger world must have felt at once daunting and exhilarating. She expressed delight at being able to join her family and to try her luck in the world, but her demission was never a matter of pure liberation. More so than with her brothers, the home remained involved in the decision of her placement and negotiated with various family members whose visions for Sally's future came into intense conflict.

In May 1929, just before her graduation, the home intercepted a letter from her father, which had been secretly delivered to Sally through a non-institutionalized school friend. It is likely that many inmates, encouraged to maintain close relationships with the children in their surrounding neighborhood, conducted unauthorized correspondence using their friends' and neighbors' addresses. Mr. Blaustein's intercepted note urged Sally to come live with him in Rochester, where he would also welcome Annie, who had just finished her yearlong stenography course. He insisted that Oscar's home near Cincinnati would be a difficult place to live, as "the distance to reach a car line to go to school or to work would be impossible" and further, that Oscar's wife was "impossible to get along with."[137] Sally's response, also intercepted by home staff, thanked her father for the two dollars, "as I was badly in need of it" and reassured him that she would not live with Oscar.[138] Upon discovering the letters, the institution's response was swift and decisive. Such secret correspondence was strictly forbidden, and the consequence was immediate suspension of Sally's privileges. Charging Blaustein with "encouraging your daughter to be deceitful," the home superintendent accused him of "nullifying all the training we have been giving her in the fourteen years she has been under our care [and] breaking down the character of your own daughter."[139] He also took Blaustein to task for maligning Oscar's character and his ability to "provide a better home for his sister than you can," and asked that he cease his interference "unless you can prove to us that you have something better for her."[140] Blaustein apologized for breaking the home's rules and begged forgiveness. He acknowledged that "Oscar and Jacob are gentlemen as far as their character is concerned" but insisted that he only wanted what was best for his daughters.[141]

While Isidore Blaustein wished for both of his daughters to join him in Rochester, Jacob and Oscar insisted that their father's home would not be appropriate for two respectable young women. Jacob explained that his father "always picked the shady place to live, for some reason or other," and characterized his father's neighborhood as a "Red Light district."[142] While their father insisted, "If they're good girls, they're going to stay good," Jacob and Oscar replied, "No way in the world are you going to bring them here."[143] The home's socialization had influenced the Blaustein brothers' sense of class and propriety, toughening their resolve that their sisters would live in a respectable neighborhood. They had learned that girls were especially vulnerable to corrupting influences, and they refused to risk the home's years of careful training. The superintendent ultimately followed Jacob and Oscar's advice, sending both girls to live with Oscar in Cincinnati. Mr. Blaustein's location in a neighborhood deemed unfavorable, and the incommensurable gulf separating his class values from his children's, were inimical to the maintenance of feminine respectability that his daughters had attained while in the home's care.

Gender norms held that girls were in need of closer supervision due to their heightened vulnerability to the outside world's racial and sexual contaminants, and benevolent leaders sought to provide guidance and support until former wards could find ultimate security through marriage. To ensure that their "graduates" found appropriate jobs and suitable places to live, the New Orleans home called on a network of supporters, from home alumni and B'nai B'rith members to board members, Honorary Matrons, and Big Sisters. The Atlanta home had a less systematic means of outsourcing the supervision of former wards, and the bulk of the work fell to the superintendents and social workers. After their demission, home staff kept in close contact with Sally and Annie to ensure that their home life and work prospects were satisfactory. After arriving at their brother's home in June, Sally and Annie wrote to the home's new superintendent, Armand Wyle and his wife, Viola, of their family's reunion and raved about their "beautiful home" and "very nice room." Sally described their joy at being reunited with their brother and his family, asking the Wyles to "please give Eleanor [their daughter], the staff and the children our love, and, of course, we send our love to you, too."[144] The Wyles replied, "[We] hope by this time you have become acclimated to the North and you will not miss our sunny South too much."[145] Superintendent Wyle's letter one month afterward asked Sally to send an update: "You see we are still interested in you and I think by this time you are beginning to be aware of the fact that the horns that I had on my head were not real horns but only long hair that needed cutting. With affectionate regards from Mrs. Wyle, Mrs. Havis, the children, and myself."[146]

A mutual affection pervades many of the letters conveyed between the former inmates and their caregivers, one that suggests that much more was on offer in the home than socialization to the community's norms. The children grew up with a sense of close affiliation with the institutional staff and the other children as an extended family, one that provided children of the poor with emotional sustenance as well as education and preparation for a productive life as true citizens of their region. Their familial relationship continued long after they left the home. In 1934 Sally invited the Wyles to her August wedding: "I am having a very small family wedding and would so love to have you come. After all, I did spend most of my life at the home and you would be just like part of my family."[147] Her invitation stands as poignant evidence of the extent to which children developed emotional bonds with the people who administered the home's care. Mrs. Wyle regretted that she could not attend the wedding but conveyed effusive best wishes: "He is a very lucky boy to have been able to capture you," she wrote, signing off, "With love in which Mr. Wyle joins me."[148]

Southern Jewish orphan homes excelled in the business of providing refined, "homelike" circumstances in which their young charges could grow into exemplary individuals and self-supporting citizens. The experiences of southern Jewish children plagued by poverty and loss illuminate institutional strategies for orphan uplift and the intricate ways in which the citizenship ideals of the region were inculcated in the home's young charges. Southern institutional structures emphasized practical education and gendered skill development, and constant exposure to the trappings of elite cultural capital helped prepare inmates for successful, post-institutional lives. Joseph Green, who left the Atlanta home in 1928, attributed his substantial success to the home's balance of regimentation and personal achievement. In their oral histories, both he and Blaustein recalled how the home's lessons in hygiene and order carried into their adult lives. Less obvious to them in retrospect were the lessons in racialized and gendered cultural citizenship that taught them to value certain kinds of work and living spaces over others, an internalized logic of class that drove Oscar and Jacob to insist that their sisters not join their father in a "Red Light district." Green eventually became one of the Atlanta home's success stories: once subject to Superintendent Feist Strauss's stern discipline, he later became a respected businessman in the Atlanta community. After completing his undergraduate degree at the University of Georgia, supported by the institution's scholarship funds, he earned a CPA and opened his own accounting firm in the 1940s. After he passed away, Green's family remained involved in the administration of the institution that helped make his rise to success possible.

As the institution became a surrogate Jewish mother, providing children with quotidian lessons in white, middle-class socialization, leisure, education, and labor, benevolent leaders clashed on efforts to provide subsidies to actual mothers who wished to raise their children in their own homes. While both institutions expressed an interest in supporting "worthy" mothers, prevailing ideals of class, race, and femininity conspired to complicate poor women's performances of maternal merit.

4

"A Very Delicate Problem"

The Plight of the Southern Agunah

One of the first interesting cases with which [I] dealt, was that of a deserted wife, an agunah. Such a matter is a very delicate problem and evokes pity for the woman. She cannot re-marry until her husband is located and gives her a "get" thereby initiating a divorce according to Jewish law.
—Rabbi Tobias Geffen, "Autobiography," 1951

The mother can so much better take care of the children and it is naturally her duty and inclination to do so, and in ninety nine out of a hundred cases wants to have her children with her if she has a means of support.
—Victor Kriegshaber, president of Atlanta's Hebrew Orphans Home, 1915

In 1914, several Jewish members of the Macon, Georgia, community appealed to the Atlanta Hebrew Orphans Home to accept custody of four children whose father had absconded to North Carolina.[1] The letters they wrote to Superintendent Ralph Sonn reveal their concern that the children's mother, Margaret Goldfarb, was ill equipped to raise her children in a manner the community considered appropriate. Following prevailing expectations for genteel understatement and discretion when it came to sensitive issues, three members of the community wrote to the home's Board of Directors. "Frankly speaking," wrote one, "these children are growing up wild and totally without any religious training."[2] In addition to their concern over the children's alleged lack of guidance, members of the Macon community highlighted the mother's failure to keep an adequately vigilant watch over her two daughters' moral upbringing.³ Worried about Mrs. Goldfarb's maternal inadequacies, particularly her inability to raise upstanding Jewish ladies, they aggressively petitioned for the orphan home's swift intervention.

Although it ran counter to official home policy to support children whose parents were living and married, the board eventually agreed to take custody of the younger three Goldfarb children. Mrs. Goldfarb's initial failure to secure a divorce from her husband was a source of significant concern for the institution, for most professional social workers and benevolent leaders at the time believed that aiding the dependents of an errant man only encouraged his irresponsibility. Yet members of the Macon community insisted that this case merited the home's attention, even if it meant bending the institution's rules. At the root of their insistence lay a profound concern for the children's upbringing. As one neighbor wrote, "We Macon people realize that the sooner the children are placed in charge of the home just so much better will be their condition."⁴ In this desertion case, as in many others in the early 1900s, the home gave into pressure from the community, because the alternative—to allow Jewish children to remain in a home with little supervision and minimal access to the guidance that would shape them into respectable, self-sufficient adults—was unthinkable. While the home's leadership remained hesitant to assume the care of children with two living and married parents, many questioned the ability of abandoned mothers to provide proper care and to model elevated cultural capital for their children.

The history of Jewish efforts on behalf of deserted wives has received thorough treatment from historian Anna Igra, who based her compelling study on the analysis of three hundred case files from the National Desertion Bureau, an organization established in 1911 in New York City.⁵ She illustrates the complex gender dynamics at the heart of Jewish efforts to reconcile what many perceived as a clash between Old World and New World values, and she situates Jewish reformers' efforts in relation to emergent public welfare ideals. However, since the formal anti-desertion movement originated in the Northeast, there exists little scholarship on desertion, and Jewish efforts to address it, in the South. The Bureau's location in New York, where Jews comprised close to 25 percent of the population by the early twentieth century, has resulted in a regionally lopsided view of the ways in which acculturated, benevolent Jews addressed the problem of "wives without husbands." Further, the abandoned Jewish women who published ads in the Jewish newspapers' "Gallery of Missing Husbands" or Yiddish personal ads pleading for their husbands' return were predominantly from northern or mid-Atlantic cities. Thus the experiences of abandoned Jewish women in the South, and benevolent efforts to help them, are less visible in the historical record.

Case files and other administrative records from southern benevolent agencies provide vital insight into the ways Jews addressed the troubling issue of desertion in spaces with comparatively small Jewish communities. These institutional records show how abandoned southern Jewish women, like Margaret Goldfarb, struggled to survive in conditions of extreme adversity, while revealing subtle change over time in the ways benevolent organizations took care of their own. While these episodes of misplaced feminine dependency and masculine recalcitrance were recurring topics of debate among Jewish social workers nationwide, the problem of wife abandonment took on special urgency in the South. Desertion signified extreme gender transgression in a region that prized strict racial segregation and white women's protection in the private home. Moreover, benevolent agencies' efforts to determine which deserted women were "worthy" of institutional subsidies, allowing them to keep their children at home, and which ones, like Goldfarb, were "not fit to care" for their own children, hinged on the mother's performance of refined femininity, the location and aesthetic conditions of her home, and her willingness to follow institutional mandates regarding her children's care. Often unsure of who was deserving of their sympathy and assistance, benevolent leaders demonstrated in their dealings with abandoned mothers their own social ambivalence and assimilationist anxieties.

A "Chained Woman": The Plight of the *Agunah*

In observant Jewish communities, the plight of the abandoned woman, or *agunah*—literally "chained woman"—has challenged scholars, religious leaders, and activists for centuries. Historically, *agunot* have struggled to sustain their religious devotion, to navigate the challenges of diasporic identity, and to maintain their cultural and religious authenticity in the face of the larger world's assimilationist demands. According to traditional Jewish law, or *halakhah*, a married woman may not remarry unless she obtains a *get*—a rabbinically mediated and approved divorce—from her husband. Only a husband can grant his wife a *get*, so a woman whose husband disappears is left with a difficult choice.[6] If she remarries civilly without a *get*, Jewish law then labels her an adulteress, and children resulting from the new marriage are considered *mamzerim*, bastards. The stigma of *mamzerut* is passed down through the generations, allowing *mamzerim* to marry only other *mamzerim*. Jewish law therefore designates all descendants of *agunot* as illegitimate and morally contaminated, yet there is no similar penalty for a man who remarries without a *get*. Nor is the man who refuses to grant his wife a *get* subject to similar stigmatization.[7]

The laws governing deserted women ironically punish them for their religious devotion, while deserters may walk free and unencumbered. Rabbi Shlomo Riskin, a leader of contemporary efforts to provide justice and support to *agunot*, writes that "a vindictive husband, or one who is unconcerned with the requirements of Jewish law, can not only deny his wife a religious divorce if he so chooses, but can also—once he has obtained a secular divorce—remarry before a justice of the peace, [forcing] his halakhically concerned wife to languish as an *agunah*."[8] Naomi Seidman, professor of Jewish culture, asserts that the laws pertaining to the *agunah* ensure that "men can easily disappear, leaving patriarchal law to guarantee their power," while their wives and children suffer in their absence.[9]

Unable to remarry without an official *get*, the *agunah*'s options were limited. Her predicament often descended into financial desperation, where religious observance and practical necessity appeared to be at odds, and this situation was often intensified in areas where Jewish community and infrastructure were sparse. *Agunot* living in rural spaces or in cities with small Jewish populations had fewer places to turn for support in tracking their errant spouses, and they had limited access to the Orthodox rabbis authorized to grant a *get*. Deserters often moved out of state and changed their names, sometimes remarrying other unsuspecting women. This was certainly the case in many southern towns, where the Jewish social networks through which errant men could be located were scarce. Having exhausted efforts to find her spouse, an *agunah* might have no choice but to remarry civilly, despite the stigma of *mamzerut* and the betrayal of her faith.

Although it is impossible to provide accurate data on the number of desertions that took place in a given time and place, since shame often prevented women from reporting their husbands' absence, scholars have shown that episodes of desertion rose substantially during times of political turmoil, economic hardship, and mass migration.[10] Certainly, such was the case with the immigration of more than two million eastern European Jews to the United States from the 1880s to the 1920s.[11] So significant were concerns about desertion that some European rabbis pressured couples to divorce before one member migrated ahead of the other. So went the logic: a man who left his family behind in the old country could not help but be tempted by the freedom and opportunities of the new.[12]

Nationwide, the stakes in combatting Jewish desertion were high. Desertion signified Jewish men's refusal to observe prevailing gender ideals, where men were to serve as breadwinners so that their wives might remain home as keepers of the hearth. Abandoned wives and children also burdened the public purse, their public dependency undermining the reputation of Jews as responsible citizens who took care of their own.[13] Since it endangered the survival and acculturation of immigrant Jewish families in the New World, desertion soon became a "predominant cause of distress," in the words of one leader, a threat to communal Jewish acceptance and cultural continuity.[14] Some social reformers even noted that desertion appeared to be more prevalent among Jews than other immigrant groups, so acculturated Jewish citizens therefore took the lead in founding a network of institutions designed to track down errant husbands and compel them to support their families.[15]

Before the creation of formal anti-desertion institutions, *agunot* found innovative ways to survive and to request help in locating their missing spouses. Women living in large northern cities often took out ads in widely circulating Yiddish newspapers, such as the *Forverts* and the *Yiddishes Tageblatt*. Among the most prominent Americanizing instruments for Jewish immigrants, Yiddish newspapers offered an opportunity for *agunot* to describe their circumstances to a broad

Jewish public and to urge errant spouses to return, to send financial support, or to file for a *get*. Further, the papers' publication in Yiddish helped conceal a communal indignity from wider public scrutiny, ensuring that Jewish manhood did not become associated with abandonment in the non-Jewish public eye. Lee K. Frankel, chair of the National Conference of Jewish Charities' Committee on Desertion, judged the Jewish press to be remarkably effective in bringing deserters to justice. "No other class of people is so fortunately circumstanced as we" to have a widely circulating press, he noted. While such newspapers "reach[ed] a class of readers who would be most apt to come into contact with deserters," their primarily northern and urban circulation made them less useful to southern *agunot*.[16] Some used the Yiddish press if they suspected that their husbands had absconded to northern urban centers, but the papers' relatively smaller circulation in the South limited their efficacy for *agunot* whose husbands fled to other southern or western towns.

In response to what appeared to be a growing need for anti-desertion reform, Jewish leaders created a department on desertion within New York's United Hebrew Charities in 1902. By 1904, the department had received more than one thousand applications for relief from *agunot* all over the country.[17] To manage the growing number of appeals from abandoned women, reformers established the National Desertion Bureau—a name that avoided naming Jews as its beneficiaries—in 1911 in New York City.[18] While the Bureau did not provide financial assistance for *agunot* or their children, it mobilized national networks of Jewish social institutions and the Yiddish press to track down errant husbands and used the full extent of civil law to compel them to support their families. By restoring the families' male breadwinners, anti-desertion reformers hoped to rebuild nuclear families headed by men, making them respectable according to the nation's dominant, middle-class standards. However, while the Bureau's central goal was to reunite families, evidence from letters to the Yiddish papers and institutional case files suggests that, for most estranged couples, reconciliation was neither desirable nor possible.

Despite its persistent efforts to locate deserters and bring them to justice, the National Desertion Bureau experienced little success in permanently reuniting families or obtaining financial support for abandoned women and children.[19] A case jointly managed by the Atlanta orphan home and the Montefiore Relief Association offers the story of Brukhe Finegold, whose husband the NDB helped locate in Texas three years after he abandoned her and their two children in Atlanta.[20] Since Mr. Finegold had remarried and had a child, Mrs. Finegold was able to prosecute him for bigamy under civil law, at which point he had no choice but to provide her a civil divorce. However, Mrs. Finegold's wish for a *get* would not be realized, as the rabbi in Dallas insisted on a $100 payment to conduct the necessary ritual. Given that her MRA case file continued off and on throughout the 1940s, it is likely that Mrs. Finegold remained single—possibly inhibited by her religious principles from remarrying—and she was never successful in gaining economic support from her estranged husband.[21]

Southern *agunot*, like Mrs. Finegold, generally had fewer resources, particularly fewer Orthodox rabbis, from whom they could procure *gitten*. One of these was Rabbi Tobias Geffen, born in Kovno in 1870, who immigrated to the United States in 1903 and made it his mission to address the "delicate problem" of wife abandonment.[22] After arriving in Atlanta in 1910 to lead the congregation of Shearith Israel, Rabbi Geffen worked tirelessly to help southern *agunot* procure *gitten* from delinquent spouses.[23] According to his autobiography, he arrived when "the presence of orthodox Rabbis was almost non-existent since six or seven southern states had none at all."[24] For many years he was one of very few Southern rabbis authorized to provide an Orthodox *get*, and he also invested untold hours and boundless ingenuity helping *agunot* locate their errant spouses.[25] In Atlanta, he befriended the county sheriff, whose presence was of significant help in convincing recalcitrant husbands to sign *gitten*, and he relied on his own tenacious investigatory efforts to locate deserters.[26] In one case, a rabbi in Missouri enlisted Geffen's help locating a deserter who had reputedly fled to Atlanta. Armed with only a small photograph of the man, the rabbi went to work asking members of the community if they recognized his face. Eventually, someone identified the man and disclosed his place of business. Rabbi Geffen and the sheriff approached the man at work and convinced him to sign the *get* or else face immediate arrest.[27] For Geffen, such work was vital to ensuring the survival and religious endurance of Orthodox women and children who otherwise faced the grim choice of starvation or the violation of their religious values. However, despite the rabbi's persistent efforts to secure justice for abandoned women, locating deserters remained difficult and costly, leaving many *agunot* and their children with few options for survival.

Unable to free themselves from their broken marriages or to find adequately remunerative work, many *agunot* appealed to benevolent institutions for aid. Most Jewish orphanages in 1900 admitted "half-orphans," the children of indigent widows or widowers, and the New Orleans home demonstrated an especially liberal admission policy. Yet the Atlanta home initially carried strict stipulations against admitting children with two living and married parents. For example, one deserted mother encountered a stern denial after seeking to admit her children to the home in 1896. The home's leaders found her case compelling, but they decided that, "both parents being alive, we could not violate our rule, to admit same, unless she would get a divorce."[28]

Early twentieth-century discussions of home policy reflect benevolent leaders' judgment that desertion provided indolent men a way to unload family responsibilities onto the shoulders of other men. Noting "the increased immigration of our co-religionists," the Atlanta home's Committee on Indenture and Discharge "recommended that the laws relative to the admission of children be made more stringent," and they urged the state to reclassify desertion as a felony rather than a misdemeanor. They feared that "applications for admission where both parents are living" reflected fathers' tendency to "leave [their] wife and children for the very purpose of placing the children in the Orphans' Home."[29] Imbedded in the home's logic was the suspicion that the new wave of immigrant coreligionists included many freeloaders who were prone to acts of extreme dishonesty in their efforts to obtain a handout. Deserting men not only committed the serious crime of leaving their families without support; they also threatened the Jewish benevolent infrastructure by contributing to its already excessive financial burden. The committee concluded with the suggestion that "there should be a positive law not to admit children where both parents are living."[30]

By the 1910s, the Atlanta home had adopted a more flexible response to desertion, gradually supplanting earlier policies that reflected the belief that desertion was a problem for family service organizations rather than for orphan homes. The relative flexibility of the Jewish orphan homes stood in stark contrast to the prevailing logic among non-Jewish agencies, which reflected social Darwinist beliefs in poverty-as-pathology and held that supporting an errant husband's wife and children only contributed to his recalcitrance. By comparison, Jewish agencies nationwide were more sympathetic to the plight of the *agunah*.[31] From 1900 to 1911, approximately 15 percent of the annual budget of Jewish charities was allocated to victims of desertion.[32] Further, despite what appeared to be a strict policy not to support children with two living and married parents, from the Atlanta orphan home's founding in 1889 until 1920, approximately 13 percent of its inmates were children of *agunot*. The 1913 annual report of the New Orleans orphan home similarly referred to rising numbers of desertions and the resulting strain on the institution's budget. New Orleans leaders gestured to the institution's "larger average population" of 166 inmates and "heavier demands made upon us from actual widows and from women with small children deserted by their husbands, all of which has effected a serious inroad upon our funds."[33] While punitive logic about a woman's fault for her husband's desertion surfaced in debates among Jewish benevolent leaders, most agreed that the welfare of abandoned Jewish wives and children could not be left to chance.

Witnessing the pernicious effects of desertion on Jewish families, Superintendent Sonn supported the criminal prosecution of deserters, and he urged the home to aid abandoned women and children: "I have advocated the subsidizing of the widowed, and even more so the abandoned, mother, in order to keep the family intact. While the suggestion was adopted in principle, it failed of execution."[34] Referring in 1905 to what was then the fairly novel practice of providing monthly subsidies to needy mothers, a practice gradually gaining legitimacy as institutional care came under increasing disapproval, Sonn noted the importance of keeping Jewish children with their mothers wherever possible. In this regard, the Atlanta home was among the vanguard in supporting mothers and their children, as most institutions began subsidy programs only after the 1909 White House Conference on the Care of Dependent Children. Mothers' subsidies—or pensions as they were called in the state adaptations that emerged in the 1910s—were designed to offer temporary support to families lacking a male breadwinner. Most southern states—including those in the Atlanta home's five-state region—were significantly slower to adopt mothers' pensions than in the West and North.[35] And while state funding was eventually made available to Jewish orphan homes in the North, the institutions of the South would rely primarily on private funding.[36] Yet the home's leaders did not find all needy mothers to be capable of raising proper Jewish citizens, and it was on this point that the home's early efforts to subsidize *agunot* may have "failed of execution."

"Not Fit to Care": The Politics of Maternal Worthiness

Margaret Goldfarb's detailed case file illuminates the ways in which gendered notions of "worthiness" figured into a southern benevolent institution's strategies for supporting an abandoned mother and her children. The Atlanta home required *agunot* to demonstrate their active pursuit of a *get* or a civil divorce before granting aid, for leaders believed that supporting the children of a married woman would enable her husband's indolence. Women who held out hope for reconciliation with their husbands or who did not actively pursue a divorce were often directed to other charities that addressed family welfare issues rather than children's needs. Goldfarb's initial failure to secure a divorce concerned the institution's leaders, as did her other transgressions of maternal merit. For instance, Goldfarb initially requested that her children be sent to the institution, so that she could continue to work in a retail store, rather than supervise the children at home while receiving a monthly subsidy. This request for her children's institutionalization ran counter to the home's definition of a good mother as one who resisted parting with her children at all costs.

Other cases of subsidized mothers reflect the home's belief that good mothers must remain at home as long as their children were too young to attend school. Reflecting the region's gendered logic of space, where respectable white women served as caregivers within the reputedly safe confines of the private home, institutional leaders expected most subsidized women to remain home and even withheld subsidies from mothers who pursued outside employment. These concerns over women's proper place were in tension with hopes that *agunot* might eventually become self-sufficient. In 1920, the vice president of the Norfolk, Virginia, Ladies Hebrew Benevolent Society, wrote to Superintendent Sonn to request a mother's subsidy for Evelyn Froug, a deserted mother of two. She asked that Mrs. Froug, "a young woman only 27 years of age," be allowed to continue working while the institution subsidized her child-care expenses. "We understand that if you subsidize the children the mother is not allowed to leave them to work, am I correct[?]" she asked, continuing, "Now Mrs. Froug is willing to work but by doing so would have to put her three year old child in a day nursery."[37] The members of the Benevolent Society believed that, "to subsidize her entirely, that is to make her entirely dependent on your aid and care, would only be the means of pauperizing her."[38] Since Froug's twelve-dollar weekly salary was "not enough to care for the two children," the Benevolent Society asked Sonn if the home could provide half of a thirty-five-dollar monthly subsidy, which would allow Froug to support her children while continuing to work. The members of the Society wished to prevent an abandoned mother "from being that most pitiful of all objects, an object of charity."[39] Sonn's response confirmed the home's policy of "requir[ing] subsidized mothers to accept only such work as would not take them away from their children."[40] However, given the Benevolent Society's provision of half the family's monthly subsidy, Sonn agreed to defer to their judgment when it came to Mrs. Froug's employment.

The Atlanta home's disapproval of mothers' employment represented a departure from the National Desertion Bureau's general policy of encouraging *agunot* to secure paid work outside their homes even if such work took them away from their children. While the Atlanta home's leadership saw such employment as a threat to children's development, workers at the Bureau encouraged *agunot* to become self-sufficient.[41] The divergent attitude toward mothers' employment suggests a regional difference in the spatial politics of gender respectability. Northern social reformers were more likely driven by a pragmatic concern for economic self-sufficiency while those in the South looked with suspicion upon a mother who would leave her children behind to pursue paid work.

Exceptions might be made when a mother's paid employment and savings were considered valuable enough to raise her family out of poverty, as in one Atlanta case in 1920, when a widow's earning potential as a salesperson gained her the home's enthusiastic support to open her own business. In this case, the home supported Fanny Ostrowsky's decision to leave her young sons in the care of a "colored maid" so that she might pursue her potentially lucrative business interests.[42] However, in contrast to Fanny Ostrowsky, whom the home's social worker considered "an attractive young woman" with an "attractively furnished" home, Margaret Goldfarb's demeanor and life circumstances initially caused the institution and its affiliates to question her capacity to raise her children in a way they considered acceptable.[43]

In contrast to prevailing sympathies for the "worthy widow," abandoned women nationwide were subject to public suspicion and scrutiny, which often suggested that they somehow deserved their plight. Some popular representations held that deserted women had failed to adapt to American ideals for wives and mothers or, on the other extreme, that they had overindulged in material consumption.[44] A 1901 open letter "To Mothers in Israel" in the English section of the *Yiddishes Tageblatt (Jewish Daily News)*, a newspaper pitched to more religiously observant Jews, suggested that some wives drove their husbands to desertion. Characterizing desertion as a more menacing social threat than alcoholism, author Eva Stern urged women to look to themselves for the reasons behind desertion. She asked, "Does it ever occur to the ... mothers of families that they are not in the family alone for the children, but for the husband, too?" She described a hypothetical woman who "met her husband with frowsy hair, the same discolored dress on as when he left, and that peculiar, worn out expression on the face that shiftless, untidy women always have."[45] In their letters to "A Bintel Brief," a Yiddish advice column published in the socialist *der Forverts (Jewish Daily Forward)*, and in discussions with social workers, deserting men often cited economic desperation, namely, the impossibility of satisfying their wives' desire to acquire the material trappings of middle-class social standing, as their reason for leaving.[46] Such critical portrayals of Jewish womanhood evinced anxiety about their roles as conduits of culture and religious authenticity to future generations of American Jews. A woman who failed to acculturate could hardly raise successful Jewish American citizens, nor could a woman who sacrificed her religious devotion for the seductive appeal of American consumer culture. The *agunah* posed an especially perplexing problem for the Jewish community: To what extent was her predicament a result of her own shortcomings, and how worthy was she of institutional support?

Abandoned women thus occupied a morally liminal position on the scale of worthiness, far below that of the blameless widow and the innocent orphan.⁴⁷

The dilemma of desertion was further complicated by eastern European gender customs, which did not always translate seamlessly to white, middle-class U.S. culture, where respectable, married women were "guardians of home and family" rather than valued wage earners.⁴⁸ Historian Susan Glenn highlights the "breadwinning partnerships" that prevailed among Jewish couples in the late nineteenth- and early twentieth-century *shtetl*, where wives' paid work enabled their husbands to study the Talmud.⁴⁹ Further, wartime upheaval throughout the Russian empire intensified the conditions under which women learned, in historian Elizabeth Reis's words, to "tailor (often literally) their skills to the marketplace" as a means of survival.⁵⁰ And while eastern European Jews traditionally celebrated men's intellectual pursuits, such unpaid activity in the United States was considered unproductive and unmanly.⁵¹ Men who repudiated their breadwinning responsibilities publicly rejected a vital principle of U.S. citizenship and violated unwritten codes of American production and consumption. While women's paid labor had comprised an essential part of family survival in eastern Europe, American gender, race, and class ideals confined the labor of white wives and mothers to the home.

Race politics in the Jim Crow South influenced a more strictly gendered logic of work dictating that respectable, white, middle-class women served as private homemakers, mothers, and consumers. The prevailing folklore of the "black beast" rapist reinforced the expectation that respectable white women remain in private spaces under male protection.⁵² Many, Jews and non-Jews alike, perceived the South as a place of potential sexual danger and racial contagion for white women. The South's predominantly agricultural economy and racialized distribution of labor also contributed to Jewish anxieties over desertion, not just as a transgression against the Jewish family, but also as a uniquely troubling crime against the region's gender ideals. Jewish men's failure to sustain their breadwinning responsibilities disrupted Jewish claims to white masculine privilege just as it brought into question the right of Jewish women to a space on the southern lady's protective pedestal. In this time and space, Jewish claims to white masculinity and white femininity could be fragile, and Jewish men's public transgressions against "respectable" breadwinning ideals threatened the hard-won legitimacy for which Jews had struggled for centuries. Not only did southern desertion stain the otherwise admirable record of Jewish citizenship and independence, it undermined Jewish men's adherence to the strictures of chivalry. By forcing their wives into the public workforce, to the detriment of their motherly duties, and by threatening their children's chances for success, deserting men jeopardized Jewish cultural authenticity and endurance. Perhaps more gravely, southern *agunot* and their children became vulnerable to the prevailing white supremacist discourse that framed the distinctive dangers of the South.

Southern characterizations of abandoned women reflected the popular iconography of *agunot* as slovenly, ignorant, and inept mothers—as women not to be trusted to raise children—often with more explicit references to their parenting defects and transgressions of racial boundaries. A 1920 case of periodic desertion in Fitzgerald, Georgia, a town approximately two hundred miles south of Atlanta with a small immigrant Jewish population and no synagogue, reveals how regional gender, race, and class assumptions influenced efforts to address desertion. Identifying himself as a leading citizen of the Jewish community, Dr. Harold Miller described both parents to Superintendent Sonn as "worthless" people "who live in the lowest nigger house."[53] His description of the family's home referred to their location in a predominantly black neighborhood as well as what he perceived to be the home's generally degraded appearance.[54] According to Miller, this was not a neighborhood suitable for raising proper Jewish citizens. He was especially outraged by what he described as the "half-witted" mother's habit of taking "the little girls along with her on her begging expeditions among black and white."[55] In Miller's opinion, the mother's public transgression of the color line threatened her young children's well-being, as did her shameful begging forays into public space. His dismay that such "expeditions" took place "among black and white" suggests the fragility of Jewish race identity as that which balanced precariously on the color line. Like other recently arrived immigrants, Jews might compromise their white legibility through their association with nonwhites.[56] Further, reasoned Miller, the girls' proximity to African Americans might train them to see themselves not as part of the racial elite, but rather as members of the racially debased masses. Perhaps more deplorable still, white gentiles who witnessed the Jewish mother's begging forays might question Jewish membership in the racial elite.

Similar cases involving *agunot* who were considered unfit mothers suggest that the home required such children to be admitted as institutional residents, where they could be supervised and educated far away from their parents' deleterious influence. This tendency impeded the home's gradual shift to mother's subsidies, a funding technique that ensured a child's continued residence with his or her mother. Institutional mothers' subsidies reflected larger national trends—like the mothers' pensions that began emerging in individual states in 1911—that increasingly valorized a mother's care in a private home over that of orphan institutions. Mothers' subsidies emerged out of growing beliefs that poor mothers lacking male providers required financial assistance as well as careful supervision in their efforts to raise the proper kinds of American citizens.[57] Since the home's founding in 1889, its leaders and administrators followed mainstream assumptions that the best place for children was with their own mothers, who were best equipped to transmit idealized American values to their children. In his 1904 annual report, Superintendent Sonn argued that "the institution is indisputably the best refuge for the parentless, probably also for the motherless. Not so for the fatherless. The children of the widow ought to stay with the mother, and the mother subsidized."[58] Five years later, having witnessed the success of mothers' subsidies, the board issued the recommendation that "whenever a mother, through subsidy, can be enabled to keep intact the family, the children of which would otherwise be admitted to the home, that said subsidy be granted."[59] Having attended the 1909 White House Conference on Dependent Children, President Simon Wolf urged the continued use of subsidies to cover the needs of impoverished children and their mothers.[60]

The Atlanta home's energetic efforts to subsidize mothers represented a radical departure from the New Orleans home's continued valorization of institutionalization. As illustrated in chapter 3, the New Orleans home's leadership believed that the institution was far and away the optimal space in which to raise the children of impoverished coreligionists. Confident in their institution's capacity to care for its district's poor or neglected children, New Orleans home administrators resisted the nation's trends toward mothers' pensions. This difference in policy reflected the institution's concern that poor mothers could not provide their children with the education and cultural capital necessary to transform them into exemplary citizens.

Crafted in the context of an intensifying eugenic faith in selective breeding and state intervention into the most intimate aspects of citizens' lives, maternal subsidies also hinged on racialized notions of citizenship in which white motherhood stood uniquely entitled to the state's financial support. Similarly, the widow and family subsidies offered through Atlanta's Jewish agencies derived their legitimacy from prevailing understandings of entitlement, whereby poor immigrant mothers were judged against high standards of middle-class respectability and careful adherence to the racial norms of their region. As benevolent Jewish leaders sought to assimilate underprivileged and unacculturated coreligionists, the economic and social improvement of immigrant Jewish motherhood was more a cultural imperative than the "cultural project" imagined by maternalist leaders of the U.S. Children's Bureau.[61] Home board members and social workers alike often held lofty expectations for Jewish motherhood that obstructed their view of the structural and cultural limitations of benevolent uplift. While the home's leadership overwhelmingly supported mothers' pensions and subsidies, they often set unattainably high standards for poor mothers' comportment.

For mothers judged incompetent, institutional subsidies were not a viable option. Although the Atlanta home initially suggested a monthly subsidy to keep the Goldfarb family intact, members of the Macon community insisted that the children be admitted into institutional custody. Morris Harris, an agent for the American Central Insurance Company and an institutional affiliate, promptly explained to Superintendent Sonn that "it would be a serious mistake to adopt the subsidy plan with these children."[62] Having familiarized himself with the case and investigated the family, Harris urged, "We Macon people realize that the sooner the children are placed in charge of the Home just so much better will be their condition."[63] Even Goldfarb's brother, Jonathan Stearn, insisted that his sister was "not fit to care for [her children]."[64]

The factors that made Goldfarb's homemaking skills and mothering style inimical to her children's successful upbringing are not explicitly detailed in the case file, and correspondence from neighbors and relatives contains coded and evasive language likely intended to shield the family's potentially disgraceful circumstances. Voicing their concerns about the children's education and religious training, Jewish members of the Macon community expressed particular skepticism of Goldfarb's ability to raise respectable young ladies. Stearn was likewise concerned that his nieces "would positively not have the proper environment that they should have and more especially being girls."[65] He believed the girls would suffer in sinister ways that would not similarly affect the boys, and he did not feel comfortable disclosing full details in the letter but preferred to do so face-to-face: "If I could see you in person I could be more explicit which I hope to see you anyhow in about 20 days." Obliquely referring to his familial insider knowledge of his sister's inadequacies, Stearn asserted, "[Mr. Harris] cannot be as explicit as I would like to if I was to see you in person."[66] While we do not have specific details of what Stearn and Harris believed were Goldfarb's parenting defects, the language in Stearn's letters suggests that something more distressing than neglect and poverty was at stake. If a grudge against his sister influenced Stearn's judgment, he and Harris both advocated for the end result that Goldfarb herself wanted: her children's immediate institutionalization. In response to these appeals, the home agreed to accept the three youngest children—two girls, ages eleven and eight, and their five-year-old brother.[67]

Less than one year later, for reasons that are not provided in the family's case file, the home's governing body voted to discharge the children back to their mother, a decision which elicited an ardent response from Macon. It is possible that several factors came into play: Mrs. Goldfarb's failure to obtain a divorce; the institution's strained budget; and the trend away from institutionalized care in favor of subsidies and foster care. However, members of the Macon community, including Goldfarb's brother, insisted that the children would fare much better under the institution's watchful gaze. Writing on behalf of other concerned members of the community, Morris Harris wrote that "to send these children back here in charge of their mother would be a very grievous mistake . . . The mother don't get along with her only brother here and lives alone."[68] Jonathan Stearn also wrote several weeks later, "I tell you emphatically that it would be cruel for you to return the children to her for she is not fit to care for them."⁶⁹ Her neighbors and family felt that Goldfarb's inadequate mothering represented a threat both to her children's general well-being and to their chances for success as upstanding Jewish citizens. Their passionate letters highlighted the importance to the children's development of a "proper environment," which they believed Goldfarb could not provide in her current circumstances.⁷⁰ Of particular concern to Stearn were his nieces, whom he believed would suffer their mother's inadequacy in especially insidious ways. These letters urging the home to retain guardianship of the Goldfarb girls had the desired effect, for the institution's leaders eventually consented to keep them until their mother obtained a divorce and remarried.

Three years later, having moved to Jacksonville, Florida, and established what she felt was a financially stable life for herself and her seventeen-year-old son, Goldfarb requested her children's return. Since her older daughter, Bessie, was sixteen and preparing to graduate from high school with training as a stenographer, Goldfarb believed that she could help contribute to the family's support. However, she discovered that financial stability alone was inadequate proof of her worthiness as a mother. She enlisted Hyman S. Jacobs, a home affiliate in Jacksonville, to write on her behalf and request the return of all three children, but Jacobs expressed skepticism about Goldfarb's capacity to supervise them. He explained to Superintendent Sonn, "The only reason the mother wants the other two children to come with Bessie is that she is afraid that the others will be lonesome when the older sister will be away from them. Mrs. Goldfarb practically admits that she will be in no position to take care of the children as she is employed as a saleslady."⁷¹ Goldfarb's affection and concern for her children's happiness were inadequate validation of her merit as a responsible caregiver.

Jacobs was primarily concerned about the fate of Goldfarb's younger daughter—rather than her even younger son—and he advised Sonn to keep both younger children at the home. He explained, "I understand that the girl is about 12 years old, and there certainly should be someone in authority to look after her during the day, and not be allowed to play around in the streets without any supervision." Jacobs confided to Sonn, "Personally, I believe it will do the children more harm than good to [live here] without the proper supervision of an older person during the daytime."⁷² Sonn agreed that the younger children should remain in the home and alluded to more sensitive issues at stake in his reasoning. He wrote, "The reserve which I am maintaining must be mysterious to you. I'll be glad to clear up the situation when I see you."[73] While these letters did not provide specific details about Mrs. Goldfarb's inadequacies, their concerns about the twelve-year-old daughter's supervision remained central to their decision not to allow the two younger children to return to their mother. We cannot know for certain the conditions of Goldfarb's home life that gave Jacobs pause, but his references to "play[ing] around in the streets" and a lack of adult supervision suggest his concern for girls' purity in spaces of potential social contamination. In Jacobs's opinion, Goldfarb was not capable of providing the maternal supervision necessary to ensure her daughter's protection from potentially destructive influences.

Southern Jewish benevolent networks placed significant emphasis on the protection and supervision of young women and girls. While all orphanages—Jewish and non-Jewish alike—paid close attention to the upbringing of "respectable" young ladies (for example, by providing training in domestic arts and carefully supervising their social activities), in the South this emphasis on respectable womanhood was especially significant. Expectations for young white women to remain well supervised, even in their own homes, derived urgency from fictive characterizations of rapacious black men who prowled the streets in search of white women. Daughters of "unworthy" *agunot* were thought to be in desperate need of rescue. Allowing them to "play around in the streets" or to burden the public purse not only created a stain on the Jewish reputation for caring for "their own," but also represented an unpardonable violation of southern chivalry. According to the home's affiliates and internal leadership, the fate of Goldfarb's children, especially her daughters, could not be left to chance in a region that prized feminine respectability and vigilantly policed the upbringing of girls.

Bessie Goldfarb graduated the following fall and was released to her mother, but only with the authorization of Goldfarb's brother. Stearn remained hesitant to offer his endorsement, explaining that his sister "has been after me for the last six weeks to write to you in reference to letting Bessie go and live with her . . . [and] I have held off as long as I could trying to put it off as long as possible." Although his was not a ringing endorsement, he confirmed that "some life there will be alright for Bessie."⁷⁴ This tepid vote of confidence satisfied the home, and Bessie was sent to Jacksonville in late November.

The younger two Goldfarb children remained in the home's care until the summer of 1921, when their mother remarried and successfully petitioned for the children's release. The home sent two affiliates to "investigate the conditions of the . . . family, and advise us, whether in your judgment it were proper to relinquish our charges to them."⁷⁵ The affiliates reported that, although her new husband was not Jewish, "he [promised] he would treat the children well and would allow [his wife] to raise the children as Jews." Further, he was "earning a good salary" and their "house is nicely furnished and in a good neighborhood." Perhaps more crucially, the affiliates described Goldfarb as "a woman of culture" who could provide a proper home for her children.⁷⁶

Since her desertion more than six years prior, Margaret Goldfarb had struggled to earn a living and to regain custody of her children, but her status as a worthy mother remained under suspicion until she married a successful breadwinner. More important to the home than her new husband's faith, or Goldfarb's success in obtaining a Jewish divorce, was her husband's ability to provide for his family so that she could remain home with the children. In the institution's reckoning, she was finally in a position to raise proper, well-supervised children protected in a "nicely furnished" home.

The Atlanta home also demonstrated concern and suspicion over abandoned mothers' capacity to manage unruly children. *Agunot* who had experienced physical abuse at the hands of their spouses were likely to receive the institution's sympathy and aid, although their capacity to manage their children might come into question. A 1912 letter from Minnie Rosenberg of the Norfolk Ladies Hebrew Benevolent Association urged Superintendent Sonn to consider the admission of the Kaufman boys, ages ten and twelve, whose father was "a fugitive from justice, and a brute of a man."⁷⁷ Rosenberg described how "he was duly arrested for beating wife and children which had been a constant habit of his, until the 'Society for the Prevention of Cruelty to Children' interceded."⁷⁸ Key to the Benevolent Society's, and later, the Council of Jewish Women's appeal, was a concern that the children's placement in the SPCC was only a temporary "emergency" solution that "would reflect very discreditably upon the Jewish community" should the children remain there.⁷⁹ Rosenberg emphasized the importance of placing the boys "in a Jewish home" as soon as possible so that their dependency would not continue to burden the gentile community.

In response to Sonn's suggestion that Mrs. Kaufman receive a subsidy to support her children at home, the concerned community members insisted that she was incapable of controlling her children, as she "had all the spirit crushed out of her" after years of abuse. Further, explained Rosenberg, "the children have seen this condition, hold the mother in absolute disrespect, their home environment having been so crude, the stronger oppressing the weak, that the dominant spirit of following the sterner sex and ignoring the weaker is the idea these children have imbibed from home conditions."⁸⁰ Having witnessed their father's abusive behavior toward their mother, the Kaufman boys appeared to be in need of the institution's intervention to help transform them into upstanding young men. The records suggest that Sonn was moved to admit one of the children, who graduated from grammar school in May 1917.⁸¹ It is unclear in the home's records what became of the other boy.

"Morally and Physically" Fit: Subsidizing the "Worthwhile" *Agunah*

In contrast to Mrs. Kaufman and Mrs. Goldfarb, whose perceived inability to care for their children disqualified them from receiving mother's subsidies, other cases reveal the institution's standards for judging an *agunah* capable of raising their own children properly. Most "worthy" *agunot* demonstrated a desire to keep their children with them at all costs, even if it meant forgoing paid employment that might offer a modicum of self-sufficiency. Mothers, like Margaret Goldfarb, who worked while their children stayed at home unsupervised, were often judged to be selfish, placing their children's needs beneath their own.

Libby Spiegel, an abandoned mother of three, received the home's sympathy when she wrote to Ralph Sonn in January 1917 to obtain a mother's subsidy. Spiegel represented herself as a woman of integrity whose primary concern was her children, and she described in detail her husband's abusiveness, alcoholism, and tendency to "lead a fast and disaffected life."⁸² Her moving depiction of her husband's physical abuse, drunkenness, and "fast" lifestyle echoed many Jewish reformers' characterizations of recalcitrant men and strengthened the legitimacy of her request for aid. Further, knowledge of her husband's abuse and immorality may have deterred the institution from urging that she reconcile with her husband as an alternative to receiving an institutional subsidy. Spiegel's poignant self-portrayal as a mother "do[ing] all in [her] power to keep [her children] together" struck a sympathetic chord, as did her desire "to give them a fair education when they get older."[83] The home granted her a six-month subsidy of fifteen dollars per week, which allowed her children to remain with her.[84]

The home's priorities in aiding worthy *agunot* are also illuminated in a Petersburg, Virginia, case where Naomi Lowenstein applied for two daughters' admission to the home in June 1924. Later correspondence reveals the home's effort to keep children with their mother as long as she was judged "morally and physically" capable of raising them. The case opened several months after Lowenstein's husband deserted the family, which included seven daughters whose ages ranged from infancy to thirteen years old. After failed efforts to locate Mr. Lowenstein, the home agreed to support the family. The means of support—whether through monthly subsidy, institutionalization, or foster care—were yet to be determined.

A letter from Mary Hardy of the Family Service League of Petersburg demonstrates how non-Jewish organizations also became involved in efforts to support Lowenstein. Hardy wrote to Superintendent Feist Strauss, "For nearly a year the Jewish People of this city have been supporting the Lowenstein family. The man deserted and although every effort has been made to locate him no one knows where he is at present." Hardy implored the home to accept the Lowenstein children into custody: "The Jewish people here have done everything in their power for this family but they feel that they cannot keep this up indefinitely. If you could arrange to take three of the little girls I think that Mrs. Lowenstein would be able to get along on the help she now receives."[85] Strauss's immediate response to Hardy suggests that he took gentile social workers' concerns seriously, particularly when it came to the welfare of poor Jewish women and children living at a remote distance from Atlanta in towns with a sparse Jewish population. Needy Jewish families required careful professional supervision, which necessitated the institution's cultivation of friendly relations with non-Jewish social workers. Evidence in the case files reveals that the home often relied on gentile social workers' professional expertise to determine which mothers were worthy of subsidies and which children would be better served by institutionalization or placement with foster parents.[86]

Strauss explained to Hardy the home's efforts to avoid "breaking up families" by "helping families to keep their children in their own homes."[87] While he might consider a gentile social worker's opinion of the family's general level of need, Strauss required a trusted Jewish affiliate to investigate the children's home life, their behavior and moral fitness, and more important, to determine whether Lowenstein was "a worthwhile mother, morally and physically, [and able] to handle her children."[88] In early November, Strauss wrote to Mrs. V. H. Nussbaum, wife of Justice Nussbaum of Norfolk, Virginia, to enlist her help in determining whether the children should be institutionalized or subsidized. Strauss wrote to Nussbaum, "There seems to be no good reason why the mother should not keep her children and care for them, if we supply part of the means and permit the Jewish people of Petersburg to supply the rest."[89]

Strauss also inquired whether "anyone of the children [is] unfit to mingle with other children well trained and morally fit, in our house, or is there a risk of tainting our present set of children morally by contact with the Lowenstein children (This is asked because of vague stories of misconduct which have reached us)."[90] The case file contains no further reference to the allegations of misconduct or their origin. Even if institutionalization was the best option for the Lowensteins, Strauss prioritized the protection of the home's current inmates from the pernicious influence of children whose "moral fitness" was in question. Just as children with contagious diseases, such as diphtheria and tuberculosis, were denied entry into the home so that they would not threaten the health of the other children, delinquency and "misconduct," especially in girls, was seen as a social contagion that would infect the other children under the home's care. While Strauss did not elaborate on the specific kinds of misconduct he meant, other case files suggest that the home was deeply suspicious of girls who exhibited signs of "sophistication," such as smoking, wearing makeup, or engaging in unsupervised socializing with boys. Before considering the Lowenstein children for admission, Strauss had to ensure that their presence would not undermine the institution's efforts to inculcate its young charges with values of respectability and good citizenship.

Nussbaum responded that Lowenstein "is thoroughly fit and capable of raising [her daughters] morally and physically but not financially."[91] The case file does not indicate how much support the Lowenstein family received or for how long, but it shows that the home did not separate the children from their mother. They judged Lowenstein a "worthwhile" mother who was capable of raising her daughters to be proper ladies. If offered financial support, Lowenstein would remain home with her children rather than venture out to work. More important, home affiliates and community members did not find a reason to question either the respectability of her neighborhood or her fitness as a mother. Although we have a limited view of how they determined a mother's worthiness, the concerns that surfaced in the Goldfarb case did not appear to be at issue here.

Some *agunot* might originally appear "worthy" of a subsidy only to lose the institution's trust and goodwill when they failed to act in what others perceived as their children's best interests. Evelyn Froug, the Norfolk mother of two who initially found ardent sympathy and support from members of the Ladies Hebrew Benevolent Society, lost the Society's goodwill when she made a desperate attempt to find her husband.[92] In 1922, having failed to secure a *get* from her wayward husband, Froug took matters into her own hands. Leaving her children in the care of her ailing mother, she went looking for her husband in Philadelphia and Baltimore. She returned home broke and empty-handed five months later, only to discover that she had fallen out of favor with the once-supportive members of the Benevolent Society. Condemned for abandoning her children and labeled "incapable of caring for them," Mrs. Froug also lost the Atlanta home's confidence in her caregiving capacities.[93] To the benevolent leaders, Froug's act of desperation evinced an unforgivable lack of consideration for her children's health and safety. Her family's monthly subsidy was discontinued and her children were promptly admitted as residents into the home, where they remained until they each graduated from high school.[94]

Southern social workers and religious and benevolent leaders approached the issue of desertion with pragmatism and creativity, sometimes bending religious and civil law as they perceived a need to preserve independent family units. In a case jointly overseen by Atlanta's Hebrew Orphans Home and the Montefiore Relief Association, a Polish immigrant experienced the sting of abandonment twice: shortly after her first marriage in 1907, and again twenty-two years later.[95] In the summer of 1929, Mrs. Frume Kellerman approached the MRA when her third husband, whom she had married in 1926, disappeared from Atlanta without a trace. Initially, Mrs. Kellerman requested the Association's help in locating her spouse, reassuring the social worker that she could manage financially. The social worker forwarded Mrs. Kellerman's description of her husband to the National Desertion Bureau and requested their assistance in locating him. In their investigation of Mr. Kellerman's insurance policy, the MRA discovered that its beneficiary was a different Mrs. Kellerman. Frume insisted to her social worker that "she was almost sure that [her husband's] former wife is now deceased" and described how his four children were being raised in a home in Russia.[96] It soon became apparent, however, that the first wife was indeed alive and had filed her own search with the National Desertion Bureau years before. In fact, the Bureau had maintained a case with the Kellerman family from 1922 through 1924 when Mr. Kellerman was trying to gather the resources to transport his family from Russia to his new home in Beaumont, Texas. A phone call to the MRA from the first Mrs. Kellerman's "horror stricken" sister confirmed that Mr. Kellerman had, indeed, abandoned his first wife in Russia, only to marry, and then abandon, another woman in Atlanta.[97]

In an unusual twist, Mr. Kellerman returned to Atlanta three months later, expressing contrition over his breach of religious and civil law and pleading for help negotiating a *get* with his first wife. According to the National Desertion Bureau, this was a simple matter of the first wife having "first claim" to Kellerman and his earnings, the second marriage being clearly "illegal." Further, warned the Bureau's chief counsel, "Mrs. Kellerman, No. 2['s] living with [Mr. Kellerman] constitutes a crime. Morally she surely has no justification for taking away a father of four children from his family."[98]

While the National Desertion Bureau threatened criminal prosecution, Atlanta's MRA sought a different solution to the problem of a man with two wives. Enlisting the help of Rabbi Geffen to negotiate a settlement with the first wife, the MRA encouraged Mr. Kellerman to provide his first wife financial remuneration in exchange for a *get*. Rabbi Geffen transmitted ten dollars to the first wife along with Kellerman's request. It is unclear whether the first Mrs. Kellerman ever responded, and, in yet another unusual twist to the conventional abandonment story, she refused to grant her husband a *get*.[99] Yet the MRA continued to support the validity of Kellerman's current family and even convinced the National Desertion Bureau to refrain from criminal prosecution despite "the legal entanglements of [Kellerman's] marital difficulties."[100] His current marriage may have transgressed religious and civil laws, wrote Federation President Ed Kahn to the National Desertion Bureau, but "breaking his [current] family relationship will not be of any aid to Mrs. Kellerman No 1."[101] It appears that the Bureau accepted this explanation and did not press charges. Despite Mr. Kellerman's bigamy and the apparent dishonesty with which he had represented himself to his wife and community, the MRA's leaders and social workers sought to preserve his marriage in the name of familial self-sufficiency during a time of extreme economic instability.

By the time the Lowenstein and Kellerman cases came to the attention of Atlanta's benevolent institutions, national standards of child welfare had shifted from nineteenth-century faith in institutions to a conviction that the private home was the optimal space for a child's socialization. The leadership of the New Orleans home steadfastly resisted this move, for they believed that poor mothers could not match the institution in providing children the necessary lessons in respectability and elevated cultural capital. They would continue to provide exemplary care and training for the children of the poor until 1946. In Atlanta, where the faith in the acculturation capacities of private homes grew alongside national trends, even the worthiest mother became subject to the institution's careful scrutiny. As they worked to ensure that *agunot* and their children did not starve or become public charges, benevolent workers and their local affiliates continued to express concern about the *agunah*'s respectability and feminine worth. Southern *agunot* were subject to particularly rigorous investigations to determine if they were the optimal caregivers for their children, and the supervision of daughters was especially critical. In Goldfarb's case, the Jewish citizens of both Macon and Jacksonville judged her to be neither a proper role model nor an able supervisor of young women until she was legally remarried and living in what they considered to be a "nice neighborhood." Goldfarb's transformation from "not fit to care" for her children to a "woman of culture" took place despite her interfaith marriage.

Although the Atlanta home originally claimed to follow a policy against supporting the children of abandoned mothers, cases like those of the Goldfarbs, Speigels, Kaufmans, Lowensteins, Frougs, and Kellermans were not unusual. While many felt that supporting a deserted woman and her children enabled an errant husband's idleness, Jewish benevolent agencies, like the orphan homes of New Orleans and Atlanta, and the Montefiore Relief Association of Atlanta, demonstrated alternative understandings of dependency. The orphan homes' commitment to serving the children of *agunot* within the southern states suggests that suspicions regarding abandoned women's inherent "unworthiness," and concerns about enabling delinquent fathers, gave way to child-protection ideals grounded in two interrelated and vital necessities: that of shrouding from the public eye the crimes of a few atypically shiftless Jewish men, and the equally pressing need to ensure that the children of poor coreligionists were brought up to be respectable citizens. Considered precariously dependent in a region where white women required the chivalrous protection of white men, *agunot* could not be left to the mercy of the gentile public purse, where the shame of their abandonment might bring into question the capacity of Jews to take care of their own.

5

"None of My Own People"

Subsidizing Jewish Motherhood in the Depression-Era South

A mother will become a beggar for her children and that [is] what I am now.
—Rebecca Weiss, Atlanta home subsidized mother, 1931

In the summer of 1935, almost six years after receiving her first subsidy check from the Hebrew Orphans Home of Atlanta to help support her two young daughters, the newly wed Rebecca Weiss Blakeney sat down to pen the last of the letters that would be included in her case file. Addressing Viola Wyle, the home's director of subsidy cases, a woman with whom she had maintained a mutually affectionate correspondence since her case opened in 1929, the once-grateful client turned defensive and resentful, excoriating what she perceived as the institution's intrusion into her personal affairs. Weiss described occasions when representatives of the home and other local welfare agencies had shared her state of dependence with the larger community of Fort Pierce, Florida. Maintaining that Jews were accustomed to "helping each other" without "let[ting] everybody know" of their coreligionists' poverty, she expressed dismay that Wyle's husband, the home's superintendent, had informed various local agencies of her family's state of need. Weiss described how a gentile social worker humiliated her by questioning her in the "presence of another gentile" to the point where she felt that "almost every gentile knew [her] business."[1] In her final letters, her appreciation for the home's generosity gave way to outrage at what she perceived as the organization's unforgiveable lack of discretion.

Weiss's marriage to a wealthy gentile, who showered her and her daughters with expensive gifts such as "a beautiful home seven other properties a 1935 Graham [Page] car and half interest in his wholesale business," offered her the means to shed the crushing stigma of institutional dependency and to ascend to the ranks of the social elite.[2] Yet this immigrant mother of two would not allow her new husband to learn of her six-year dependence on the orphan home. She sent her final letters through an intermediary and begged Wyle not to try to locate her. For Weiss, being Jewish, foreign-born, and temporarily poor mattered little to her new husband, but institutional dependence signified an unforgivable stain on her past, one that endangered her newfound prosperity and happiness. According to Weiss, "What a man don't know don't hurt me," and she intended to keep her relationship with the home a secret.[3]

Although Weiss appreciated the home's enduring generosity, she expressed relief in her freedom from institutional charity: "I am just so happy that we have everything that is not given to us as a charity. I really deserve to be happy after many years of struggle and humiliation."[4] What was humiliating about her years as a subsidized mother, and why didn't she share her frustrations earlier with Wyle, the woman she characterized as "the best friend [she] ever had"?[5] Her six-year experience as a subsidized widowed mother, supported by an agency that took pride in its status as a benevolent protector of impoverished Jewish mothers and children, was fraught with contradictions and searing complexities, many of which challenged Weiss's understandings of respectable Jewish womanhood and caused her to resent the institution's intrusion into her personal affairs. Rather than maintain the friendship that emerged out of her desperate need, this former recipient of the home's aid wrote one final letter to Viola Wyle, reassuring her that "she was Jewish still."[6] Then she and her children disappeared from the home's records.

Considered in the context of her relationship with the Hebrew Orphans Home of Atlanta during the Depression, Weiss's letters and the meticulous case record compiled by Viola and Armand Wyle tell a story that helps flesh out the contours of southern Jewish uplift and the ambivalence that often accompanied the relationship between the benevolent institution and its needy clients. As demonstrated in earlier chapters, the process of supporting the poor immigrant Jewish masses was anything but straightforward and uniform, and the extension of *gemilut hasadim* to half-orphans and their mothers was especially fraught with the tensions, contradictions, and performance anxieties of Jewish charity. By the late 1920s, the institution's earlier intentions of supporting poor or abandoned mothers had given way to an emphasis on subsidizing children only, and Weiss's case provides a close look at the impact of this shift on poor mother's struggles to get by on little to no income in a failing economy. Yet Weiss's relatively generous monthly subsidy of sixty dollars, combined with Wyle's unflagging efforts to provide support to Weiss and her daughters, suggest the depth of the institution's commitment to the support of poor families considered "worthy." For it was not simply the safety and stability of Weiss's small family at stake in the home's decision to offer financial and emotional support. In the minds of the leaders who managed and negotiated the home's vision for social uplift, the legitimacy of Jewish cultural citizenship rested on their ability to prevent their poorest coreligionists from becoming a burden to the public purse and to provide them the means of becoming respectably self-sustaining.

Gemilut hasadim was part of a broader system of institutional magnanimity through which relatively privileged Jewish benefactors conveyed the lessons of exemplary citizenship to their needy coreligionists. Children of foreign-born, widowed Jewish mothers required spiritual and material support and protection from conversion, starvation, and the public stain of charity. But perhaps more important, they required education in the ways of being appropriately Jewish in the post-Reconstruction South, a process that entailed the vigilant collaboration of social workers, benevolent leaders, and community members. Most crucially, this project to impart the values of cultural citizenship demanded the cooperation of the subsidized mothers themselves. For Jewish mothers, cultural citizenship relied heavily on the accumulation of middle-class cultural capital, their fluency in the daily performance of respectability and emulation of middle-class, white ideals of production and consumption. As Weiss's story reveals, even the worthiest mothers received careful institutional scrutiny and discipline, as their strategies for their own and their children's uplift often diverged considerably from the aspirations of the benevolent institution.

"My All Existence and Future Depend on You": Reading Ambivalent Intimacies in the Case File

One month after her case opened, and just weeks after the stock market crash triggered the nation's descent into financial depression, Rebecca Weiss composed her second letter to Viola Wyle. Having discovered that she and her two young daughters, ages eight and five, would be displaced out of her in-laws' home, the widowed immigrant wrote to the one person who she believed could help her. "Dear Mrs. Wyle!" she began her letter, "Now where I will move? My all existence and future depend on you."[7] Emphasizing her grief and profound sense of isolation, she continued, "Dear Mrs. Wyle I know you won't forget me. Otherwise I will starve and nobody would know about it . . . I have no husband and no brothers to help me I just have to depend on good people for my children sake." She closed her letter with an appeal to Wyle's friendship as well as a reminder that she requested charity only reluctantly and on behalf of her children: "My girls sending you *lots* of *kisses*."[8] These letters from a foreign-born, widowed mother to a U.S.-born and educated social worker marked the beginning of an emotionally intimate friendship that complicates prevailing assumptions about the client–social worker relationships that existed in the 1920 and 1930s.

Weiss's case opened officially in September 1929, and Viola Wyle, the wife of the home's new superintendent, Armand Wyle, served as Weiss's first professional representative from the home. Appointed in January 1929 after the unexpected death of Superintendent Feist Strauss, the Wyles received "a whole-hearted Southern welcome" at the board's annual meeting.[9] Both Armand and Viola had received training in modern, "scientific" social work methodology at Jewish orphan homes in Cleveland and New York. Upon arrival, the couple insisted on working as a team. While past superintendents' wives had often been assigned as the home "matrons," Viola Wyle assumed the more professional title of "social service worker" and took command of the institution's foster care and mothers' pension procedures.

Wyle was one of a growing number of female professionals employed in the field of social welfare. Beginning in the 1920s, Atlanta's network of Jewish benevolent institutions began hiring professionally trained female workers to gather data and to supervise the composition of case files on the families they served. In 1925, the home hired Anita Bolotin as their first "after care worker," whose primary purpose was "to visit families here and throughout the district and to ascertain whether the children are being properly taken care of and the family conditions are satisfactory."[10] Bolotin worked for the home for three or four years before moving to Chicago to continue her career as a social worker.[11] Atlanta's Federation of Jewish Charities—an umbrella organization established in 1906 as part of a national effort to consolidate and streamline the many independent Jewish charitable institutions—likewise employed a caseworker to supervise its subsidized families. Rose Goldstein, a Polish immigrant who had served as secretary of Atlanta's Montefiore Relief Association for several years, was promoted to director of case work in 1933.[12]

Educated women like Bolotin, Goldstein, and Wyle forged their careers at the intersection of national transformations of social welfare work as a "scientific" discipline and women's increasing professionalization in reform work relating to mothers and children.[13] The forty-nine-year-old mother of a grown daughter, Wyle was able to devote her full attention to this demanding position. Although Wyle assumed her new responsibilities as social service worker immediately upon arrival, the 1930 Census suggests that her position may have been instituted on a trial basis. While her husband, Armand, was listed as the home superintendent, Viola was listed simply as "wife" and her occupation as "none." At that time, the home's matron was Frannie Pinsky, a thirty-eight-year-old immigrant from Poland. The 1930 Census lists nineteen institutional inmates, indicating that the majority of the home's eighty-four wards were being subsidized in their own homes or fostered with well-off local families.[14] Indeed, Viola Wyle was largely responsible for the home's efforts to phase out what many saw as the antiquated practice of institutionalizing dependent children.

It is largely through Wyle's eyes and her professionally trained sensibilities, in the form of the case records she compiled on each of her clients, that we receive the most detailed descriptions of Rebecca Weiss and her interactions with the home. Although Wyle did not always place copies of her own letters to clients in the case file, she maintained a thorough narrative, in which she described her appraisal of Weiss and her children and recorded her visits to Fort Pierce. Karen Tice's work on the professionalization of social work warns of the ways in which case files reduce a client's experiences to those "facts" considered relevant by the caseworker.[15] We must also attend to the silences in each file, which contains only those items—"scientific" case records, personal letters, receipts, ledgers, children's report cards, and so forth—that the social worker considered relevant to the client's case. While case records offer a limited distillation of a client's life into fragments of professionally relevant partial truths, the voices of the clients are nevertheless, in Gunja SenGupta's words, "muffled but not mute."[16] Fortunately, whether out of sentimental or professional instincts (or a combination of both), Wyle preserved in the case file many of the handwritten letters she received from Rebecca Weiss. And while Weiss ostensibly embraced the familial intimacy that emerged between herself and her social worker, addressing Wyle as "the best friend she ever had," she also chafed under what she perceived as the home's inconsistent policies and unwelcome intrusion into affairs she felt were private.[17] We must consider her professions of friendship and intimacy in the context of the vast social and cultural gulf that separated Weiss from her "best friend."

Although the new breed of female professional sought to distance herself from her nineteenth-century, untrained, volunteer, "friendly visitor" origins, Wyle's interactions with Weiss reveal that remnants of earlier practices, in the form of an intimate, sometimes familial affect, persisted. The ambivalence of this intimacy surfaced episodically but nowhere more starkly than in Weiss's final letters where she criticized the home, and Wyle indirectly, for compromising her privacy and threatening her dignity. While Roy Lubove argues that the professionalization of social work successfully avoided the "fiction of friendship," the six-year relationship of these women suggests that the transition from untrained friendly visitor to professional social worker was far from complete by the mid-1930s.[18] Indeed, Wyle's relationships with other subsidized mothers and with institutional inmates demonstrate a similarly warm maternal affect that comprised a crucial component of the home's efforts to provide for poor mothers and children.

The letters that Weiss sent to Wyle help trace the former's efforts to ascend to the middle class through the acquisition of elite cultural capital as well as the latter's reflections on her client's "worthiness" as a mother and recipient of institutional support. From this narrative and the letters that passed between the two women, we may also glimpse the home's ambivalence about mothers' dependency and the institution's sometimes erratic strategies for improving clients' life conditions. This well-documented case file thus enables an in-depth exploration of the complex priorities of Jewish benevolence in the Depression-era South, where the path to respectability and the acquisition of cultural citizenship were far from linear or transparent.

Conflicting Data: Client Self-Invention and the Politics of Respectability

The home's case narrative provides Viola Wyle's assessment of Weiss's past and present family life, the condition of her and her children, and other vital factors contributing to the family's institutional evaluation. Shortly after the home's board accepted the Weiss children as wards and offered them a fifty-dollar monthly subsidy for their upkeep, Wyle paid a visit to the family in November 1929 and recorded her observations in detail. Although the subsidy was designated for the children's upkeep only, Wyle's primary focus was on the worthiness of their mother.

Wyle wrote in her case narrative that Weiss was born in Austria in 1903 and met her husband, Jacob, an educated, skilled craftsman, in Belgium during the First World War. After being gassed in combat, Jacob never made a full recovery. He died five years after migrating with his wife to the United States and was "buried by the Jewish Orthodox Community" in Galveston, Texas.[19] Shortly after his death, Weiss, her two young daughters, and her in-laws moved to Fort Pierce, Florida, in the hopes of making a living from a small poultry farm. With the business struggling and her father-in-law's health failing, Weiss applied to the Florida Jewish Welfare Bureau for help. Since the Bureau could offer only nominal financial aid, a representative from that institution referred the case to the Atlanta orphan home.

In addition to providing the basic details of Weiss's life, Wyle also made several more subjective observations about the family's financial circumstances and emulation of a genteel lifestyle. Wyle observed, for example, that Weiss was "handicapped because of her lack of knowledge of English" but nevertheless possessed a "rather pleasing accent."

Wyle also described her new client as "neat," "attractive," and "refined" and was similarly impressed with Weiss's in-laws.[20] She observed that her father-in-law was a well-educated and cultured man who spoke four languages and "was to be admired for his grit and perseverance."[21] She described Rebecca's mother-in-law as "a woman who has been accustomed to better things in life . . . She and her husband have lost everything they ever possessed although during the boom they were worth $50,000.00 . . . They are proud and are not willing to let the community know of their plight."[22] Weiss's two children, Millie and Anna, also made a favorable impression. In response to what was likely a carefully choreographed showcasing of the children's musical abilities, Wyle reported, "Both children appear to be talented, the older one sings and plays the piano and the younger one, Anna, dances exceptionally well." She left the Weiss home impressed that both girls were "well-trained . . . having lived in refined surroundings."[23] According to Wyle's professional assessment, Rebecca Weiss and her family were not "paupers," the pathologically impoverished, but rather respectable, educated people who had temporarily fallen on hard times.[24] Their hesitance to seek charitable assistance, combined with their demeanor of refinement and education, stood as evidence of their internalization of elevated cultural capital and made the Weiss children appear worthy of generous institutional support. As a reflection of this favorable first impression, the home increased the family's monthly subsidy to sixty dollars per month.

Immigration and Census records provide additional details about Weiss's life. The passenger list for the SS *Aquitania*, the ship on which Rebecca and Jacob sailed from Southampton to New York in 1921, indicates that the couple's final destination was Galveston, Texas, a port city of note for the "Galveston Plan" that channeled over ten thousand Jewish immigrants to the southwestern and western regions of the United States from 1907 to 1914.[25] These earlier efforts to establish Jewish communities throughout the western United States made Galveston a welcoming home even for religiously observant Jewish immigrants. Given their ostensible commitment to their faith, it seems surprising that Weiss and her in-laws chose to relocate to Fort Pierce, a city lacking in Jewish infrastructure and community, but it is likely that business opportunities were among their primary considerations.

According to the SS *Aquitania*'s passenger list, Jacob was thirty-six and Rebecca twenty-three at the time of their arrival, which would make her five years older than the home's listed birth date of 1903. Later Census records contribute to the uncertainty of her age. The 1935 Florida State Census reports her age as forty-one, placing her date of birth in 1894. The conflicting data from immigration and Census records suggest that Weiss may have manipulated the details of her earlier life as she sought to maximize her success in her new home. Certainly she wished to obtain the approval and goodwill of her social worker and the benevolent institution she represented, so she may have adjusted her birth date to appear younger than she was, twenty-six at the time of her first encounter with the home, rather than thirty-one or thirty-five.

Weiss's efforts to navigate the complexities of cultural citizenship may also have influenced the way she described her national origins. The SS *Aquitania* passenger list describes Rebecca and Jacob as "Polish" in the categories for both "Race or People" and "Nationality or Citizenship," yet Weiss later told Wyle that she was Austrian. Further, the SS *Aquitania* carried several other passengers described as "Hebrew" in the category "Race or People," which begs the question of why the Weisses, described alternatively as observant and Orthodox in their case file, were not similarly classified in the ship's records. Weiss did not leave behind an explanation for these inconsistencies, so it is impossible to know for certain what motivated her decision to self-define as Polish in the early instance of her migration, and eight years later to tell her social worker she was Austrian. Certainly Poland's partitioning by the imperial powers of Austro–Hungary and Russia complicated Polish citizenry, and Weiss may have spent significant parts of her life in the Austria-governed territories.[26] Yet her shifting terms of self-identification point to her awareness of the complex interdependencies of nationality, religion, and cultural citizenship.

Social workers' detection of clients' particularities in language, religious observation, and standards of domesticity and consumption proved influential in the evaluation of their clients' potential for a seamless transition to independence and success. Other case files from the period confirm that a family's national origins carried significant weight in the home's budgeting decisions, demonstrating a tight correlation between clients' nationality and social workers' perceptions of cultural capital and potential for citizenship. Faced with an influx of immigrants from the Jewish Pale of Settlement, the primarily U.S.-born, central European–descended social workers and institutional leaders often disparagingly characterized their immigrant clients as foreign "strangers" and "Russian refugees."

Some foreign-born, subsidized mothers were considered worthier than others. The Miner case in North Carolina involved a family of French descent whose head-of-household died in 1930, leaving his wife and two children indigent. As in the Weiss case, Mrs. Miner's characterization as a "refined" and educated woman of French, rather than eastern European, descent supported the institution's evaluation of her worthiness.[27] Many acculturated Jewish reformers were less likely to grant eastern European and Sephardic newcomers the same institutional generosity accorded to families who, like the Miners and Weisses, claimed to hail from putatively more civilized and modern European nations. Given the weight that benevolent leaders and social workers accorded one's national origins, families may have misrepresented their nationality in an effort to sway institutional (and larger social) sentiment in their favor. During her travels, Rebecca Weiss likely became aware of growing prejudice against eastern European immigrants, perhaps telling Viola Wyle she was Austrian so she would appear more cosmopolitan and assimilable than her Polish origins would have suggested.[28]

The inconsistencies among the "facts" of Rebecca Weiss's life stand as testament to the complexity of the benevolent relationship. The recipients of benevolence were active participants in the effort to find a sense of belonging in their new home, and they were not always as cooperative and transparent as their social workers hoped. Warring ideals of cultural citizenship were at the heart of these inconsistencies in the data, and they provide fertile soil for investigation into the means by which loving kindness was distributed.

"Unusual Circumstances": Children's Subsidies and Cultural Capital

Prior chapters addressed how southern Jewish benevolent institutions cultivated elevated cultural capital—the system of knowledge and daily habits that signified class mobility—among their beneficiaries. In this place and time, successful emulation of cultural capital legitimized one's belonging in the middle-class white citizenry. Southern orphan home inmates could be carefully supervised as well as insulated from exposure to potentially contaminating influences such as impoverished and foreign-born parents whose homes and lifestyles were incompatible with the home's vision of success. Yet subsidized children lived with their mothers and were thus further out of reach of the institution's influences and supervision. Children whose mothers had already internalized the lessons of class sophistication were often given generous subsidies so that they could maintain their relatively high standards of living. Often this meant additional funding to hire "colored help" or to pay for children's enrichment activities, such as summer camp and music and dance lessons, even in times of extreme financial strain.

Although the Atlanta home's leadership originally intended subsidies to support impoverished mothers as well as their children, the period between the 1910s and the Depression witnessed a gradual shift in policy where subsidies were increasingly designated for needy children only.[29] By the mid-1920s, mothers' needs were disappearing from the home's calculation for determining monthly subsidies, and many subsidized mothers felt pulled between efforts to make ends meet while following institutional mandates to remain home with their children. Further, in an effort to encourage families to become self-supporting, the home deducted all family earnings from their monthly subsidies. While this practice was intended to cultivate a sense of self-sufficiency among subsidized families, it had the unintended consequence of encouraging parents to under-report—or to avoid reporting—their earnings.

The home's trend away from supporting mothers' needs was in part a result of the consolidation of the city's charitable Jewish network under the umbrella of the Atlanta Federation of Jewish Charities. Federation President Ed Kahn praised the streamlining effect of federating the Jewish charities into a single entity, arguing that "duplication, overlapping, [and] little cooperation among agencies" had earlier rendered the city's Jewish philanthropy ineffectual and unscientific.[30] One result of this consolidation of charities was the division of support for needy Jewish citizens into two categories: "child welfare" for orphans and half-orphans—overseen by the home—and "family services"—managed by the Montefiore Relief Association, the Federation's "Family Welfare

Unit."³¹ The distribution of charitable responsibility was far from seamless, and leaders often clashed over where exactly the line between mothers and their children could be drawn.

Correspondence between Leo Hexter, executive secretary of Atlanta's Federation, and philanthropic administrators at peer institutions in other cities demonstrates a growing recognition that the home's subsidies were inconsistently—and sometimes inequitably—administered. In a 1924 letter to the Federation of Jewish Charities of Pittsburgh, Hexter expressed his dissatisfaction with the "small pittance" given to widows and suggested that the Atlanta Federation and home share the cost of supporting mothers as well as their half-orphan children.³² Weeks later, Hexter wrote to Superintendent Sonn to suggest "a solution to the perplexing problem of adequate subsidy for local widows and children."³³ Within one year, leaders of the two institutions had agreed to a policy by which the home would receive funding from the Federation to cover the cost of "adult care of subsidy children."³⁴ While the new policy was a success for those cases managed jointly by the two organizations, it appears that those managed solely by the orphan home did not receive additional support to cover indigent parents' needs.

The transition away from providing for mothers as well as children also took place concurrently with the growing legitimacy of mothers' pensions nationwide. The 1909 White House Conference on the Care of Dependent Children helped crystallize the belief that home life was preferable to institutionalization for children's development, and good mothers were central to this ideal. The nation's first foray into welfare benefits, mothers' pensions originated in western, less industrialized states like Iowa and Arizona, with Illinois leading the way in 1911. By 1920, forty states had adopted mothers' pensions.³⁵ Many of the southern states lagged behind this national trend, with Georgia and South Carolina adopting programs only after federal incentives were offered in 1935. While Florida was among the earlier southern states to adopt mothers' pensions in the late 1910s, it does not appear that Weiss pursued such support before her relationship with the Atlanta home.

Despite the financial hardship of the Depression, the home still managed to provide comparatively generous monthly support to particular Jewish families. The home's justification for offering limited assistance to certain children and generous aid to others illuminates the extent to which notions of class and cultural capital were shaped on the larger social terrain in which these benevolent efforts took place. Considered alongside her ostensible demeanor of refinement and her family's standard of living, Weiss's widowhood contributed to her superior position on the scale of moral standing compared to other dependent women such as divorced or deserted mothers. As illustrated in chapter 4, these others often fell into a morally suspect category in which it was assumed that they somehow deserved their plight.[36] As a "neat, refined little woman" who worked to forge friendships with her respectable Jewish and non-Jewish neighbors, Weiss was an ideal recipient of the home's sympathy and support. Her generous subsidy of sixty dollars per month reflected Wyle's positive assessment of the family's chances for future advancement and her confidence that Weiss would cooperate with the home's mandates when it came to raising her children.

The home's Board of Control decided to allocate a generous subsidy to the Weiss children in part because, like the Miners, they had previously enjoyed a middle-class lifestyle and demonstrated an appreciation of the finer things in life. In the Miners' case, the board approved a high subsidy due to the family's "unusual circumstances," namely, their formerly high standard of living. The board considered it "worthwhile not to too drastically reduce the present standard of living, even though the proposed budget is higher than the usual amount allowed to indigent families."[37] In this case, the family's refinement and their location in a "good neighborhood" contributed to the home's decision to grant them a generous monthly subsidy. As in the Miner case, Weiss's presumed national origins may have reinforced institutional belief in her potential to obtain favorable status in a community strictly regimented by notions of respectability and citizenship in which one's cosmopolitanism and "pleasing accent" could be influential in framing one's chances for class escalation. Thus the decision to subsidize children involved more than budgetary concerns; it signified an effort to ensure that Jewish children retained their high standard of living even in times of financial hardship. Despite their poverty, the Miners' and Weisses' emulation of class ideals consistent with the benevolent institution's vision for social uplift stood as a powerful refutation to anti-Semitic claims of innate Jewish backwardness and cultural ignorance.

Jewish Mothers and the "Advantages of Home Life"

Although the home's Depression-era policy designated subsidies as strictly for children and not their mothers, the records caseworkers left behind evince the importance these institutions ascribed to an idealized performance of Jewish motherhood. As demonstrated in earlier chapters, a mother's worthiness depended in large part on her concern for her children's well-being and willingness to place their needs before her own, but perhaps just as important was her comportment as a model of refined ladyhood. Although Weiss's children and in-laws made a positive first impression on the home's social worker, and although the subsidy would be only for the children, its allocation ultimately hinged on Weiss's merit as indisputably "worthy." It was therefore her own performance of respectable femininity and motherly devotion that determined her children's degree of entitlement to the institution's aid.

The influence of a respectable motherly figure was crucial to the successful uplift of the southern Jewish poor. While the two southern Jewish orphan homes diverged in their policies on orphan care—one gradually placing orphans in private homes and the other favoring institutional life—both looked to the Jewish mother as a vital conduit of culture to future Jewish citizens. While the New Orleans home originally provided aid and housing to widows, they did not support foster care or children's subsidies. Instead, they offered their wards Honorary Matrons and "Big Sisters" to serve as provisional mothers and role models. Typically the wives of wealthy board members, Honorary Matrons offered a modicum of motherly care while providing inmates with guidance in the gendered accumulation of cultural capital and the experience of inclusion in New Orleans high society.

Despite her professional training as a social worker, Viola Wyle herself became a model of idealized Jewish motherhood to many who entered the Atlanta home, as well as to the many subsidized mothers and children throughout the region. Weiss fondly addressed Wyle as a motherly figure in many of her letters, as did other subsidized mothers who looked to Wyle for personal advice and support. Former institutional wards, like the Blaustein and Green children, some of whom had left the institution before the Wyles' 1929 appointment, developed a warm and familial relationship with the couple. The Atlanta home case files are full of letters and greeting cards addressed warmly to Mrs. Wyle, the mother for which many of these orphaned and half-orphaned children had always longed. When she died suddenly in 1944, the home's president wrote to former clients and inmates, eulogizing her as "a mother to many."

From the outset of her career at the Atlanta home, Wyle took charge of visiting subsidized and foster children throughout the home's region as well as following up on the lives of all former inmates. She maintained an active correspondence with the home's subsidized mothers and former wards, embarked on regular trips to visit children living with their mothers outside of Atlanta, kept detailed records of their circumstances, and reported back to the board at monthly meetings. It was also largely through her efforts to bolster adherence to national standards of modern social work that the Atlanta home ended its policy of institutionalized care by 1931. Having attended the White House Conferences on Children and Youth in 1909 and 1919, Wyle believed in what President Roosevelt had extolled as the "advantages of home life" to destitute children. Wyle took to heart the Conferences' message about the dangers of institutionalization to children's emotional and intellectual development, and she led efforts to find suitable Jewish foster homes for all remaining inmates in an effort to phase out the outmoded system of institutionalized care. At the 1931 annual board meeting, Armand Wyle declared with pride that the success in phasing out the home's boarding policy was "due to the unexpected and wholehearted response to our appeals to the latent and actual motherhood of Atlanta Jewish women."[38]

Viola Wyle conducted careful investigations of prospective foster parents—with particularly vigilant observation of mothers—in the Atlanta area. Children accepted as wards were rarely allowed to remain in their home cities unless it was determined that their own mothers were capable of caring for them, in which case they were subsidized. Children placed in foster homes were either full orphans, children who had lost their mothers, or those whose families were judged incapable of raising them in a way the home deemed acceptable. Traces of Wyle's perception of a proper home as well as an ideal mother appeared throughout her annual reports, where she detailed her efforts to investigate prospective foster families. She described in 1931 how a family's entire history received careful scrutiny before an orphan could be placed in their home. Even as she sought out safe and loving homes, Wyle looked for foster parents who could convey the appropriate class values to their young and often foreign-born charges. Beyond providing mere financial security, prospective foster families had to demonstrate the trappings of good taste as well as a non-excessive engagement with modern consumer culture. Wyle explained with pride that "most of their homes are owned by our foster parents and have either a piano, victrola or radio, and sometimes have all three [and] many of them maintain automobiles."[39] Foster parents' suitability therefore rested in large part upon their possession of material things judged (in this case, by Wyle) to be genteel, and their emulation of elite cultural capital in private, domestic space. Since it was middle-class women who increasingly served as consumer representatives on behalf of their families, foster mothers assumed a primary role in creating a domestic ethos of "good taste" while providing the nourishment and love that orphaned children required. In Wyle's eyes, good mothers were good consumers, their cultivation of taste and domestic order critical to a family's access to middle-class respectability, and ultimately their legibility as fully realized citizens.

Unlike foster mothers, who were relatively privileged and predominantly U.S.-born, most subsidized mothers were poor and foreign-born. The latter could not afford many of the commodities that signified class security, so the institution developed alternative means of judging subsidized mothers' suitability for the momentous task of raising the proper kind of Jewish citizens. Case records demonstrate the complexities of institutional faith in maternal competence. In the early 1900s, when the home first instituted its policy of offering monthly subsidies to divorced or widowed mothers considered "worthy," the institution's mother-centered rhetoric was tempered by suspicions of poor mothers who might exploit their children in order to obtain an institutional subsidy. As was the case with many *agunot*, a mother was worthy inasmuch as she could serve as a guide—rather than an impediment—to her children's upward mobility. The result of institutional ambivalence about poor mothers was an unofficial sliding scale of worthiness, with orphaned children at the top, followed by widows who demonstrated a solid grasp of middle-class cultural capital and motherly devotion. On a much lower tier were abandoned or divorced mothers, who were often suspected of having caused their marriages to fail. The institution demonstrated a belief that children were innocent and deserving of at least a chance to succeed. Women were less deserving unless they demonstrated that they were worthy mothers, capable of transmitting proper class values as well as love and assiduous care to their children.[40]

Efforts to improve the southern Jewish masses dictated that poor mothers' bodies in particular receive special scrutiny regarding their appearance and comportment. An Atlanta home case file from the 1930s described one mother as "a woman of about fifty. At the time of our first interview she appeared highly nervous and despondent. Her appearance was untidy and she was very poorly clad."[41] A Russian immigrant mother living in Savannah, Georgia, made the following unfavorable first impression: "Mrs. Bergmann is a little over forty years of age, rather stout, untidy and unclean. Claims to be healthy although very badly in need of dental attention."[42] Case records from as late as the 1950s characterized mothers in similarly unflattering ways, often describing them as "feeble-minded" and "unclean."[43]

The Depression witnessed the rise of a popular radio show, *The Goldbergs*, whose central character, Molly Goldberg, exemplified the respectable Jewish mother.[44] Her domestic virtue appealed to a vast audience, and her successful simultaneous embodiment of U.S. patriotism and Jewish authenticity served as a model for Jewish women. While hers was a characterization designed, in literary scholar Donald Weber's words, "to soften the jagged edges of alienation" experienced by Jews in the United States, other popular representations posed the Jewish mother as uneducated, culturally backward, and a threat to her people's social and political integration.[45] Although storylines and characters varied, the central message remained the same: the proper performance of Jewish motherhood lay at the center of the Jewish people's successful integration into mainstream America. The Jewish mother walked a tightrope stretched over two craters of extreme inadequacy: on one side was her family's failure to emulate a convincing performance of American citizenship; on the other was "over-assimilation," the unthinkable loss of a legible Jewish identity itself.

Jewish notions of motherhood's colossal role in Americanization were complicated by the nation's shifting citizenship ideals. By the 1920s, eugenic theories of racial perfection had taken hold in the popular imagination as a scientifically sound solution to what many perceived as the "degeneration" of the "race," and the refined, educated, native-born white mother was pivotal to the nation's progress.[46] Eugenicist celebrations of the chaste and untainted white female body resonated in a region whose social structure hinged on the vigilant protection of white women from attack from racially suspect men. By the 1930s, the ossification of the color line provided the bulwark for a white identity whose legitimacy was based on comparison to racialized outsiders and white women's containment and protection in the venerated bourgeois home.[47] Southern Jewish efforts to self-define therefore demanded precise adherence to the very norms that equated whiteness with the political power, civic entitlement, and the protections of full citizenship. Light skin alone was inadequate to legitimate one's membership in the ruling caste; full cultural citizenship required a subject's vigilant adherence to racialized class and gender ideals, a genteel performance always awaiting validation from an indistinguishable judge.

Weiss would feel the burden of these maternal ideals as she discovered the difficulty of determining where a child's needs began and a mother's ended. By the 1930s, the home's subsidies were for children's needs only, but it was ultimately their mothers who remained on trial for the duration of their children's institutional dependence.[48] During visits to homes of subsidized children, caseworkers and institutional affiliates from benevolent organizations across the country scrutinized mothers' child-rearing and housekeeping abilities as well as their personal comportment. Although Weiss's letters offer proof of her awareness of the institution's unspoken and unwritten priorities, clients often became objects for careful analysis in a non-reciprocal relationship of investigation and regulation.[49] Case records confirm that the institutional gaze extended deep into the private lives of its beneficiaries. Such vigilant surveillance was of vital importance to benevolent leaders' sense of control over the project of uplifting the foreign-born Jewish masses.

Institutional Surveillance and the Worthy Widow

The home's records indicate that Weiss received many institutionally affiliated visitors despite her six-hundred-mile distance from Atlanta.

The Wyles separately visited every year while Weiss received a subsidy. Other professional institutional visitors in Fort Pierce included the gentile social worker mentioned disparagingly in Weiss's letters, Mrs. Meredith, from the Federal Emergency Relief Association, and Ms. Lois Dobrin of the Jewish Welfare Bureau. As representatives of institutions from which Weiss received financial aid at some point, these trained investigators carefully observed and evaluated her family's home, surroundings, behavior, and health.

Yet these professionally trained visitors were not the only people to observe, evaluate, and manage the institution's subsidized mothers. As the practice of granting mothers' subsidies geographically dispersed the home's clientele base, caseworkers devised innovative ways of tracking and recording the progress and behaviors of institutional dependents. As in the case of Margaret Goldfarb, whose home in Jacksonville was too far away for Ralph Sonn to visit, the home relied on the judgment of local affiliates to determine whether she was capable of supervising her children. Institutional leaders often asked local rabbis or members of B'nai B'rith, the National Council of Jewish Women, or benevolent societies to visit subsidized families and report back on their condition.

In Rebecca Weiss's case, the home maintained an active correspondence with Mr. Sidney Cohen, a B'nai B'rith affiliate and one of Weiss's neighbors who agreed to observe the family and offer his assistance when necessary. Volunteers like Cohen were deputized as temporary social workers who kept in contact with clients and reported to the institution on the state of their neighborhoods, homes, and the condition of the individuals occupying those homes. Although she did not openly express her resentment of this supervision until her final letters to Viola Wyle, Weiss chafed at the institution's sometimes unpredictable modes of surveillance.

The relationship between Wyle and Weiss offers insight into the competing and often-contradictory constructions of feminine respectability that stood at the heart of the institution's mission. The struggle to help Jewish immigrants find their place in the southern landscape meant impressing on them the importance of intricate codes of behavior through which one self-identified as "refined" by middle-class, white standards. Of primary importance in this project was the docile cooperation of the mother, who in turn held the power to convey proper codes of behavior to her children so that they might become acceptable representatives of Jewishness to mainstream society. Mothers had to be watched and monitored in order to guarantee that their children received the proper upbringing, thereby ensuring the full inclusion of future generations of Jews.

While she was under the home's care, Weiss's letters suggest her comprehension of the institution's priorities and hence her ability, in turn, to scrutinize and judge her own audience. Her writings and actions reveal her to be an astute observer of the institution's expectations for mothers of subsidized children. Because they reflect at times a thorough understanding of the way the home operated, her letters provide a glimpse into the institution's sometimes convoluted strategies for supporting needy coreligionists. Weiss's ardent expressions of social intimacy and loyalty suggest that Wyle became a motherly figure and confidante to whom Weiss poured out her heart in times of strain. After receiving her first check, she wrote a warmly appreciative letter to Wyle, expressing her reluctance to accept money "when I don't earn it" and hoping to meet Wyle and "have a heart to heart talk."[50] Having initially succeeded in representing herself as a pious woman whose devotion to her children drove her pursuit of charitable assistance, she avoided identification with the notorious "pauper" whose dependence might become a chronic burden to the community.[51] She initially demonstrated unwavering trust in Wyle's directives, and her letters document her efforts to follow guidelines regarding the care of her daughters. Her act of seeking advice and approval from Wyle contributed to her self-fashioning as one sincerely trying to conform to the institution's wishes.

Yet Weiss's dependence on the institution no doubt influenced the "truth" value of her letters to Wyle. While she expressed great affection for and referred to Wyle as her "best friend," Weiss's written words must be evaluated in the context of her state of dependence for survival upon the institution that Wyle represented. While these illuminating firsthand accounts of Weiss's subjectivity shed valuable light on the negotiation of citizenship for a southern Jewish immigrant, we must consider the extent to which the author of the texts withheld information or constructed her narrative in a way consistent with her perception of institutional priorities. While she received the home's aid, Weiss crafted her letters to Wyle in ways meant to convey a sense of her worthiness and high moral standing. Weiss came to understand which emotions she could express to her benevolent friend and which ones had to remain hidden.

Jewish benevolent leaders struggled during the Depression to combat the stigma of pauperism among coreligionists because such association threatened collective Jewish cultural citizenship. Maintaining an appearance of middle-class identity by constructing proper neighborhoods and clean, orderly Jewish homes was paramount in efforts to rescue and to protect needy Jewish mothers and children. Yet social and economic realities curbed immigrant women's abilities to conform to the benevolent institutions' often demanding ideals. For Weiss and other institutionally subsidized widows, observance of the region's cultural and social norms was crucial to her access to the unequivocal respectability for which she longed.

"None of My Own People": Cultural Estrangement in the Jim Crow South

Living in relative isolation from other Jewish immigrants only heightened Weiss's perceptions of her own difference from those around her. Very soon after her first meeting with Wyle, her letters convey the depth of her loneliness and longing for a benevolent home: "You all have been so kind to me. Never in my li[f]e will I forget that. I don't know what I would do if you stop helping me financially before I have any means of supporting us. I haven't got none of my own people in this country to look after me."[52] It seems that the presence nearby of her deceased husband's parents and siblings did little to assuage her sense of alienation. Weiss appealed to Wyle as the only one she could turn to for compassion: "Please excuse me for pouring out my troubles to you but I haven't got nobody to talk to and if I keep to myself I will break down."[53]

In an undated case report, Wyle noted that Weiss "deplores the fact that [her children] have no companions of their own age and that there is a great deal of prejudice in a small town and that she prefers to keep them at home with her."[54] Weiss possessed a keen awareness of her difference from the general Fort Pierce community and wished for her children to grow up with others of a similar background. It is unclear whether the "prejudice" in this passage referred to the community's anti-Semitism or to a general suspicion of immigrants. It was possibly a combination of both that made Weiss feel like an outsider and drove her to seek relocation elsewhere, for later references to the Fort Pierce Jewish community suggest that Weiss's poverty made her feel like a stranger among her comparatively well-off coreligionists. She expressed a desire to move to Atlanta, "where my girls would get a proper education."[55] Despite her sense of cultural and religious alienation in Fort Pierce and her many requests to relocate her family to Atlanta, the home refused to move a "dependent family" to a city experiencing its own financial instability, not to mention one with prejudices of its own.[56]

Weiss's early interactions with the home brought to light her concern for fostering Jewish ritual observance and education. Many of her early letters exhibited anxiety over how to raise observant Jewish girls in a city with little Jewish infrastructure. She worried about the lack of a synagogue in Fort Pierce and asked how to provide for her daughters' religious education, reporting in October 1929 that her children "don't know what Jewish means living among Gentile."[57] She lamented, "On Sundays they always ask me why they don't go to Sunday school like the other children. Once they went and came back so excited [and] they don't really know what they are and that hurts and worry me bad."[58] A case report from September 1934 described Weiss's joy at having obtained a Hebrew book from one of her neighbors. She used it to offer her children some degree of religious education, "teaching them to the best of her ability." Such efforts proved that Weiss was, in Wyle's words, "very ambitious for the future of her children" and anxious to retain their distinctly Jewish identity.[59]

"A Beggar for Her Children": Production and Consumption in the Southern Jewish Home

Institutional expectations regarding proper motherly comportment limited subsidized women's opportunities for social and financial independence. The erosion of financial provisions for mothers was not accompanied by a commensurate relaxing of standards of maternal worthiness, and the institution held fast to the belief that a good mother remained home with her children until they were old enough to attend school. Mothers of school-aged children might pursue part-time employment as long as they could be home when their children returned from school, but adequately remunerative part-time work was increasingly scarce as the impact of the economic depression and unemployment deepened through the 1930s.

Weiss's status as a foreign-born widow who was "not good acquainted with the English language" made it difficult to find "any decent position" in her town.[60] Even if she had possessed the necessary language skills, there were few job openings in the white-collar trades.[61] In early 1930, several of Wyle's letters inquired if Weiss had had any luck securing a job, as "the [tourist] season is now on."[62] Since both of Weiss's children were in school during the day, Wyle believed that she could secure paid employment without compromising her children's physical and moral safety. Weiss provided Wyle a detailed account of her efforts, describing how "all [hotels] took colored help. There is one job open in a Chinese laundry. They pay $9 a week from 7pm to 6am. This is the best I can get in this town."[63]

Emphasizing her distance from the "colored" hotel workers, Weiss found herself too white to obtain work in the city's unskilled trades. By describing the "Chinese laundry" job's low pay and grueling hours, she persuaded her benefactor that the position was unacceptable. Its long evening hours would have deprived her children of their mother's care, a fact Weiss knew would not sit well with the home. Further, proximity to Chinese, particularly as her employers, would have undermined Weiss's racial privilege. While her note highlighted the unfeasibility of the laundry job, Weiss nevertheless signaled her good faith effort to find employment, and she closed her letter by asking, "Would you advise me to go to Miami?"[64]

Unspoken yet understood was Weiss's failure to seek employment in domestic labor, as such work was considered primarily the realm of black women.[65] Historian Tera Hunter describes how the South's depressed wages, lagging technology, and rigid segregation conspired to prevent even educated black women for obtaining "respectable" or professional employment. Characterized as innately corrupt, black women were excluded from the protective category of "lady." The exclusionary trope dictated both that black women would be wage earners in white homes and that they would receive the lowest wages for the most toilsome and contemptible work.[66] For certainly no southern white lady—even an immigrant Jewish one—would seek a position in domestic labor, even if her children's livelihood depended on it.

Only recently introduced to the South's social hierarchies, Weiss demonstrated an intimate knowledge of this racial logic of work. Her case file, and the letters contained therein, evince the clarity with which she perceived herself as a consumer, rather than a performer, of domestic labor. Similar unspoken refusals by southern Jewish women to seek employment as domestic servants appeared in other Atlanta cases of this time period; and the home did not encourage subsidized Jewish mothers, regardless of their need, to seek jobs as domestic workers.[67] Such implicit but nevertheless determined maintenance of racial boundaries contributed to the construction of Jewish cultural citizenship. For leaders of the home to allow their coreligionists, however poor, to become maids for southern white gentiles was to allow Jewish identity to stray dangerously outside the realm of intelligible white privilege.

Weiss continued seeking work but experienced little success until she accepted a part-time factory job in the winter of 1931, but her triumph turned out to be a mixed blessing. When Armand Wyle paid an unannounced visit, he found only "the two children at home in care of a colored maid."[68] His report from the visit suggests that Weiss had failed to inform him about her job or of her decision to hire a maid. The same report described what he perceived as Weiss's duplicitous rendering of her financial situation, and he recommended that her subsidy be reduced. While they had encouraged Weiss to find part-time work, the Wyles opposed the employment of a maid to supervise the children so that Weiss could work at a factory. It is possible that the Wyles did not believe the factory job justified the additional child-care expense, or that they did not approve of Weiss's delegating her maternal duties to a "colored maid." They were also frustrated at Weiss's failure to inform them of her paid employment. Particularly during this time of economic struggle, benevolent institutions monitored more closely the ways in which clients sought social stability and economic improvement.

Armand Wyle's criticism underscores the quandary in which Weiss found herself, where her own well-being was placed at odds with that of her daughters. She discovered that she could not become a wage earner without losing all or part of her children's subsidy, but she could not adequately provide for herself without paid employment. The following year's visit from Armand Wyle revealed that Weiss defiantly continued to work part-time in the canning factory and to retain the services of a maid. Her refusal to disclose her earnings or to admit to hiring a servant suggest that she knew such information would jeopardize her children's subsidy. The home's mandates placed Weiss in the uncomfortable position of trying to balance an institutional ideal of worthy motherhood with her own vision for her family's survival.

Weiss's letters to Viola Wyle reveal her often less-than-subtle rebellion against the values imposed on her and proves that recipients of home subsidies were not simply docile bodies on whom the codes of proper Jewish comportment could be written. Her actions also suggest her determination to forge her own path out of poverty, regardless of the institution's directives. Attempting to justify her furtiveness about her job, she wrote a desperate letter to Viola Wyle explaining how she needed things for herself and had only meant to work "a few hours a day." She then promised to follow Armand's mandate to quit working, to make peace with her in-laws, and to concentrate her energies on raising healthy children: "I am doing everything in my power to make them healthy [and] well-behaved and will do everything to educate them. A mother will become a beggar for her children and that [is] what I am now."[69] Invoking the sacrifices of a universalized motherhood ideal, Weiss disparaged what she perceived as the home's unrealizable standards. She emphasized the injustice of granting subsidies only to children, leaving mothers to fend for themselves.

Weiss's deliberate defiance of the Wyles' mandates to remain home with her children and to dismiss her maid suggests her comprehension of larger systems of social and cultural capital in the Depression-era South. It is likely that she had learned enough about racial hierarchy during her ten-year residence to recognize the legitimizing power of a white woman's prerogative to hire a black maid. Although she was a poor widow who struggled to speak English (notwithstanding her "pleasing" accent), her ability to hire a black woman to clean her house and to watch her children helped bolster her status as a white southerner. Within this regional context, black domestic servants were considered vital to white families' respectable standard of living. Indeed, Tera Hunter cites the widespread southern notion that "no white family ever did its own laundry."[70] As illustrated in previous chapters, performing an intelligible white identity in the Jim Crow South depended in part upon one's appropriate placement within a racialized hierarchy of work and consumption.

If the Wyles' northern origins influenced their perceptions of Weiss's survival strategies, they would not have allowed other subsidized families to use home funding to hire domestic servants. Only two years earlier, the Miners' comparatively generous subsidy included a five-dollar weekly allowance to employ an African American maid who had lived with the family for several years.[71] The decision to allow the Miners to retain the services of a maid suggests the extent to which preserving a family's elevated cultural capital required careful observation of the dominant racial order. Perhaps the impact of a few years of economic depression on the institution's budget had made such expenditures seem extravagant. It is also likely that the Wyles considered a servant unnecessary for a family who had not employed one previously.

Underlying these restrictions on work and child care loomed the suspicion that mothers worked for "selfish" reasons, to enhance their wardrobes or to finance evening entertainment.[72] Indeed, Weiss's case file contains references to her in-laws' allegations that she misappropriated money toward purchases like rouge and other "articles for personal adornment."[73] Concern about women's misuse of money reveals the depth of the conflicts between women's realities and benevolent institutional priorities. Making themselves attractive was both a practical and a psychic strategy, for many widowed or abandoned women sought to attract new husbands as well as to maintain an appearance of respectable femininity. Yet benevolent institutions frowned on such a transgression of ideal self-sacrificing motherhood, and the possibility that a respectable Jewish mother was anything but a self-abnegating "beggar for her children."

Weiss also subtly contested institutional imperatives when it came to educating her children. She considered her daughters' education in music and dance to be crucial to their future success. For a few years Millie was able to take free piano lessons, but the case record reports her grandmother paying one dollar per week in 1932. Weiss also went to significant lengths to obtain the home's financial support for dance lessons for Anna. By September 1934, she paid $1.50 per week for dance and piano lessons combined. The value of these lessons to Weiss is illustrated in her adamant refusal to discontinue them when she lost most of her subsidy check in 1934. Although Wyle advised her to cease the children's dance and piano lessons until she could get out of debt, the records confirm that Weiss did not heed this advice. Proficiency playing the parlor piano, with its accompanying aura of genteel leisure and entertainment, was considered just one of many "conspicuously consumed" things through which immigrants broadcast their access to class privilege.[74] Weiss considered the lessons vital to her daughters' social escalation, and she was willing to sacrifice the family's economic security, and the approval of her social worker, to retain them.

Weiss's dedicated consumption of things perceived as cultured and refined suggests her understanding of the ways in which southern cultural citizenship was enacted on a stage set with genteel gender, racial, and class norms. While her poverty, religious difference, and foreign upbringing may have set her apart from mainstream ideals of cultural citizenship, she struggled to emulate middle-class respectability by providing high-class forms of leisure for her children and hiring a "colored maid" to govern her domestic space. Consumption of such goods and labor helped distinguish her family as cultured and refined, thus distancing them from the racially suspect individuals whose poverty they shared.

"I Am Jewish Still": Intermarriage and Jewish Authenticity

It was shortly after Armand Wyle's troublesome 1932 visit that Weiss's handwritten letters to Viola Wyle ceased. The next letter to appear was dated July 1935, when she briefly resumed contact, and then her case was closed. It was only through local institutional informants and Weiss's former neighbor, Mrs. Myers, that Viola Wyle learned of her client's marriage to a wealthy gentile businessman. The news of her client's good fortune pleased Wyle, but she expressed consternation that Weiss "did not write to us telling us of her marriage particularly since she professed so much affection for me personally and repeatedly expressed her appreciation for what we were doing for her and her children."[75]

It was at this point in the relationship that Weiss reversed the dynamic of critique that had characterized her association with the home for almost six years. Having obtained financial security and hence independence from the institutional gaze, Weiss found herself in a position where she could manage the dissemination of her personal information. Perhaps her feelings of genuine friendship for Wyle motivated her to explain herself, to confess her true feelings about her experience as an institutional dependent. She may also have felt the need to confess to Wyle some of the weighty information that she had previously withheld.

Certainly one motivation in particular governed Weiss's decision to disclose her story to Wyle: her desire to relate with pride her success story as one risen from the depths of poverty and alienation into the ranks of class privilege and respectability. When the newly wed Mrs. Rebecca Blakeney finally wrote to Wyle on July 4, 1935, she sent the letter through her former neighbor so that her location would remain unknown. Her last two letters reveal her desire to earn her former social worker's approval. In a tone that alternated between elation and defensiveness, she justified her seemingly hasty actions with the successful result. Having finally found an end to her poverty and dependence, she had ascended to the height of respectability as a consumer of fine new clothes instead of secondhand things given through others' goodwill. She described the happiness of "hav[ing] things we haven't had for so many years . . . [such as] expensive school dresses [and] no more dime store dresses or hand me down dresses." She also referred to her husband's social legitimacy as a member of the Masons and "several other clubs."[76]

In addition to defending her seemingly rash and secretive behavior as necessary to her family's economic stability and class ascension, Weiss also addressed what she perceived as Wyle's fears of the erosion of the family's Jewishness. Her letter described her new husband's contentment "not [to] interfere in my religion" and that of her girls: "My children will attend Jewish Sunday school just the same and I am Jewish still."[77] Although her husband was "like a real father" to the girls, Weiss promised that their incorporation into a gentile household would not interfere with their Jewish upbringing. Reflecting what Laura Levitt observes as the liberal assimilationist project of fashioning Jewishness "as simply a matter of individual faith," Weiss assured Wyle that she had obtained respectability and wealth without compromising her spiritual or cultural authenticity.[78]

She insisted in her final letters to Wyle that she saw no inconsistency in her efforts to remain Jewish while becoming the wife of a prominent gentile businessman. Indeed, Matthew Frye Jacobson argues that "'difference' among the former white races diminished" starting in the 1920s as "race itself was recast with color."[79] Yet the defensive tone with which the newly wed Rebecca Blakeney composed her letter, along with her effort to address the unasked question of her and her daughters' spiritual preservation, suggest that she was uncertain about the future of her Jewish particularity. Even years before she married Mr. Blakeney, Weiss was slowly recognizing the incongruity of Jewishness, and its accompanying cultural particularity, with assimilation to the social norms of her community. Once a treasured component of her identity, faithful religious observance became less tenable given her social aspirations. The scarcity of others like her—"refined" observant Jews—in addition to the absence of an Orthodox community in Fort Pierce, had earlier forestalled her efforts to maintain religious traditions and to cultivate an observant lifestyle in her children. Eventually her appeals for help obtaining Hebrew instruction gave way to requests for piano and dance lessons as she realized the impact of the latter in shaping her girls into respectable young women. Perhaps her religious orthodoxy seemed a small price to pay for financial and social security for herself and her daughters.[80] Given her class ascension and betrothal to a man whose whiteness and social status effaced her cultural liminality, Weiss insisted that she and her daughters would remain Jewish, but her very insistence suggests that she herself was unsure if such a thing was possible.

"I Do Not Belong to This Kind of Woman": Institutional Dependency and Sexual Shame

While Weiss may have understood her Jewishness to be a simple difference of religion, she viewed her relationship with the orphan home differently. In her final letter, Weiss implored Wyle not to try to locate her, insisting that her failure to disclose the family's new address was a necessary means of concealing her past dependence from her new husband.[81] Weiss's desperation to hide her relationship with the home suggests her perception of institutional dependence as gravely threatening to her social escalation. She begged Wyle not to tell anyone of her dependence on the home for fear that such knowledge would "spoil everything" for her and the girls. "Nowadays what a man don't know don't hurt me," she explained.[82] Weiss believed that her past dependence imperiled the respectable ladyhood on which her fragile claims to privilege were based.

Her location in the Depression-era South necessitated that Weiss hide her past state of dependence because such association carried the moral stigma of "pauperism," a classification gravely threatening to her membership in the southern white gentility to which she aspired.[83] The Depression intensified the stigma of charitable "hand-outs," strengthening the link between financial struggle and personal failure. Immigration restrictions barring those judged "Likely to Become a Public Charge" further marked dependency as that which excluded one from national admission and citizenship.[84] Believing that her dependence on private charity threatened the stability of her performance as a white, southern, middle-class lady, Weiss disavowed her reliance on the home.

Weiss's final letter suggests the discursive linkage of institutional dependence with the racialized stigma of sexual exploitation and a belief that her reliance on charity had compromised her moral standing. Hesitant to "take money when I don't earn it," Weiss had early on echoed dominant notions of respectability, which emphasized individual independence and self-reliance. Her final letters demonstrate her comprehension of the dangers of dependency to sexualize and to threaten the female aid recipient's moral standing. In light of southern chivalric codes, needy women without male protectors appeared in constant danger of defilement.[85]

Since geographical distance had placed Weiss outside the range of the institution's protection, and the Wyles had repeatedly refused to allow Weiss to move to Atlanta, she found herself subject to the unwanted attentions of the home's trusted affiliate, Sidney Cohen. Acknowledging that she had praised his magnanimity in earlier letters, Weiss described how Cohen's generosity veiled his romantic interests and his desire for her to "stay single and become his mistress."[86] According to Weiss, Cohen had made repeated efforts to purchase her affections with gifts, monetary support, and his close connections with the home's administration. When she announced her intention to marry, Cohen protested that it would not be in the best interest of Weiss or her daughters. As one of the home's volunteer informants, Cohen represented to Weiss yet another example of the institution's misdirected intrusion into her and her children's lives. Her hesitance to report Cohen's advances reflected her comprehension of the institution's priorities as well as her fear of threatening her children's subsidy. Insisting to Wyle, "I do not belong to this kind of woman," the kind who would participate in an affair with a married man, Weiss simultaneously chastised the institution for its failure to protect her and reasserted her claim to an ascendant feminine respectability. Having held her moral ground against Cohen's advances while complying with what she perceived as the home's intrusive demands, Weiss felt she had earned her newfound liberation from the shame of charity.

Her final letter offers a rare glimpse of an institutional client's self-conscious efforts to exude cooperation and gratefulness, even in the face of humiliation, in order to continue receiving institutional support for her children. Although she expressed appreciation for Wyle's personal attention and friendship, Weiss described in detail her sense of betrayal by Armand Wyle and numerous others associated with the home. The once outwardly docile and grateful recipient of aid confessed her resentment at the institution for its intrusion into her affairs, and, more significantly, the public disclosure of her dependence to non-Jews. She described how Armand had "run all over telling everybody that he have to have some money for me for my children and that was not enough that every Jew in town knew all about me he went to Mrs. Meredith a gentile a anti-semite [who] hates the sight of a Jew and asked her to watch . . . how I am behaving myself."[87] She also explained her decision not to complain about this incident to Viola Wyle earlier: "I was not free to tell you that before for fear that I will be too frank and might hurt my children but I know I am at liberty to tell everything that [has] hurt me for so long."[88] Weiss's docile performance as an institutional client had masked her indignation at her subordination to and surveillance by the benevolent coreligionists who claimed to know best how to help her. For years Weiss had stifled her outrage that the community knew of "her business," particularly her poverty and reliance on charity for survival. Her final letter also suggests that Weiss perceived the institution's power to delegate its supervisory authority to local volunteers, Jewish and gentile alike, as the greatest insult to her respectability.

When the newly wed Rebecca Blakeney sat down to write her final letter to her friend Viola Wyle, she no doubt struggled for the words with which to explain her seeming betrayal of the truth, her abrupt departure and secrecy. Looking beyond her constraints as one whose native language was not English, we can appreciate the difficulty she faced as she explained the reasons for her seemingly rash behavior. Given her almost-six-year dependence on the Atlanta home, her transformation from an impoverished widow, alienated from her southern setting, to the wife of a prosperous businessman, bears a striking resemblance to traditional rags-to-riches stories that may have populated her children's storybooks.

Weiss's efforts to escape her poverty and to find acceptance took place within a matrix of citizenship structured around a gendered and racialized logic of production and consumption. Her struggle illuminates the ambivalent role of benevolent uplift in the process of converting impoverished immigrants into proper representations of southern Jewishness, authentically raced citizens in a region of strict segregation and naturalized violence. Instead of asking whether Jewishness served as an identifier of racial difference in a particular time and place, Weiss's story enables exploration of the ways in which the region's regulatory ideals forged unique southern Jewish subjectivities. Weiss's racial, national, and class transformations occurred side by side and simultaneously, each influencing the other and none in isolation. As illustrated in Weiss's insistence that she did "not belong to this type of woman," understandings of race had constructed the boundaries by which she learned to know herself by what she was not.

Weiss's case file and the letters contained therein open up a window onto the ways in which southern Jewish cultural citizenship was imagined and attained. Her aspirations to a standard of living she considered respectable were not always compatible with the directives set forth by the home. Recognizing the high stakes involved in following institutional mandates, Weiss spent almost six years negotiating a difficult path between upholding her own ambitious and observing the home's vision for her uplift. As she struggled to represent herself and her daughters as worthy of the institution's financial assistance, she also fought to counteract the stigma of institutional dependence.

Adherence to the South's ruling ideologies and ideals for white middle-class cultural capital was a necessary step in realizing this dream of material and social success. Like Rachel Ferrera in the following chapter, Weiss's comprehension of the trope of southern ladyhood required that a "colored maid" preserve order in her home and, more important, guarantee her own distance from the demeaning labor associated with black femininity. Since that historical time and place rendered respectable, white femininity as dependent on a public performance of gentility, many poor, foreign-born Jewish women sacrificed financial stability to hire black maids, for they had learned that certain types of domestic labor had the power to inscribe racial degradation onto those who performed it.

Despite her foreign birth, Rebecca Weiss learned enough about the complex identity politics of her new home to enact for her benefactors what she felt was an intelligible production of respectable Jewish motherhood. Her story of confession and deceit, of devotion and betrayal, further illuminates some of the ways in which southern Jewish claims to citizenship involved a complicated tangle of gender role contestation, class incongruity, and race ambivalence. The fact that Weiss's strategies for escaping her poverty often came into conflict with institutional directives suggests the intricate nature of efforts to protect worthy Jewish mothers and children from poverty and cultural degradation. Ultimately, this subsidized mother's success in achieving the respectable life to which she aspired depended on extricating herself from what she felt was the stigmatizing shame of charity as well as her ability to balance with dignity the multifarious cultural forces vying for her acceptance, to sacrifice her religious orthodoxy and ethnic particularity in the name of practical necessity.

6

Sex, Race, and Consumption

Southern Sephardim and the Politics of Benevolence

In New York City's population of some 1,500,000 Jews, there are 40,000 souls who are almost as alien to their kinsmen as are the negroes to the average white Southerner.
—Louis M. Hacker, 1926

Race is not just a conception; it is also a perception.
—Matthew Frye Jacobson, 1998

In the summer of 1929 the struggle of an immigrant *agunah* caught the attention of Atlanta's benevolent leaders. It appeared that the woman's husband had fled to Los Angeles one month prior, leaving her alone with five children, and their situation was becoming dire. But upon closer investigation, it became clear that the husband, Victor Ferrera, had left temporarily to pursue a business lead and, falling ill, had been hospitalized in California. Despite Rachel Ferrera's claims that her family was starving in the absence of a steady means of support, the social worker found her and her children immaculate and well dressed, the home neatly furnished and kept spotless by an African American maid.

Further complicating the case was the family's status as foreign-born Sephardim, whose perceived cultural and religious difference contributed to their Ashkenazic social worker's suspicions about their worthiness and capacity for full belonging. Victor's "Oriental habits," Rachel's "extravagance," and what she learned about the couple's sexual incompatibilities caught the social worker's attention and were recorded in ways that further illuminate the boundaries of cultural citizenship in the Jewish South. Southern taxonomies of race placed some immigrant

Sephardim perilously close to the indeterminate color line delineating insider from outsider, and case files provide evidence of the ways in which assumptions about Sephardic difference framed social workers' diagnoses of their institutional clients. Sephardic immigrants' negotiations with benevolent agencies therefore provide insight into the logic by which southern Jews used benevolence to navigate a shifting and treacherous racial terrain. Considered alongside the cases of other Sephardic recipients of charitable aid in Atlanta, the Ferrera case provides a window onto the complex dialectic of benevolent uplift and the sometimes subtle ways in which interethnic Jewish differences mapped onto the racial landscapes of Depression-era Atlanta.

From 1899 to 1925, between twenty-five and thirty thousand Sephardim—descended from Jews who lived on the Iberian Peninsula prior to the expulsions of the late fifteenth century—arrived in the United States. In contrast to the earlier wave of Sephardim who arrived in the Americas during colonial times, most who migrated during the twentieth century were poor and possessed only minimal education.[1] This second wave of Sephardic immigrants came to the Americas not as a result of religious persecution, but rather through a combination of social and political factors.[2] Turkey's wars with Russia, Italy, and the Balkans led to increasing instability, as did the conscription laws of 1908, which granted Jews the same civil rights and responsibilities as other Turks. Unable to avoid conscription, those who left were mostly poor, uneducated men whose wives, sisters, and daughters followed shortly afterward.[3]

The majority settled in New York, drawn to the city's substantial Jewish infrastructure. In 1926, just two years after passage of the Johnson Reed Act—effectively shutting the doors to future immigration—the New York Jewish Federation commissioned economic historian Louis Hacker to study the impact of Sephardic migration on Jewish life in the city. Citing a "mode of life that . . . differs radically from Occidental manners and points of view," Hacker asserted that Sephardic immigrants were "set apart from New York Jewry by religious, linguistic, and psychological differences that vitiate any attempts at mutual understanding."[4] Echoing claims to women's "elevation" as a key component of civilized masculinity, Hacker highlighted "the inferior status of their women folk" as further evidence of Sephardic primitiveness.[5] Further, his analogy comparing the cultural alienation between New York's Sephardim and Ashkenazim to that between "negroes" and "the average white Southerner" derived its coherence from prevailing understandings of the South as the location of an unequivocal system of racial bifurcation.

It was to the South that Hacker looked for a racial epistemology to frame his assertions of Jewish authenticity. While comparing Sephardic particularity to visible race difference, he associated New York's Ashkenazim with the privileges of whiteness and at least the *potential* to access the rights and protections of citizenship. He concluded that New York's Sephardim, like southern blacks, were "alien" to the values of American independence and that their path to acculturation would be significantly more difficult than that pursued by Ashkenazic immigrants. For Hacker, and for many other acculturated, U.S.-born Jews, Sephardim were alien subjects, whose tenuous legibility as Jews complicated the uplift efforts of even the most devoted adherents of *gemilut hasadim*.

Although ideals of charity and loving kindness commanded Jews to "take care of their own," Hacker's comments evince the challenges of invoking a united and culturally homogenous "Jewish community" and the prevalence of what historian Aviva Ben-Ur describes as "coethnic recognition failure" among Jewish Americans in the early twentieth century. According to Ben-Ur, Ashkenazim often disparagingly identified their Sephardic coreligionists as "Turks" and denied any commonality with those newcomers who arrived speaking Spanish, Greek, or Turkish, in addition to Ladino—a hybrid language comprised of Hebrew and medieval Spanish—instead of Yiddish, and practicing Judaism in ways that appeared alien.[6] As Hacker's words suggest, acculturated Jews faced a quandary in classifying Sephardic newcomers as Jewish when they appeared at best unfamiliar, at worst culturally "Oriental" and "alien" to the values of American citizenship.[7]

Yet established Jewish benevolent agencies still reached out to these newcomers, for to do otherwise was to leave their acculturation to chance and to threaten the civic entitlement of all Jews. Leaders in *gemilut hasadim* internalized the prevailing logic that placed all, regardless of linguistic, cultural, and religious differences, into the totalizing category of "Jew," and they recognized that their shared peoplehood bound their fates together. They saw that their own successful performance of

American belonging hinged on their ability to minimize the poverty and visible cultural difference of even their most backward coreligionists. Thus loving kindness remained of critical value to Jewish efforts to ensure that these most foreign of immigrants learned to become self-sufficient in their new surroundings and to reflect a positive image of Jewishness to the larger world.

As we have seen, location in the South had significant consequences for the benevolent uplift imperative as well as for the ways in which new immigrants sought to self-define. Jewishness in the South distinguished itself from its northern and western counterparts in its calculated and proscribed juxtaposition to blackness. For, as Hacker's article suggests, it was only in *relation* to and against the supposed degradation of blackness that southern whiteness constructed itself as unquestioningly ascendant in the social order. Like their eastern European, immigrant "kinsmen," Sephardic newcomers arrived in the South as virtual strangers to the racial order of Jim Crow and its accompanying culture of ambivalent intimacy, and their very survival depended on their ability to navigate this unfamiliar cultural landscape. Fashioning oneself as a full citizen also involved complex negotiations around their acculturated coreligionists' perceptions of "foreign" accents, "dusky" skin tones, and perhaps most significant, "alien" ideas about sex, gender, and consumption.

Sephardim in the South

Historian Yitzchak Kerem hypothesizes that the few Sephardim who migrated to southern cities at the turn of the twentieth century did so because of the familiar climate and positive reports from Greek Orthodox neighbors who had settled there successfully.[8] By the early 1900s, Montgomery, Alabama, boasted a thriving and prosperous Jewish community—complete with both a Reform and an Orthodox congregation—that drew a steady stream of Sephardic young men from the Isle of Rhodes. Most settled in the Five Points area among the other Jewish immigrants.[9]

Many Sephardic immigrants who originally settled in Montgomery were later attracted to Atlanta for its larger size and comparatively greater economic opportunities. The history of Atlanta's Sephardic congregation, Or V'Shalom (Light and Peace), describes how Montgomery supplied the city's first Sephardic citizens, Victor Avzaradel and Ezra Tourial, in 1906.[10] Tourial soon became a successful businessman, overseeing both the Majestic Shoe Company and a laundry business. He also achieved prominence as a leader of the Sephardic community, serving as president of Or V'Shalom and establishing a free loan society. He quickly earned the respect of the city's elite Ashkenazim, which enabled him to serve on the boards of the Hebrew Orphans Home, the Montefiore Relief Association, and the Federation of Jewish Charities, where he helped represent the needs of the growing Sephardic community.[11]

While such openly derogatory characterizations as Louis Hacker's were rare in southern cities that held a significantly smaller Sephardic population, Ashkenazim, U.S.-born and foreign-born alike, nevertheless expressed their skepticism of the former's Jewish authenticity. One of the first Sephardic women to live in Atlanta, Rebecca Amiel, noted that her inability to speak Yiddish made it difficult for her Ashkenazic neighbors to believe that she was Jewish.[12] Steven Hertzberg describes the less than hospitable relations between Atlanta's Sephardim and their coreligionists: while "Ashkenazim were suspicious of the swarthy complexioned newcomers from the Levant," he explained, "the Sephardim reciprocated with aloofness, partly in an attempt to maintain their self-respect but also out of an impoverished hidalgo's sense of inner superiority."[13] The new Sephardic southerners therefore found themselves culturally, religiously, and linguistically at odds with their more established coreligionists.

By the time Victor and Rachel Ferrera emigrated from Turkey in the 1910s, approximately 150 Sephardim were living in Atlanta, at the time one of the South's largest populations of Sephardic immigrants. The community had grown to almost twice the size of Montgomery's and included immigrants from the Isle of Rhodes, Turkey, Crete, Bodrum, and Izmir.[14] Despite the two-hundred-mile distance between them, ties of culture and kinship linked the Sephardim of both cities. Rachel's sister lived in Montgomery, and over the course of her decade-long relationship with Atlanta's Montefiore Relief Association—the city's

Jewish family welfare organization—the Ferreras would often consider relocating to Montgomery to be closer to family and possible business opportunities.

The family's case opened officially the summer or 1929, several months before the stock market crash, and the family continued receiving aid from the MRA off and on until the late thirties. When Rachel first approached the MRA for help, the administrators requested information about the family from Ezra Tourial, by then a leading member of the Sephardic community.[15] He confirmed that they were "worthy," thereby cementing his collaboration with the largely Ashkenazic Atlanta Jewish Federation.[16] Social workers from the MRA and the orphan home would continue to look to Tourial for advice and support as they worked to help the Ferreras and other indigent Sephardic families back on their feet.[17]

As we have seen, the confidential nature of institutional case files makes them particularly valuable as a lens on competing ideals of cultural citizenship and cultural capital that were negotiated between social workers and their clients. Since it was the caseworker's duty to establish and then to eliminate the roots of a family's poverty and cultural alienation, she recorded every factor she felt might inhibit her clients' success as self-sufficient and respectable citizens. The case files therefore convey a rich and detailed sense of the ways predominantly Ashkenazic social workers, like the MRA's Rose Goldstein and the orphan home's Viola Wyle, detected and analyzed the perceived differences of their Sephardic clients and how these clients in turn struggled to survive in conditions of dire poverty. As in Rebecca Weiss's case, social uplift efforts were not always a linear matter of lifting a family out of poverty or teaching them the trappings of elite cultural capital. Rather, immigrant families sometimes actively resisted benevolent agency's efforts to impose their own versions of assimilation and independence, preferring instead to integrate the habits of their Old Country with the social and cultural dictates of their new home.

According to the family's case file, Victor and Rachel both came from well-off families in Turkey, they were married in 1913 in Constantinople when Rachel was eighteen and Victor was thirty-three, and, by means and routes that are not disclosed, arrived in Atlanta several years thereafter.[18] The 1920 Census lists the couple as living at 89 Woodward

Avenue, an area populated by Greek and Italian families. At that time, Victor was proprietor of a hat factory, and their three children ranged in age from one to six.[19] The family became prominent in Atlanta's Sephardic community, as evidenced by Rachel's role as cofounder and president of the city's Nessah Israel (Eternal Israel) Society, a charitable organization of Sephardic women, in 1920.[20] Among the Sisterhood's many charitable efforts were contributions to the Atlanta Hebrew Orphans Home, the Red Cross, and Or V'Shalom. In an odd twist of fate, the organization that Rachel Ferrera helped found would also subsidize the Federation of Jewish Charities, in whose institutional archives her family's voluminous case file remains to this day.[21]

By the late 1920s, the Ferreras had fallen into debt as Victor found it increasingly difficult to make a living in the hat-making and cleaning business. Struggling to support their growing family on Victor's unpredictable salary, they moved with their five children to Richardson Street, a working-class neighborhood with significantly fewer foreign-born families.[22] This long-running case is notable for its limited focus on the children, for, as the case evolved, the parents' troubles consumed most of the social worker's energies, generating deep anxieties about the family's chances for economic independence and success. The MRA originally classified the Ferreras as a desertion case, as Goldstein (and possibly Rachel Ferrera herself) suspected that Victor had absconded permanently to the West Coast. Having followed a friend's advice to seek employment in Los Angeles, where well-paying skilled jobs were rumored to be plentiful, Victor was unable to secure enough work to support himself. He took ill and required hospitalization before returning to his family in August at the MRA's expense.

In her first interview with Victor, Goldstein learned of the couple's tumultuous marriage and their efforts three years prior to obtain a *get* from the city's Sephardic rabbi.[23] At his urging, the couple had agreed to reconcile, but throughout their relationship with the MRA, their case file documents continuous marital instability and discord. While the social worker presumed that their greatest difficulty was intimate incompatibility, issues of sexual dysfunction and infidelity were inextricable from the couple's seemingly irreconcilable differences in social and cultural comportment and their divergent efforts to adjust to the customs of their adoptive homeland.

Seeing Race: Characterizing the "Semitic Type"

Like the eastern Europeans concurrently fleeing political persecution, the Sephardic immigrants experienced the extreme poverty that led many of them to the doors of local Jewish charitable organizations. In the Ferreras' case, the Atlanta Montefiore Relief Association extended a helping hand in the form of monthly subsidies and assistance securing employment for Victor. Opened in 1896, and named for the eminent Sephardic philanthropist Moses Montefiore, the MRA comprised what Ed Kahn, director of the Atlanta Federation of Jewish Charities, described as the Federation's "Family Welfare Unit."[24] One of the Federation's charter members, the MRA not only provided financial support to needy families and individuals, but it also engaged professional social workers to help guide them on a path to independence and acculturation.

One of these professionals was Rose Goldstein, employed as the Association's secretary during the 1920s until she was promoted to caseworker in 1933.[25] Goldstein's relationship with the Ferreras, which began several years before she was officially appointed as a caseworker, suggests that the Federation and its constituent member organizations may have struggled to accommodate the volume of family need for professional guidance and supervision as well as financial support. Having migrated from Poland in 1910, Goldstein would have been well acquainted with the intricacies of acculturation.[26] Although the MRA hired more workers as the needs and population of the community grew, Goldstein's eventual position as director of case work ensured her contact with most of the families served during her tenure, and many of the case files therefore bear the distinct signature of her professional insights.

Appearance ranked high among the most important characteristics for social workers, for being "seen" as a citizen required strict adherence to a prescribed code of white aesthetics and respectability. The fact that case files from both the Atlanta orphan home and the Montefiore Relief Association described their Sephardic clients as "W" for "white" might lead one to believe that social workers viewed Sephardim as racially uncomplicated. The "W" used for all their clients suggests social workers' perception that their designation as similarly "Jewish" bound Sephardim and Ashkenazim together in the eyes of the larger world. Beyond this initial classification, however, other visible indicators of race—including but not limited to body type and complexion—invited careful evaluation from Ashkenazic caseworkers.

Despite their universal designation as "W" in the case records, the vigilance with which social workers evaluated the appearance and skin tone of their Sephardic clients suggests the former's perception of an essential Sephardic difference as well as a possible correlation between judgments of racial difference and moral and intellectual inferiority. To the contemporary viewer, photos from institutional records betray scant evidence of Sephardim's supposedly darker skin tones, but one must bear in mind the influence of racial epistemologies on the ways in which difference is "seen" in a given time and place. In Matthew Frye Jacobson's words, "Race is not just a conception; it is also a perception."[27] Case files, memoirs, and institutional records bear witness to a general perception of Sephardic immigrants as both dark and foreign, regardless of how the contemporary observer might see them. While Ashkenazic social workers, like Rose Goldstein, went to great lengths to describe the skin tone—from "ruddy" or "swarthy" to "light"—of their Sephardic clients, they rarely made such judgments for Ashkenazim. According to Goldstein's notes after meeting the Ferreras, Rachel and her five children were all "attractive," as they possessed blue eyes, blond hair, and light skin. Victor received a less flattering description as "dark complected [and] apparently overweight." Further, noted Goldstein, he spoke "with a decided foreign accent."[28] Future case notes would confirm her impression of Victor as less intelligent, less refined, and less capable than his wife and children of adapting to cultural norms.

Another, unnamed, MRA social worker recorded a similarly detailed description of the physical appearance of her new clients, the Valensis, in 1930. Having emigrated from the Isle of Rhodes, the Valensis applied to the MRA for assistance during Mr. Valensi's convalescence from a heart illness. The caseworker offered the following description of Mr. Valensi: "Tall, angular . . . dark complexioned, [with] small brown eyes. His features are small . . . [he was] dressed neatly and seems to have taken pride in his appearance . . . speaks with a distinct Spanish accent." Eva Valensi, she wrote, "is [of] medium height and rather fleshy. She has brown hair, fair complexion. Her features are large and coarse. Her eyes are large brown . . . W[oman] is neat about her person as well as her household [and] tak[es] upon herself all household duties. She is active, intelligent, and seems willing to cooperate."[29] Despite the social worker's positive first impressions of the family, she noted Mr. Valensi's "distinct" accent as well as the darkness of his skin. Only Eva, who possessed a "fair complexion," was described as "intelligent."

The Lopez family received similar scrutiny. Mr. Lopez's death in February 1929 prompted Rose Goldstein's first home visit, after which she described the appearance of her new clients. Born in 1891 in Constantinople, Lenora Lopez was small in stature, thirty-eight years old, five foot two, 110 pounds, and had "black hair and eyes; [and a] ruddy complexion." In describing Lenora's four children, Goldstein's classifications of skin tone ranged from "dark" to "ruddy" to "pale." In Goldstein's opinion, it was only the "pale" child, a boy of five, who "seem[ed] especially bright for his age."[30] No other family members' intellect received such high praise.[31] Goldstein also described finding "numerous members of the Sephardic community in [the Lopez] house," many of whom "had contributed direct[ly] to W[oman] as that is the custom among their people to render gifts in the form of cash, if family is in need."[32] She noted that the "family is living in a fair neighborhood which is made up almost completely of Sephardic people." Although her characterization suggested that such a neighborhood could not aspire to be anything better than "fair," the social worker seemed gratified to know that the "family [was] well thought of among Sephardic Jews."[33]

Even these reports of a "fair" neighborhood and a family's social stability could not shake Goldstein's suspicion of her clients' difference. On another visit, she found the family eating a lunch consisting of "dishes known to them but foreign to visitor."[34] Another visit found Lenora "and children at the table, partaking of a supposedly wholesome lunch, which consisted of some Spanish dishes, including vegetables and meats. Mother and children appeared cheerful and seemed to enjoy their meal; invited V[isitor] to eat with them. V[isitor] waited until W[oman] completed her meal, in the meantime, spoke to the children regarding their school and general activities."[35] The social worker's refusal to join the family for dinner suggests her sense of her clients' cultural difference and inferiority. Even in the context of this very clean home—which, unlike many Sephardic homes depicted in case files, was never described as less than spotless—the caseworker could not bring herself to eat such "foreign" food.

Professional judgments on family members' supposedly darker complexions also influenced social workers' assessment of clients' sexuality. Later in her interactions with the Lopez family, Goldstein described in depth the appearance of the two oldest girls, ages seventeen and fifteen: "Muriel is attractive. She is of the Semitic type. She is quiet and reticent, and has an air of sophistication about her." Judy, the younger daughter, was "also very attractive, and . . . of the Semitic type. She is reserved, but more talkative and alert than Muriel."[36] Goldstein's description suggests her perception of Muriel, the oldest and the only Lopez child born outside the United States, as slightly less respectable than her siblings. In the early twentieth century, "sophistication" was not considered an attribute for teenage girls, but was rather a veiled reference to a girl's advanced sexual maturity and potential for delinquency. Although later records revealed Muriel to be a virtuous young woman who socialized primarily with other girls, Goldstein's suspicions about her sexual maturity continued to manifest themselves in her reports.[37] Goldstein did not invest the same time commenting on the younger brother's appearance, reflecting popular beliefs that young women's appearance was vital to their future success. Further, their younger brother's "pale" skin, combined with his presumed unusual intelligence, gave him, in Goldstein's assessment, a distinct advantage in obtaining independence and respectability. The exoticizing label of "Semitic type" suggests Goldstein's presumption of the girls' foreignness; they were "attractive" young women only *despite* their difference.

Goldstein paid similarly close attention to the complexions of members of the Ferrera family, describing the five "children [as] attractive, apparently [their] health [is] good, quite playful and alert . . . All the children have the same coloring, blue eyes, blond hair, fair complexion."[38] Her initial impressions of the children and their mother's attractiveness would influence her assessment of their potential for success. Yet despite her careful scrutiny of the children's appearance, Goldstein would spend most of her time managing Rachel and Victor's marital tribulations.

"The Crux of the Situation Is Sexual": Intimacy, Consumption, and Dependency in the Sephardic Family

The challenges of Jewish authenticity and "coethnic recognition failure" manifested themselves in the ways social workers diagnosed the roots of a family's problems. Based on data in the case records, Sephardic immigrants appeared to be at a disadvantage due to their poverty, their limited education and opportunities for economic success, and what their Ashkenazic coreligionists perceived as their darker complexions and unfamiliar habits and behaviors. Presumptions of her clients' exoticism influenced Goldstein's approach to her Sephardic clients' problems and inflected the solutions she proposed.

Goldstein recorded her impressions of the Ferreras' struggle to become self-sufficient, highlighting what she perceived as Rachel's extravagance and Victor's foreign, Old World behaviors, and she kept a careful record of her observations about the couple's intimate relationship. She recorded Victor's reflections on his wife: "In the past when he could not provide her demands [for money] she would beat him and hit the children threatening divorce, but on account of being madly in love with her he could not make up his mind to leave her."[39] Victor "claim[ed] to love his wife 'more than he loves himself'" but described her as "a very selfish person" who often "banished him from their bed."[40] He confided to Goldstein his inability to satisfy his wife's desire for money and her tendency to "tease" him sexually. Noting that Victor "admits to masturbation, and claims that he would restrain from sexual relationship if wife would do her share," Goldstein eventually suggested that the couple invest in a separate bed "so that there will be plenty of room in the house." Yet Rachel "refuse[d] to sleep in other bed unless [Victor] gives up the feather mattress on which they are accustomed to sleep."[41]

For her part, Rachel reported that her husband threatened to "get her pregnant if she made him angry," and Goldstein commiserated with her over Victor's sexual coerciveness.[42] Recognizing that Rachel's multiple pregnancies and self-induced miscarriages were contributing to marital discord, she put her in touch with a nurse "for instructions in contraceptive methods."[43] Yet it became clear that the unplanned pregnancies were only part of the problem. Goldstein later recorded Rachel's "friendly attitudes towards [the boarder] Mr. G.," and documented

Victor's struggle to come to terms with allegations of his wife's affair.[44] Long after Mr. G. moved out of the family's home, Victor continued to notice the appearance of mysterious gifts, such as "a half a gallon of caviar in the icebox," and to hear reports of his wife consorting with Mr. G., but he felt powerless to fight the romantic sway of this charming, French-born "home breaker."[45]

In a private meeting with Goldstein, Rachel explained that "no one knows what she has to contend with; that if she did not seek recreation she would be in an insane asylum." Claiming that "their home life revolves around sex," Rachel insisted that her active social life was vital to her mental health. She exclaimed, "'Send me a married woman and I'll tell her what I have to put up with.' She said that she cannot stand it any longer from him . . . that before she can get money from him, she has to satisfy him sexually."[46] After two years of working with the Ferreras, Goldstein diagnosed the couple's problem—indeed, the whole family's dependency. She noted in the case file, "The crux of the situation is sexual."[47]

The Ferreras were not the only couple whose intimate life was implicated in their family's struggles with dependency. Another couple from Turkey, Mr. and Mrs. Mendes, also received Goldstein's careful scrutiny and analysis. In this case, however, Goldstein determined that the couple's "sex life has been congenial."[48] When Mrs. Mendes was advised by her doctor not to have more children because of a heart condition, Goldstein praised Mr. Mendes for being "most considerate of her" by not insisting on intercourse more than several times a month.[49] The Mendes case opened within one year of the Ferreras', and Goldstein similarly characterized Mrs. Mendes as "very refined and very charming."[50] Yet despite the couple's immigrant status, Goldstein did not experience similar difficulties helping the couple negotiate a path to independence.

For the Ferreras, problems of intimacy appeared closely linked to their irreconcilable views on consumption. Goldstein noted that Rachel spent significant money and time maintaining her own and the children's appearance, according to Victor, "always wanting to dress above her means . . . anything that is stylish she wants to be the first one to have it" and "demand[ing] that the children have the most expensive clothing."[51] She also valued domestic appearances, investing the family's scant income in fine furnishings, and, even when the family could not afford food, she employed a servant. Goldstein's favorable first impressions of the Ferrera home as "neatly furnished and well-kept" suggest that she appreciated the time, attention, and money Rachel spent on personal and domestic upkeep:

> [The] living room has piano, center table, chairs. Dining room has suite of furniture, also oriental tapestry hanging on the wall. Both living room and dining room have carpets on the floors. 2 bedrooms contain 2 beds in each room, dressers, tables, and chairs. Kitchen equipped with cabinet gas range, coal stove, ice box. Bathroom has enamel bathtub, stationary, heating apparatus for hot water. W[oman] showed her Maytag Washing machine and claimed that same means a saving to her. Furniture bears evidence of having been in the house for a number of years; none of it is fancy but seems to be in good condition.[52]

Despite her appreciation for Rachel's good taste and attractive appearance, Goldstein became increasingly concerned by her client's excessive spending on clothing, home furnishings, music lessons for her children, and entertainment. On Goldstein's advice, Rachel returned much of their new furniture, but refused to part with the piano. In a way similar to Rebecca Weiss's resolute attachment to costly commodities, Rachel retained what she perceived as a vital symbol of respectable middle-class leisure and perhaps a reminder of her family's former economic prosperity. Throughout their client–social worker relationship, Rachel resisted the social worker's recommendations for cost-cutting, and the latter eventually decided to "work through [Victor], giving him $ directly for bills, etc." rather than risk seeing the MRA's funds mishandled by Rachel.[53]

While Goldstein was critical of Rachel's extravagance, Victor's problems were equally concerning, because they confirmed his foreignness and stubborn incapacity to adapt to the ways of his new home. While Rachel threw herself with abandon into the modern world of consumption, in which women shored up their family's respectability by accumulating objects with which to beautify themselves and their homes, Victor exhibited retrograde ideas about consumption, production, and the roles of men and women in a modern society. It was his practice, reflecting traditions in Turkey, to purchase and occasionally prepare the family's food, rather than cede control over the family budget to his wife. He explained to Goldstein that he could not entrust the shopping to his wife for fear that she would spend the money on gambling and clothing, allowing the children to go hungry. Rachel often expressed resentment at Victor's allocation of family income for expensive foods. Purchasing groceries may have been Victor's way of maintaining control over some aspect of the family's consumption since he was unable to serve as the home's provider. Although Goldstein condemned his "Oriental habit" that clashed with prevailing beliefs that grocery shopping was women's work, she allowed him to continue doing so as a way of protecting the MRA's subsidy from Rachel's fiscal irresponsibility.[54]

Goldstein's narrative of the couple's tumultuous intimate life highlights the interrelated nature of gender and consumption, racial intelligibility and cultural capital. These concepts were tightly linked in the minds of the Ferreras, as well as in Goldstein's diagnosis of their troubles. She and Rachel believed that Victor retained too many of the folkways of his Turkish homeland. In addition to purchasing the family's food, he exerted tight control over the activities of his wife and daughters and tried to restrict them to the home. On the other hand, Rachel and her social worker shared the opinion that women should be encouraged to socialize both inside and outside their homes. While Rachel allowed her daughters to socialize with young men, Victor resisted by trying to keep the girls at home. Goldstein labeled his behavior as "tyrannical" and "Oriental," and tried through her meetings with Victor to instill a more modern sensibility.

Although Victor's Old World assumptions about gender, sex, and consumption made Goldstein's efforts to improve the family's circumstances more challenging, Rachel's excessive consumption posed a more immediate threat to the family's stability. Since she could not stay within what Goldstein perceived as a reasonable budget, she placed her family's independence and economic security in jeopardy. According to Goldstein, Rachel's "selfishness" drove her need for such activities as card-playing, riding in cars with unmarried men, throwing parties, and shopping on credit, all of which prevented her from becoming a good mother by MRA standards.

That Goldstein saw fit to record her impressions of the couple's most intimate issues—including what she characterized as Victor's "sexual dysfunction" and occasionally coercive behavior toward his wife, and Rachel's multiple miscarriages and her suspected infidelity with Mr. G.—suggests that the Ferreras' sexual (mis)conduct was of considerable concern to the social worker and influential in her plans for the family's transition to independence. Of equal importance to the couple's assimilation to the larger culture was correcting what Goldstein considered their discordant efforts to navigate the local gender and class norms that clashed with assumptions imported from their homeland. While Victor "seemed to be living in Constantinople rather than in Atlanta, GA.," Rachel threw herself with abandon into her role as a modern American woman by purchasing fashionable clothing, fine home furnishings, and engaging in costly forms of leisure.[55] In contrast to other Sephardic institutional clients, Rachel eventually abandoned many of the traditional Sephardic religious rituals and stopped attending Or V'Shalom, the Sephardic synagogue, in favor of Ahavath Achim, a synagogue for Orthodox Ashkenazim. Rachel also encouraged her girls to socialize primarily with Ashkenazic children, a fact Goldstein took as proof "that the children are rising to a higher standard."[56] Sephardic neighbors occasionally reported to the MRA what they perceived as Rachel's inappropriately extravagant behavior, evincing the disdain with which fellow Sephardim may have perceived Rachel's efforts to disassociate herself from her immigrant community.[57] While Victor's consumer habits rendered him backwards and unassimilable in the eyes of his social worker, Rachel's signified excessive materialism and "selfishness." Both approaches were distressing to the social worker whose job it was to guide them to a self-supporting and respectable existence in Depression-era Atlanta.

Racial Geographies and Sephardic Identity

The institutional case files also provide clues into the complex relationship between immigrant Sephardic identity and southern ideals of race. Filtered through the gaze of professional social workers, the case files nevertheless shed light on the complex ways in which Sephardic immigrants struggled to self-define racially. Taken together, these stories of economic struggle and acculturation reveal variegated translations of the region's notions of class respectability and racial propriety as immigrants tried to negotiate an intricate and shifting color line.

Racial politics were of significant concern to the social worker who oversaw the Atlanta orphan home's subsidy case of the recently widowed Eva Satori of Atlanta. The unnamed social worker—most likely the recently appointed Viola Wyle—recorded some difficulty in her efforts to convince the family to adhere to what she perceived as acceptable racial comportment. The trouble began in May 1929 when the Satori boys, ages fifteen and thirteen, began to spend their after-school time in and around their cousin's Decatur Street shoe shop. The social worker described the boys' habit of being "somewhere on the streets" near the shop while their mother worked from one to ten-thirty each night. Further investigation that fall found the younger boy with "a colored man in charge of the store" while the owner was out to lunch.[58] It was common practice throughout the South for Jewish shopkeepers to employ African Americans, and even for African Americans to be among their primary customers.[59] While such spaces of inter-racial commerce were common, they nevertheless raised concern among the benevolent workers whose job it was to train Jewish immigrants, particularly children, in the intricacies of proper social conduct.

The social worker expressed her disapproval of this arrangement by speaking to Eva Satori the following day about "the inadvisability of having her send the boys to the Decatur Street store."[60] The store's location near the city's red light district and its proximity to a predominantly black and immigrant neighborhood no doubt fueled the social worker's concerns.[61] Furthermore, the social worker disapproved of the boys' supervision by a black man. While social workers often did not object to families employing black women as caretakers within a family's home when mothers recovered from illness, in the Satori case, it appears that gender, race, and geography conspired to create a combination the social worker believed detrimental to the proper education and socialization of Jewish children. Their location on Decatur Street, a neighborhood in which many working-class and poor Atlantans of all races lived, worked, and socialized, was determined to be inimical to the boys' development into ideal citizens.

It is likely that Mrs. Satori did not take the social worker's concerns to heart, for one month later, the latter found the younger boy outside the cousin's shop, this time "sitting on the street talking to some of the neighborhood negroes." In addition to keeping what in the worker's opinion was questionable company, the boy "looked dirty and said that [his] mother [had] instructed him to go to [the] store after school."[62] Once again the social worker noted the child's geographical and racial displacement and reacted by summoning Mrs. Satori to her office. This time the social worker threatened dire consequences should she fail to heed the institution's instructions and choose "to have the boys on Decatur Street." She stated that "our organization would have to take care of these boys" and would "withdraw our subsidy" if Satori failed to cooperate.[63] Full cooperation meant that this widowed mother of two would "remain at home and be there when the boys return from school every afternoon." Furthermore, the social worker arranged for the younger boy to visit the orphan home each day after school to play with the children, and she arranged for both boys to join the home's Boy Scout troop as well as their Tuesday Hebrew class.[64]

For the social worker, absorption into the institutional home's carefully regulated social life was far preferable to the boys' socialization on Decatur Street. As we saw earlier, the home's ability to expose children to approved forms of recreation alongside other white children was considered critical to underprivileged children's development into useful citizens. The home offered training in the values of cleanliness, order, and thrift, while Decatur Street appeared to the social worker to be a place of dirt and danger, of racial and sexual disorder. The social worker therefore served as an enforcer of the "rituals of separation" so vital to the production of authentic Americans.[65] According to her logic, Jewish immigrants might earn a livelihood on Decatur Street by selling their goods and services to its residents, but Jewish children, whether Sephardic or Ashkenazic, could not be allowed to view the area as their rightful place. Social mingling with African Americans, regardless of their class or level of education, was considered a dire threat to the children's racial purity as the idealized "white posts" of Ralph Sonn's invocation. It is unclear in the case record how Mrs. Satori continued earning a living after this meeting, but it appears that she agreed to follow the social worker's orders. To have done otherwise would have meant the home's reconsideration of her "worthiness," which could have led to the end of her subsidy, or worse, the loss of her children to the institution's custody.

The social worker in the Valensi case did not have to resort to such coercive measures to induce the family to conform to the region's logic of racial separation. After an encouraging first impression, the worker seemed even more impressed with this Sephardic immigrant family after meeting Mrs. Valensi's younger sister, Hannah, who Mr. and Mrs. Valensi were raising like a daughter. The case report from the meeting described Hannah as "pleasing to talk to [and] attractive," a poised young lady with great potential. In response to the worker's query regarding Hannah's deferred position in school, Hannah "explained of being one year behind in school because of the [family] taking her to New York about four years ago at which time they thought they might settle there." Hannah continued, describing how she "could not tolerate going to school with the negroes and therefore did not go to school at all in New York. She resumed school only upon her return to Atlanta."[66]

While her family's origins lay in Italy, Hannah's comments suggest her awareness of racial politics in the United States as well as regional differences in black–white relations. Hannah believed that relocation in the South would afford her greater distance from what she perceived as undesirable company. Furthermore, it seems that this young woman rested her self-definition in part on her ability to distinguish herself from racially debased Others, to perform her race as different from and superior to black schoolchildren. She could not achieve this separation in the context of an integrated school system and felt she had to move South to find the racial order she desired.

The social worker's comments reveal little of her opinions of Hannah's story, but the fact that she considered Hannah "pleasing to talk to" suggests that she found nothing troublesome about Hannah's demeanor. Especially considering the importance with which Jewish social workers invested immigrant children's public education, we can assume that wishing not to keep company with "negroes" was an attitude that the social worker understood and perhaps shared. Otherwise, the worker would most likely have characterized Hannah's decision not to attend school as "lazy" or perhaps "prejudiced."

A similar episode appeared in the Ferreras' case file in January 1930. In an effort to make the family self-supporting, Goldstein suggested that they relocate to Montgomery to operate a lunch stand. However, after talking with the business's former proprietor, the couple "did not think the place suitable" for several reasons. The Ferreras had discovered that the unpredictable business "meant a hard living." Furthermore, Rachel explained to Goldstein that "she could not undertake to do the cooking and that her husband does not like to work with negroes as he cannot get along with them."[67] It is unclear whether the people to whom Rachel referred were to be the business's employees or its patrons. Regardless, the couple decided not to purchase the lunch stand even if it meant possible self-sufficiency, because they did not want to risk the racial contamination that such close proximity to blackness threatened. Nor did Goldstein criticize their decision—at least not in their case file—implying that her appreciation for racial order surpassed her ambition to find permanent employment for the family. Even in the dire economic conditions of the Depression, this family's resistance to accepting work was based in a racial logic that the social worker appeared to understand and respect.

"Them Were Her Children": The Ambivalent Intimacy of Domestic Help

Although their clients' adherence to a creed of white supremacy generally aided social workers in their uplift efforts, it was possible for families to push the limits of racial privilege too far. As we have seen, Jewish social workers found that many subsidized families, Ashkenazic and Sephardic alike, hired African American maids for laundry, housework, and occasionally for child care. Although it was common even for poor, white southerners to employ black domestic workers, social workers often perceived this practice as an inappropriate investment of institutional funds. In some cases, such as in the event of a subsidized mother's illness, social workers sanctioned part-time domestic help. For example, the Mendes family first approached the MRA in 1928 after Mrs. Mendes fell ill and was admitted to a sanatorium. The MRA granted Mr. Mendes a weekly stipend so that his three children could receive daytime supervision from "a competent maid."[68] Once Mrs. Mendes regained her health and returned home, she was expected to resume full responsibility for the care of her children.

While employing a maid for child care was usually frowned on unless a mother was ill, both the orphan home and MRA often allowed subsidized families to employ part-time laundresses to spare mothers what was thought to be toilsome and degrading work. However, benevolent institutions usually disapproved of the employment of cooks, general housekeepers, or caregivers. Both institutions supported clients who retained servants even over their social workers' objections. As in the case of Rebecca Weiss, there is evidence that other clients risked institutional good graces by hiding their servants when social workers paid home visits. That subsidized women took such monumental risks, and often were caught in the act, like Weiss, suggests the significance with which they invested the labor of black domestic workers.

Analyzing the ideals of racial, gender, and class entitlement that informed this propensity is neither uncomplicated nor straightforward. On the most practical level, even poor women desired help with their housework and therefore hired the cheapest labor available to them. Particularly in the South, intertwined constructions of race and gender conspired to force black women into the most demeaning and strenuous jobs, such as laundry, child care, cooking, and general cleaning.[69] It was also distinctly a privilege of racial caste that enabled even the most impoverished white women to hire domestic servants. Given southern white efforts to maintain strict public separation between black and white, hiring a black maid helped signify one's racial location as unquestionably white. American studies scholar Phyllis Palmer describes how the presence of a black domestic worker reaffirmed the purity and middle-class refinement of her employer. Delegating the most tedious and undervalued domestic labor to black women helped establish an employer's distance from such corrupting and degrading work, and hence her proximity to white, middle-class gentility.[70] For a southern, Jewish, foreign-born woman, hiring a black female servant may well have seemed a necessary step in the process of becoming a true southern lady. It is therefore not surprising that subsidized Jewish women risked their benevolent organizations' goodwill in order to assume an elevated position in the racial hierarchy, a position that their class status, and often their foreign origins, rendered elusive.

As in other cases, the presence of a domestic servant in the Lopez household became a contentious issue for social worker and client.

During the course of several home visits, Goldstein noted finding a "colored maid" performing various chores such as cooking and ironing. In April 1929 she recommended that Mrs. Lopez "dispense with services of the maid" to save money, but later visits revealed that her client did not heed this advice. During an August visit the worker "found the place clean. W[oman] states that she is doing her general cleaning herself, [and] in this way she is able to bank the additional income." Yet several years later, a surprise visit revealed "the maid . . . washing the clothes." The caseworker reported that Lopez, "who is always conscious of V[isitor]'s finding a maid in the house, remarked that all the maid does is wash the clothes which she cannot do as she is not well."[71] Although Lopez claimed to be suffering with "nervousness," the case file documents the social worker's continued skepticism of her client's integrity.

Rachel Ferrera was similarly insistent about retaining the services of a maid even while she received institutional support. Goldstein recorded that "W[oman] keeps a colored maid in the house on account of being weak. Pays her $3 a week. Maid has been with her for several years and understands her circumstances, and is willing to be of service to her and work for a small salary."[72] Goldstein's early "Plan Suggested" included moving the family to more affordable housing, returning Victor from Los Angeles, and discharging the maid. In July Goldstein authorized the family to hire the same maid, Betsy Williams, to do the wash and ironing temporarily while Rachel recovered from a miscarriage. As with the Lopez family, hiring a domestic servant was allowed in cases of a mother's infirmity but was otherwise considered an unaffordable luxury.

Although Rachel reported dismissing Mrs. Williams on July 31, "as her week was up," a later visit revealed that she had rehired her without Goldstein's knowledge. Goldstein visited the home to find "maid with [daughters] Esther and Pearl on porch. Maid says that she assists Mrs. F with her laundry. This evening [Rachel] asked that she stay with the children while she and her husband go down town."[73] This tension between the social worker's expectations for frugality and Rachel's desire for domestic help would continue throughout the MRA's relationship with the Ferreras. A month later, when Rachel complained to Goldstein about making ends meet, the latter advised her to keep within her budget, "that it does not take into consideration music lessons for Simon, nor clothing nor maid service."[74] Goldstein later recorded her suspicions regarding what she perceived as Rachel's dishonesty: "Although worker occasionally sees maid in the house W[oman] still contends that she only comes in twice a week to do her washing and ironing, which she is physically unable to do and for which she pays $1.50 per week."[75]

Goldstein's visit to the Ferrera home in February 1931 allowed her to speak to Betsy Williams concerning her relationship with the family. Since Rachel had gone to Montgomery with one of her daughters, Williams was caring for the other children and "had given them dinner, which consisted of cabbage." "Seeing the interest the maid was taking in the children," Goldstein initiated a conversation, inquiring about her plans for the children's dinner and asking "how long she had been there."[76] According to Goldstein, Williams replied, "Them were her children, and that she had raised them," while working for the family steadily for the past twelve years. Williams also described working for the family "for nothing" when they lacked money to pay her.[77] Such was her ostensible devotion to the family that Williams occasionally sent her own daughter to clean for the Ferreras when she could not do so herself. During another home visit while Rachel was away, Goldstein recorded the following exchange:

> Maid showed V[isitor] how well she ironed. She said that for the past few months she has not been working regularly, and only comes in about three times a week to do the washing and ironing. She comes whenever she wants to as W[oman] only pays her for the laundry. Maid complained of finding it hard since W[oman] can not employ her full time. She said that she does not earn as much as she used to when she worked regularly. Maid said that when she was working full time, W[oman] would go out a great deal, but now W[oman] keeps busy doing her housework. W[oman] only goes out when maid comes to do the washing.[78]

Although filtered through Goldstein's perspective, the record of these encounters offers rare insight into the ambivalently intimate relationship between a southern domestic worker and her employing Jewish immigrant family. The paradox of this interracial symbiosis placed

Williams's professions of devotion to the Ferreras and her alleged willingness to work "for nothing"—even during a time of great economic hardship—in juxtaposition to the Ferreras' earlier protestations against "working with Negroes."[79] Like the southern orphan homes' dependence on the affective and physical exertions of black women employed as nursemaids and cooks, here was a relationship based simultaneously on interdependence and disavowal. Williams had likely forged a close relationship with the Ferreras during their twelve-year acquaintance, and the family might have compensated Williams for her work with food and clothing, as Rachel was an accomplished seamstress. The exchanges also suggest Williams's efforts to cover for Rachel by explaining her own presence as an exigent, temporary measure, or by insisting that Rachel "only goes out when [she] comes to do the washing" so that the children were not left unsupervised. Certainly such relationships were not uncommon in the Jim Crow South, where, as we have seen, Jews and African Americans often made common cause in their efforts to survive economically turbulent times.[80]

Goldstein's depiction of Williams bears a striking resemblance to popular narratives of the loyal and self-abnegating black servant whose devotion to her white family superseded her attachment to her own. Emerging in the wake of Reconstruction, the "mammy" ideal reinforced Lost Cause justification of black servitude by insisting on the compassion and generosity of white masters and employers.[81] This pervasive story may have provided Williams a conveniently legible narrative to convince a skeptical social worker of her devotion in order to avoid the further institutional scrutiny that might have resulted in her dismissal.

Also likely is the possibility that Ferrera and Williams were savvy enough to have discussed ahead of time their plan of action in case Goldstein found the latter working in a capacity other than as a part-time laundress. Williams would have recognized that her continued employment in the Ferrera household was contingent on the social worker's belief that she often worked "for nothing" and chiefly did the family's laundry. We cannot know for certain whether Williams received a consistent wage for her labor while working for the Ferreras. Yet she remained with the family throughout their relationship with the MRA, a fact that confirms both Rachel's belief that Williams's work was a critical component of the family's survival and Williams's perception that working for the Ferreras was worth her time.

Goldstein held many private discussions with Rachel over her apparent misuse of the institution's funds for "selfish purposes." Although Goldstein diagnosed Victor as "delusional and nervous," she was more troubled by his assertions that his wife continued to employ domestic help and to play poker while Williams watched the children.[82] Goldstein considered these allegations serious enough to warrant a discussion with Rachel, in which she "advise[d her] that the organization can not function in her behalf unless she cooperates with our plan." Rachel's reply to this veiled threat surprised Goldstein: "She did not pretend any more of not having a maid, however, said that should she be forced to discharge the maid she will leave home." When Goldstein asked "whether she would give up her children for the sake of satisfying her own desires," Rachel's answer confirmed Goldstein's suspicions that she was "primarily interested in herself." According to Goldstein's case report, Rachel "will not conceive of giving up her comforts and offers many excuses why she can't do without a maid."[83] After another visit revealed Williams doing general housework and caring for the children, Goldstein recorded Rachel's insistence that she could "live on bread and water just so she had a maid."[84] The social worker diagnosed Rachel's "mania for a maid" as part of her overall "selfish character."[85]

Rachel's defiant reply—her willingness to abandon her family should she be deprived of Williams's services—provided the trump card against which Goldstein and the MRA were powerless. Goldstein's professional judgment held Rachel to be "more to blame for their marital disharmony" than Victor, but her abandonment would have sent the family hurtling into cultural chaos.[86] While she diagnosed Rachel as "selfish" and dishonest, Goldstein knew that her influence on the children provided a necessary counterpart to Victor's retrograde ideas and "Oriental habits." Rachel might not be an ideal mother by the MRA's standards, but her refinement and elevated sense of cultural capital were of great value to her children's successful upbringing.

After the same visit, Goldstein reported that "W[oman] was dressed very nicely, face all fixed up. House was clean; children looked all well and happy." When Rachel complained that the family did not have enough to eat, Goldstein suggested that "the money she spends for [the] maid she could use for food." She also told Rachel "that V[isitor] will not call to see her again until she changes her mode of living," but this turned out to be an empty threat.[87] The MRA continued supporting the family, and Goldstein continued her visits, despite Rachel's stubborn defiance.

"Easily Swayed by Gossip": Superstition, Cultural Capital, and Client Rebellion

Clients' clashes with social workers and instances of rebellion against institutional prescriptions offer the opportunity to scrutinize the ways in which Sephardic southerners struggled to self-define. While case files issue from the social worker's point of view, filtered through the latter's perceptions of clients' foreignness and cultural backwardness, a close reading illuminates moments when clients fought to control the benevolent relationship in ways that challenged their social workers and the institutions they served. For example, the Atlanta orphan home's social worker noticed Eva Satori's mutual affection for her distant cousin and urged them to consider marriage, but they refused due to what the social worker perceived as an irrational "superstition." Since the man in question possessed the same first name as Satori's father, the couple feared that—if they married—a curse would threaten their lives. However, what appeared to the social worker as her client's stubborn adherence to "family tradition and superstition" may have been an effort to preserve a modicum of independence.[88] While the social worker hoped that marriage would allow her client to live independent of the home's assistance, Satori may have seen marriage as an imposition on her personal autonomy.

Adina Castanada similarly frustrated her social worker by seeking medical care from a doctor recommended by her neighbors rather than the MRA's preferred doctor at Grady Memorial Hospital. The case report described with frustration Castanada's habit of missing her appointments at Grady. Castanada explained "that she has more faith in Dr. Petway and that the Grady doctors were not helping her."[89] North Carolinian Frank E. Petway was likely not Jewish, and it is unclear why he was the preferred physician for Castanada and her friends.[90] It is possible that some institutional clients resented being sent to a hospital that catered to the city's indigent.[91] The social worker's report dismissed Castanada as "easily swayed by gossip of neighbors," but it appears that she was able to see the doctor of her choice.[92] In this case, as in Eva Satori's, the client's desire for privacy, independence, and the power to make her own decisions came into conflict with the social worker's sense of scientific efficiency and rationality. Although their preferences were ultimately dismissed as "superstitious" stubbornness, these clients were able to obtain a small measure of independence from the interference of their social workers and the benevolent agencies that supported them.

Evidence from the case files implies that Rachel Ferrera may have been little more than an extravagant, poker-playing, selfish woman who engaged in illicit relations with her boarder. But the institution continued supporting her, just as the orphan home continued supporting Rebecca Weiss even after she defied the Wyles' instructions. Records of subsidized immigrant mothers' resistance evince the complexity of southern Jewish struggles for survival and cultural citizenship in conditions of dire poverty. For Rachel and Rebecca, emulating high cultural capital required a combination of practices that often stood at odds with their social worker's vision for their families' improvement. It meant dressing themselves and their children well, even when nourishing food was lacking. They also maintained clean, tastefully decorated homes and worked to distance themselves and their children from low or debasing cultural influences.

Further, the presence of African American women in their homes was especially vital as a means of guaranteeing their own distance from the toilsome labor that threatened to "blacken," physically and socially, those who performed it. Efforts to understand why a "colored maid" could be of such importance to impoverished mothers must center in part on the mothers' perceptions of their families' (as well as their individual) survival and chances for social escalation. Stories of subsidized women's "mania for a maid" reveal clients' perceptions that servants were necessary not only to maintain order in the home but also to signal the family's social standing. Since the southern convergence of race, gender, and work conspired to designate domestic labor as uniquely black women's work, the presence of African American maids—in institutional as well as private spaces—helped elevate the employers' racial status by underscoring their distance from blackness.

Despite Rachel Ferrera's resistance to her social worker's orders, and Goldstein's diagnosis of her as "primarily interested in herself," the MRA continued to support the family throughout the 1930s. The institution's loyalty suggests that Goldstein may have seen more potential in the family than she expressed in her reports. While the Ferreras may not have been ideal parents, they managed to keep their children well clothed, neat, educated, and cultured, and, despite their poverty, Rachel and her children set forth an image of dignity and refinement. While they were under the MRA's care, the Ferrera children were never reported roaming the streets, associating with people deemed inappropriate company, or engaging in illicit or dishonest practices. In other words, they were well-bred, "light-skinned" Jewish children with significant potential for developing into respectable citizens. As with other Jewish philanthropic institutions whose central motive was to create upstanding models of Jewish citizenship, the MRA may have seen in the Ferrera children a worthwhile investment of their time and money. Indeed, the Ferrera boys would both grow up to serve in the U.S. military during World War II, alongside the three formerly subsidized Mendes boys.[93]

Rachel Ferrera's insistence on hiring a maid, purchasing music lessons for her children, and securing fine clothes and leisure time for herself suggests a deeper story about her sense of class propriety as well as her understanding of her proper place in a relationship of production and consumption. Indeed, consumption served as a key site on which suspicious race, gender, and sexual differences converged. During a time of extreme poverty and economic instability, social workers understandably took an interest in the ways their clients spent their subsidies, as evidenced by the battles that raged between social workers and ostensibly undisciplined or spendthrift clients. Yet the stories in the case files suggest that more than the clients' mere survival was at stake in these confrontations. That otherwise private matters like home décor, food consumption, and sexual conflict were subject to the social worker's scrutiny demonstrates that successful incorporation into the citizenry demanded a meticulously staged performance of respectability and adherence to prevailing social norms. Certainly some case files provide a view—straight to the bedroom in the Ferreras' case—for scholars interested in the ways that these norms of belonging took shape. This and other cases suggest that a client's rebellions against benevolent institutional imperatives often occurred in protest against the narrow confinements of her racial ascription as a Sephardic, Jewish noncitizen dependent on private charity for her survival. Rebelling against characterizations of Sephardim as irrational, uncultured, and ignorant, Rachel Ferrera was determined to exemplify culture and refinement. Her efforts to obtain a high standard of living provide us a window onto a foreign-born woman's interpretation of privileged cultural citizenship in Depression-era Atlanta.

Conclusion

Loving Kindness and Its Legacies

A few years ago, the *Journal for the Scientific Study of Religion* released a study, conducted by economist Mark Ottoni-Wilhelm, comparing the charitable giving of U.S. families representing various religious communities. Ottoni-Wilhelm concluded that Jewish families demonstrated exceptional generosity, and he explained the difference in part as a result of the traditional association of Jewishness with charity.[1] So goes the circular logic: more Jews give generously to charity because they understand charity as an essential part of being Jewish. Certainly this logic has merit, and the legacy of this impulse runs deep. As this book has shown, Jewish benevolence nationwide has been characterized by its liberality and longevity. But the roots of Jewish benevolent exceptionalism, or "excess" in Laura Levitt's words, are inextricable from the circumstances of struggle and social coercion under which Jews have historically tried to fashion "themselves and their Jewishness into something familiar."[2] Benevolence has long constituted a critical part of Jewish efforts to become legible to the larger world, to be "like everybody else, only more so."[3]

The ambivalence at the heart of loving kindness is eloquently expressed in the seal of the nation's first Hebrew Benevolent Society. Forged in silver in 1784 in Charleston, the angel of death wielding an hourglass in one hand and a scythe in the other evoked the tension between self-sacrifice and self-interest, between life-prolonging charity on one hand and death on the other. From the first American Jewish settlements, these tensions shaped the politics of loving kindness—"that pride of race and character" in Benjamin Franklin Jonas's words—framing collective belonging for a people whose rights to the full benefits of juridical and symbolic citizenship were perennially in question.

And yet, after the Civil War, this dynamic of struggle and contestation was most pronounced in the Jim Crow South, a place where adherence to the strictures of the color line dictated the terms of belonging and where perceived Jewish difference—religious, cultural, linguistic, and historical—placed Jews in an unpredictable relationship to those volatile terms. While Jews nationwide constructed a benevolent empire that reached throughout even the smallest communities, in the South the performance of benevolence was no less than a matter of survival. Benevolence served as a means for established members of this minoritized community to control the process of meaning-making by which authentic citizens were known. The Jews of the South therefore became paragons of benevolence in large part because they needed to "take care of their own" in order to navigate the region's precarious racial terrain.

This book contributes to scholarship on racial and ethnic identity by showing that belonging in the South was not just a matter of imitating whiteness; it required a complex staging of one's membership in an ostensibly united community of chivalrous men and respectable ladies. In the Jewish South, benevolence and honor—concepts infused simultaneously with gendered and racialized meaning—were inseparable, and immigrant Jews had to learn to navigate an unfamiliar political and cultural climate in which particular modes of etiquette and collective memory were essential. Their exceptional performance of *gemilut hasadim* gave southern Jews a means of proving not just their capacity to "take care of their own"; it provided irrefutable proof of their belonging in a narrative of southern transcendence.

The South's Jewish orphan homes therefore stood as exemplars of "the good work," raising the children of poor brethren to a level of cultural citizenship unavailable to most of their parents, and training them for lives of prosperity and service to their communities. But the very process of transmitting cultural citizenship to less fortunate brethren lent itself to coercion and inequality, reinforcing rather than challenging the social norms that placed some people into the category of "citizen" while others remained on the outside looking in. Southern Jews struggled to remain in the former category, and their "good work" helped to ensure that the larger world would judge them worthy of all the privileges, rights, and protections of full belonging.

Studying racialized citizenship through the lens of benevolence offers us a nuanced sense of how race was seen, understood, and managed among southern Jews at a time of significant social, political, economic, and cultural instability. Minoritized members of a community strictly regimented by racial exclusion learned how to shape themselves collectively as members of the powerful race. This meant that benevolent leaders and social workers tried to help their indigent coreligionists reflect the values of white privilege so that the "least of them" would not "cover them all in shame," in Mary Antin's words. This dynamic was present in all locations that Jews called home but was more intense in a region that defined citizenship through racial exclusion. True citizens of the South, those who could participate openly in the political process and pursue economic, social, and political success were unequivocally white. Southern Jewish benevolent negotiations bring to the fore the many complex and ambivalent attitudes that guided the effort to "take care of their own." Race, therefore, was not just about skin color but involved a whole array of performances related to making oneself intelligible as a citizen rather than an outsider. Class, sexuality, and gender norms conspired to produce race; conspicuously consuming things deemed genteel and avoiding certain kinds of manual labor helped some impoverished clients fashion themselves into southern ladies.

The use of confidential, previously hidden sources illuminates the micropolitics of acculturation and cultural/symbolic modes of citizenship and belonging. Since racial knowledge was communicated through sometimes subtly coded language and practices that are not explicitly "about" race, interpreting these sources must be an interdisciplinary project, one that draws from literary analysis as well as social history. Cultural studies provides a critical lens on how meanings are made in space and time, questioning beyond the surface of a text to delve into the complex inner workings of power and inequality that by necessity frame, for instance, the social worker's interpretation of her efforts to convince an errant client to abide by her recommendations. Attention to discourse and accompanying systems of representation allows us to locate moments of complexity and polyvalence, places where mechanisms of power switch direction or work against what may appear on the surface as an actor's own best interests.

These rich sources also reveal immigrant clients' efforts to access the trappings of respectability and to emulate privilege through carefully choreographed consumption and elite outward appearances, evincing the complexity of maximizing one's civic entitlements in the context of poverty and social alienation. Indigent immigrant clients' negotiations with their social workers provide valuable insights into the logic by which southern Jews used benevolence to navigate a shifting and treacherous social terrain. Ultimately, the complex dialectic of benevolent uplift teaches us about the multifarious ways in which individuals understand themselves as members of communities, exposing the sometimes subtle ways in which interethnic Jewish differences mapped onto the racial landscapes of the South. Regional ideals of cultural citizenship and the surrounding epistemologies of race in which they were embedded inflected the delivery of loving kindness to impoverished brethren and shaped the way these immigrant newcomers negotiated the terms of their belonging. Their stories remind us that the path to becoming a true citizen was never a straightforward matter of sacrificing "Old World" ways for new. Rather, historical subjects strained under the weight of their region's multilayered folkways, often making significant sacrifices, to prove themselves worthy of full inclusion in the dominant culture. And today we witness the persistence of these benevolent legacies, and the significance of collective memory to the formation of exemplary citizens.

NOTES

NOTES TO THE INTRODUCTION
1. Of the fifty-one children living in the home when the 1920 U.S. Census was taken, thirteen were listed as foreign-born. This figure did not include children who remained home with their single or widowed mothers and received monthly subsidies. The Census taker originally listed all parents' origins as "unknown" but later added in the margins the foreign-born children's nations of origin. Corresponding case files reveal that many more of these parents—well over half—were of foreign origin.
2. Ralph A. Sonn, Annual Report to the Home's Board of Trustees, December 31, 1917, Atlanta Hebrew Orphans Home–Jewish Educational Loan Fund (hereafter cited as JELF), Annual Reports, Series I, Container II, Ida Pearle & Joseph Cuba Archives and Genealogy Center, William Breman Museum, Jewish Federation of Greater Atlanta, Atlanta, Georgia (hereafter cited as BCA).
3. See Steve Oney's thorough account of the trial, *And the Dead Shall Rise: The Murder of Mary Phagan and the Lynching of Leo Frank* (New York: Pantheon, 2003).
4. Tom Watson used the "Jew Pervert" moniker to refer to Frank on several occasion in *Watson's Magazine*. See, for example, the September 1915 (21:5) issue. See also *Tom Watson's Jeffersonian*, April 23, 1914 (11:17), 9, wherein Watson describes Frank as a "lustful brute" and "lascivious simian." For a detailed analysis of the "black beast" rapist stereotype, see George Frederickson, *The Black Image in the White Mind: The Debate on Afro-American Character and Destiny, 1817–1914* (New York: Harper Torchbooks, 1971).
5. Harry Golden, *Our Southern Landsman* (New York: Putnam, 1974), 86–88.
6. For examples of recent scholarship on charity as a means of promoting ideals of American citizenship, see Cybelle Fox, *Three Worlds of Relief: Race, Immigration, and the American Welfare State from the Progressive Era to the New Deal* (Princeton: Princeton University Press, 2012); Reena Sigman Friedman, *These Are Our Children: Jewish Orphanages in the United States, 1880–1925* (Hanover: University Press of New England for Brandeis University Press, 1994); and Alex Stepick, Terry Rey, and Sarah J. Mahler, eds., *Churches and Charity in the Immigrant City: Religion, Immigration, and Civic Engagement in Miami* (New Brunswick: Rutgers University Press, 2009).

7. Golden, *Our Southern Landsman*, 19.
8. Immanuel Kant, *Groundwork for the Metaphysics of Morals* (Cambridge: Cambridge University Press, 1997), 25.
9. For estimates on the southern Jewish population, see Robert N. Rosen, *The Jewish Confederates* (Columbia: University of South Carolina Press, 2000), 25.
10. Rayford Whittingham Logan, *The Negro in American Life and Thought: The Nadir, 1877–1901* (New York: Dial Press, 1954). While Logan claimed 1901 as the "nadir's" conclusion, more recent scholarship, including work by John Hope Franklin and Henry Arthur Callis, argues that the period of most concentrated racial violence extended into the 1920s. Since many instances of vigilante violence went unreported, precise statistics on the number of people murdered are elusive. Evelyn Brooks Higginbotham estimates that between the years 1884 and 1900 lynch mobs murdered more than 2,500 African Americans, and William Fitzhugh Brundage estimates that 3,220 people were lynched between 1880 and 1930, with an estimated 80 percent of lynchings taking place in the South. See Higginbotham, *Righteous Discontent: The Women's Movement in the Black Baptist Church, 1880–1920* (Cambridge: Harvard University Press, 1993), 4; Brundage, *Lynching in the New South: Georgia and Virginia, 1880–1930* (Urbana: University of Illinois Press, 1993), 8; Estelle Freedman, *Redefining Rape: Sexual Violence in the Era of Suffrage and Segregation* (Cambridge: Harvard University Press, 2013), 97. Ida B. Wells calculated that 728 black southerners were lynched between 1886 and 1892. See "Southern Horrors: Lynch Law in All Its Phases," *New York Age*, June 25, 1892. The creators of the Charles Chesnutt digital archive (http://www.chesnutt archive.org/classroom/lynchingstat.html) estimate that 4,743 lynchings took place between 1882 and 1968 and that African Americans comprised 72.7 percent of the victims.
11. Clive Webb, *Fight against Fear: Southern Jews and Black Civil Rights* (Athens: University of Georgia Press, 2001), 20–21.
12. Recent research addressing American Jewish benevolence includes Dianne Ashton, *Rebecca Gratz: Women and Judaism in Antebellum America* (Detroit: Wayne State University Press, 1997); Marjorie N. Feld, *Lillian Wald: A Biography* (Chapel Hill: University of North Carolina Press, 2008); Mary McCune, *Charity Work as Nation-Building: American Jewish Women and the Crises in Europe and Palestine, 1914–1930* (Columbus: Ohio State University, 2000); and Beth Wenger, *New York Jews and the Great Depression: Uncertain Promise* (New Haven: Yale University Press, 1996).
13. See Leonard Dinnerstein and Mary Dale Palsson, eds., *Jews in the South* (Baton Rouge: Louisiana State University Press, 1973). The Southern Jewish Historical Society was established in 1977 "to move southern Jewish history from the margins of the American Jewish narrative into the mainstream" and has since helped generate a rich multitude of new scholarship on the Jewish South.
14. Gary Phillip Zola, "The Ascendancy of Reform Judaism in the American South," and Robert N. Rosen, "Jewish Confederates," in *Jewish Roots in Southern Soil: A*

New History, ed. Marcie Cohen Ferris and Mark Greenberg (Waltham: Brandeis University Press, 2006).
15. In *The Southerner as American: Jewish Style* (Cincinnati: American Jewish Archives, 1996), Mark K. Bauman argues that "Jews in the South were influenced by the regional subculture in a relatively marginal fashion" (5).
16. Eric Goldstein, "How Southern Is Southern Jewish History?" Biennial Scholars' Conference in American Jewish History (Charleston, S.C., 2006), 3–5.
17. John Hope Franklin and Charles Grier Sellers, *The Southerner as American* (New York: E. P. Dutton, 1960) address how "Lost Cause" mythologies influence the production of southern history. Bryan Edward Stone argues in *The Chosen Folks: Jews on the Frontiers of Texas* (Austin: University of Texas Press, 2010) that "the frontier need not be a physical or geographical place but rather a set of ideas that gives meaning to physical reality" (3). I similarly address "both literal and figurative significance" of space to Jewish identity formation. For an excellent analysis of region's impact on racial and ethnic identity, see A. Yvette Huginnie, "A New Hero Comes to Town: The Anglo Mining Engineer and 'Mexican Labor' as Contested Terrain in Southeastern Arizona, 1880–1920," *New Mexico Historical Review* 69:4 (October 1994), 323–344; and Linda Gordon, *The Great Arizona Orphan Abduction* (Cambridge: Harvard University Press, 1999). Also, Mike DeWitt's documentary *Delta Jews* (PBS, 1999) investigates the impact of location in "the South of the South" on Jewish culture, politics, and community in the Mississippi Delta.
18. Lisa Lowe argues that "it is through the terrain of national culture that the individual subject is politically formed as the American citizen" in *Immigrant Acts: On Asian American Cultural Politics* (Durham: Duke University Press, 1996), 3. See also Jennifer Rae Greeson's assertion that "knowing about our South is part of knowing what it means to be American" in *Our South: Geographic Fantasy and the Rise of National Literature* (Cambridge: Harvard University Press, 2010), 1.
19. See Grace Elizabeth Hale, *Making Whiteness: The Culture of Segregation in the South* (Chapel Hill: University of North Carolina Press, 1998); William Fitzhugh Brundage, *Where These Memories Grow: History, Memory, and Southern Identity* (Chapel Hill: University of North Carolina Press, 2000).
20. Renato Rosaldo, "Cultural Citizenship," Hemispheric Institute Encuentro, http://hemisphericinstitute.org/. See also "Cultural Citizenship and Educational Democracy," *Cultural Anthropology* 9:3 (August 1994), 402–411.
21. See, for example, Aihwa Ong, "Cultural Citizenship as Subject-Making: Immigrants Negotiate Racial and Cultural Boundaries in the United States," *Current Anthropology* 37:5 (December 1996), 737–762; and Arlene Davila, *Latino Spin: Public Image and the Whitewashing of Race* (New York: New York University Press, 2008).
22. Lowe, *Immigrant Acts*, 2.
23. Rabbi Sara Paasche-Orlow, "Acts of Kindness," *Jewish Education News*, Spring 2001, published by the Coalition for the Advancement of Jewish Education, Boston, Massachusetts.

24. Matthew Frye Jacobson, *Special Sorrows: The Diasporic Imagination of Irish, Polish, and Jewish Immigrants in the United States* (Cambridge: Harvard University Press, 1995).
25. New Orleans Association for the Relief of Jewish Widows and Orphans (hereafter cited as ARJWO), 1856 Minutes, 12, Microfilm, Jacob Rader Marcus American Jewish Archives, Hebrew Union College, Cincinnati, Ohio (hereafter cited as AJA).
26. Wilbur J. Cash, *The Mind of the South* (New York: Knopf, 1941), xlvii.
27. *Jewish South* (Atlanta), December 14, 1877, 6. The article was likely authored by editor Rabbi E. M. B. Browne. See Janice Rothschild Blumberg, *Prophet in a Time of Priests: Rabbi "Alphabet" Browne, 1845–1929* (Baltimore: Apprentice House, 2012).
28. Ibid.
29. Gunja SenGupta, *From Slavery to Poverty: The Racial Origins of Welfare in New York, 1840–1918* (New York: New York University Press, 2009), 20.
30. Hale, *Making Whiteness*, 53.
31. Pierre Bourdieu, *Distinction: A Social Critique of the Judgment of Taste*, trans. Richard Nice (New York: Routledge, 1984).
32. Matthew Frye Jacobson, *Whiteness of a Different Color: European Immigrants and the Alchemy of Race* (Cambridge: Harvard University Press, 1998), 3.
33. Eric Goldstein, *The Price of Whiteness: Jews, Race, and American Identity* (Princeton: Princeton University Press, 2006), 41–50. See also Karen Brodkin, *How Jews Became White Folks and What That Says about Race in America* (New Brunswick: Rutgers University Press, 1998); and Michael Omi and Howard Winant, *Racial Formation in the United States: From the 1960s to the 1990s* (New York: Routledge and Kegan Paul, 1986).
34. Leonard Rogoff asserts that their liminal position on a racial spectrum made Jews a "racial tabula rasa upon which anything could be written" in "Is the Jew White? The Racial Place of the Southern Jew," *American Jewish History* 85:3 (1997), 195. See also George Bornstein, *The Colors of Zion: Blacks, Jews, and Irish from 1845 to 1945* (Cambridge: Harvard University Press, 2011), 45–46. Bornstein describes Abernethy's reliance on William Z. Ripley's influential text, *The Races of Europe: A Sociological Study* (New York: D. Appleton and Co., 1899).
35. Mary M. Ryan, *The Grammar of Good Intentions: Race and the Antebellum Culture of Benevolence* (Ithaca: Cornell University Press, 2003), 192.
36. Ibid., 4.
37. Lawrence Schenbeck, *Racial Uplift and American Music, 1878–1943* (Jackson: University Press of Mississippi, 2011), 4.
38. Higginbotham, *Righteous Discontent*, 17–18; Kevin Gaines, *Uplifting the Race: Black Leadership, Politics, and Culture in the Twentieth Century* (Chapel Hill: University of North Carolina Press, 1996), xiv–xv, 2–4, 20–21.
39. Higginbotham, *Righteous Discontent*, 14, 18, 186–188.

40. Mary Antin to Simon Wolf, 1914, 25th Anniversary Celebration of the Hebrew Orphans Home of Atlanta, JELF, Series I, Container 2, Folder 2, BCA.
41. Roy Lubove, *The Professional Altruist: The Emergence of Social Work as a Career, 1880–1930* (Cambridge: Harvard University Press, 1965).
42. Louis Althusser, "Ideology and Ideological State Apparatuses (Notes towards an Investigation)," in *Lenin and Philosophy, and Other Essays*, trans. Ben Brewster (London: New Left Books, 1971).
43. Helen Heran Jun, *The Race for Citizenship: Black Orientalism and Asian Uplift from Pre-emancipation to Neoliberal America* (New York: New York University Press, 2011), 3.
44. Laura Levitt, "Impossible Assimilations, American Liberalism, and Jewish Difference: Revisiting Jewish Secularism," *American Quarterly* 59:3 (September 2007), 808–809.
45. See Karla Goldman's discussion of the "ambivalent" project of benevolent uplift in "Kaufman Kohler and the Ambivalence of Reform Judaism," *American Jewish History* 79:4 (1990), 447–499, and an unpublished paper titled "Ambivalent Benevolence: Female Jewish Philanthropy and the Immigrant Jew," presented at the Berkshire Conference for Women's History, 1994.
46. William Edward Burghardt DuBois, *Black Reconstruction in America, 1860–1880* (New York: Free Press, 1998), 700.
47. Pierre Bourdieu and Jean-Claude Passeron, "Cultural Reproduction and Social Reproduction," in *Knowledge, Education, and Cultural Change: Papers in the Sociology of Education*, ed. Richard K. Brown (London: Tavistock, 1973).
48. See Michael Omi and Howard Winant's pivotal text *Racial Formation in the United States*.
49. For example, see Charlotte Perkins Gilman: "Feminism, College Education, and the Birth Rate," *Forerunner* 6 (October 1915), 259–261. She and other writers called for women to take control over their reproduction through judicious, scientifically informed selection of mates. See also Lydia Kingsmill Commander, *The American Idea* (New York: A. S. Barnes and Co., 1907); and Victoria Woodhull, "To Women Who Have an Interest in Humanity, Present and Future: Personal Greeting," *Woodhull and Claflin's Weekly*, October 31, 1874.
50. Jennifer Ritterhouse, *Growing Up Jim Crow: How Black and White Southern Children Learned Race* (Chapel Hill: University of North Carolina Press, 2006), 55.
51. See Freedman, *Redefining Rape*, particularly chapter 5, "The Racialization of Rape and Lynching," 89–103; Frederickson, *The Black Image in the White Mind*; Martha Hodes, *White Women, Black Men: Illicit Sex in the Nineteenth-Century South* (New Haven: Yale University Press, 1997); Robyn Wiegman, *American Anatomies: Theorizing Race and Gender* (Durham: Duke University Press, 1995); Jacqueline Dowd Hall, "'The Mind That Burns in Each Body': Women, Rape, and Racial Violence," in *Powers of Desire: The Politics of Sexuality*, ed. Sharon Thompson, Christine Stansell, and Ann Barr Snitow (New York: Monthly

Review Press, 1983); and Jonathan Markovitz, *Legacies of Lynching: Racial Violence and Memory* (Minneapolis: University of Minnesota Press, 2004).
52. Katherine Van Wormer, David W. Jackson, and Charletta Sudduth, *The Maid Narratives: Black Domestics and White Families in the Jim Crow South* (Baton Rouge: Louisiana State University Press, 2012), 38–40.
53. This book benefits from several decades of exemplary scholarship on the lives of Jewish women, including: Jeanne E. Abrams, *Jewish Women Pioneering the Frontier Trail: A History in the American West* (New York: New York University Press, 2007); Joyce Antler, *The Journey Home: How Jewish Women Shaped Modern America* (New York: Free Press, 1997), and Adler, ed., *Talking Back: Images of Jewish Women in American Popular Culture* (Hanover: University Press of New England for Brandeis University Press, 1998); Charlotte Baum, *The Jewish Woman in America* (New York: Dial Press, 1976); Rose Laub Coser, Laura S. Anker, and Andrew J. Perrin, eds., *Women of Courage: Jewish and Italian Immigrant Women in New York* (Westport, CT: Greenwood Press, 1999); Elizabeth Ewen, *Immigrant Women in the Land of Dollars: Life and Culture on the Lower East Side, 1890–1925* (New York: Monthly Review Press, 1985); Kathy Freidman-Kasaba, *Memories of Migration: Gender, Ethnicity, and Work in the Lives of Jewish and Italian Women in New York, 1870–1924* (Albany: State University of New York Press, 1996); Susan Glenn, *Daughters of the Shtetl: Life and Labor in the Immigrant* Generation (Ithaca: Cornell University Press, 1990); Karla Goldman, *Beyond the Synagogue Gallery: Finding a Place for Women in American Judaism* (Cambridge: Harvard University Press, 2000); Paula Hyman, *Gender and Assimilation in Modern Jewish History: The Roles and Representation of Women* (Seattle: University of Washington Press, 1995); Paula E. Hyman and Deborah Dash Moore, eds., *Jewish Women in America: An Historical Encyclopedia* (New York: Routledge Press, 1997); Marion A. Kaplan, *The Making of the Jewish Middle Class: Women, Family, and Identity in Imperial Germany* (New York: Oxford University Press, 1991); Melissa Klapper, *Ballots, Babies, and Banners of Peace: American Jewish Women's Activism, 1890–1940* (New York: New York University Press, 2013); Riv Ellen Prell, *Fighting to Become Americans: Jews, Gender, and the Anxiety of Assimilation* (Boston: Beacon Press, 1999); Sydney Stahl Weinberg, *The World of Our Mothers: The Lives of Jewish Immigrant Women* (Chapel Hill: University of North Carolina Press, 1988).

NOTES TO CHAPTER 1

1. Thomas J. Tobias, *The Hebrew Orphan Society of Charleston, S.C., Founded 1801: An Historical Sketch* (Charleston: The Society, 1957).
2. In *Strangers within the Gate City: The Jews of Atlanta, 1845–1915* (Philadelphia: Jewish Publication Society, 1978), Steven Hertzberg estimates that "approximately half of the 2,700 Jews in the United States in 1820 lived below the Mason–Dixon line" and that this percentage fell to 14 percent (32,000 out of 230,000) in 1878 and to 5 percent in 1907 (3). The Union of American Hebrew Congregations released "Statistics of the Jews in the United States" in 1880, suggesting that 28,579 Jews

lived in the eleven states of the former Confederacy in 1878 out of a total 230,257 Jews in the United States, or roughly 12 percent. According to Robert N. Rosen, in 1860, between twenty and twenty-five thousand Jews lived in the eleven states of the Confederacy, with eight thousand concentrated in Louisiana. See *The Jewish Confederates*, 25, 34; Jacob Rader Marcus, *To Count a People: American Jewish Population Data, 1585–1984* (Lanham, MD: University Press of America, 1990).
3. Beth S. Wenger, *History Lessons: The Creation of American Jewish Heritage* (Princeton: Princeton University Press, 2010), 4.
4. See Jacobson, *Special Sorrows*.
5. Constitution of Charleston Hebrew Orphan Society, 1801, Jewish Heritage Collection at the College of Charleston, Addlestone Library, Charleston, South Carolina (hereafter cited as JHC).
6. Ibid.
7. George Stern, Esq., Oration for the 28th Anniversary of the New Orleans Association for the Relief of Jewish Widows and Orphans, March 25, 1883, 11, AJA.
8. Ibid.; and Jacob Clavius Levy, Oration for the 33rd Anniversary of the Charleston Hebrew Orphan Society, November 5, 1834, 20, JHC.
9. See Aviva Ben-Ur, *Sephardic Jews in America: A Diasporic History* (New York: New York University Press, 2009).
10. Citing *Publications of the American Jewish Historical Society* (50:34), Jacob Rader Marcus estimated that in 1790, three hundred Jews lived in South Carolina and one hundred lived in Georgia. See Marcus, *To Count a People*, 203, 49.
11. Charles P. Daly, *The Settlement of the Jews in North America* (New York: P. Cowen, 1893), 4. Judge Daly compiled this history in recognition of the fiftieth anniversary of what he believed to be the first Jewish benevolent institution in the nation, the New York Hebrew Benevolent Society. Within a decade, Barnett A. Elzas discovered the original seal of Charleston's Hebrew Benevolent Society, which confirmed the Society's formation in 1784. See Barnett A. Elzas, *Story of a Long Lost Seal: Proves the Age of the Hebrew Benevolent Society* (n.p., 1900).
12. Peter Stuyvesant to Dutch West India Co, September 22, 1654, quoted in Paul Finkelman, "How the Jews Won the Right to Remain in New Netherland," in *New Essays in American Jewish History: Commemorating the Sixtieth Anniversary of the Founding of the American Jewish Archives* (Cincinnati: American Jewish Archives of Hebrew Union College–Jewish Institute of Religion, 2010), 28–29; and Sandra Cumings Malamed, *The Jews in Early America: A Chronicle of Good Taste and Good Deeds* (McKinleyville, CA: Fithian Press, 2003), 20–22.
13. Finkelman, "How the Jews Won the Right to Remain in New Netherland," 27–28.
14. Dutch West India Co. to Peter Stuyvesant, April 26, 1655, quoted in ibid., 29–30.
15. Yitzchok Levine, "The Jewish Settlement of Savannah, Georgia," *Glimpses into American Jewish History*, part 10 (TheJewishPress.com, January 2006), 1–2. See also Malamed, *The Jews in Early America*, 95–96.
16. Marcus estimated the 1790 Jewish populations of New York and Pennsylvania to be 350 and 250, respectively, in *To Count a People*, 139, 183. On the role of

synagogues in the development of a charitable Jewish infrastructure, see Oscar Handlin, *Adventure in Freedom: Three Hundred Years of Jewish Life in America* (New York: McGraw-Hill, 1954), 59–79.

17. Beth Elohim followed the establishment of synagogues in New York City, Newport, Rhode Island, and Savannah, Georgia. See James Hagy, "This Happy Land," in *A Portion of the People: Three Hundred Years of Southern Jewish Life*, ed. Dale Rosengarten and Theodore Rosengarten (Columbia: University of South Carolina Press in association with McKissick Museum, 2002), 90–93. Jonathan D. Sarna traces the emergence and development of the nation's first synagogues in *American Judaism: A History* (New Haven: Yale University Press, 2004).

18. Gerald Sorin, *A Time for Building: The Third Migration, 1880–1920* (Baltimore: Johns Hopkins University Press, 1992), suggests a Jewish population of 1,350 in 1790 (7), but Tobias, *The Hebrew Orphan Society of Charleston*, cites a number closer to 2,500 (v).

19. Preamble of the Report of the 1870 Committee on Revision, quoted in Barnett A. Elzas, *The Jews of South Carolina, from the Earliest Times to the Present Day* (Philadelphia: J. B. Lippincott, 1905), 283–284.

20. Peter McCandless, *Slavery, Disease, and Suffering in the Southern Lowcountry* (New York: Cambridge University Press, 2011), 9.

21. Ibid., 106–107. See also *New York Times*, September 18, 1871, which lists each Charleston outbreak and the numbers of dead, where available.

22. Tobias, *The Hebrew Orphan Society of Charleston*, 3.

23. Clarence A. Spencer, "Evolution of Southern Benevolent Societies with Emphasis on Alabama," *Journal of the Alabama Academy of Science* 58:1 (1987), 2.

24. Eli Evans, preface of *A Portion of the People*, xvi. In *A Time for Building*, Gerald Sorin estimates a Jewish population of 1600.

25. John E. Murray, *The Charleston Orphan House: Children's Lives in the First Public Orphanage in America* (Chicago: University of Chicago Press, 2013).

26. Save for a brief period during the 1860s, the Society did not provide institutional housing for orphans. See Levy, 1834, 3, 4, JHC. In 1860, writes Tobias, "the Society voted to convert its building into an orphan house . . . a marked change from the traditional system of maintaining its wards in private homes." Upon the onset of the Civil War, the use of the building as an orphanage was abandoned. Tobias, *The Hebrew Orphan Society of Charleston*, 16–17.

27. Murray, *The Charleston Orphan Home*, 37–38.

28. Levy, 1834, 8, JHC. Arthur Hertzberg observed that, by mid-century, New York alone contained approximately fifty Jewish benevolent and social organizations whose membership surpassed that of the synagogues. See Hertzberg, *The Jews in America: Four Centuries of an Uneasy Encounter* (New York: Simon and Schuster, 1989), 115–116.

29. Levy, 1834, 19–20, JHC.

30. Constitution of Hebrew Orphan Society, 1801, JHC.

31. Jacobson, *Special Sorrows*, 59.

32. Myer Moses, "Oration, Delivered before the Hebrew Orphan Society, on the 15th Day of October, 1806" (published 1807), 6, JHC.
33. Ibid., 6.
34. Ibid., 13–14.
35. Ibid., 15.
36. Levy, 1834, 8–9, JHC.
37. Ibid., 9.
38. Goldstein, *The Price of Whiteness*, 17–18.
39. Peter Wood, *Black Majority: Negroes in Colonial South Carolina from 1670 through the Stono Rebellion* (New York: Knopf, 1974); Jack Bass and W. Scott Poole, *The Palmetto State: The Making of Modern South Carolina* (Charleston: University of South Carolina Press, 2009).
40. Southern Jews who could afford to own slaves did, and those who did not rarely questioned the ethical validity of slavery. See Rosen, *The Jewish Confederates*, 15–16; Leonard Dinnerstein and Mary Dale Palsson, *Jews in the South* (Baton Rouge: Louisiana State University Press, 1973), 9–10; Howard Rabinowitz, "Nativism, Bigotry, and Anti-Semitism in the South," in *Dixie Diaspora: An Anthology of Southern Jewish History*, ed. Mark K. Bauman (Tuscaloosa: University of Alabama Press, 2006), 279.
41. Moses, 1806, 17, JHC.
42. Levy, 1834, 9, JHC.
43. Ibid., 11.
44. Quoted from the IOBB mission in Cornelia Wilhelm, *The Independent Orders of B'nai B'rith and True Sisters: Pioneers of a New Jewish Identity, 1843–1914*, trans. Alan L. Nothnagle and Sarah Wobick-Segev (Detroit: Wayne State University Press, 2011), 28. See also Deborah Dash Moore, *B'nai B'rith and the Challenge of Ethnic Leadership* (Albany: State University of New York Press, 1981); and Sarna, *American Judaism*, 88–91.
45. Howard M. Sachar, *A History of the Jews in America* (New York: Knopf, 1992), 70–71; and Wilhelm, *The Independent Orders of B'nai B'rith and True Sisters*, 61–65.
46. Malamed, *The Jews in Early America*, 96. See "By-Laws of the Union Society," in *Proceedings of the 108th Anniversary of the Union Society*, vol. 108 (Savannah, GA: Union Society, 1858), 3.
47. Sheftall's son, Mordecai, served as Society president during the Revolutionary War. See Rev. Willard Preston, "Extract from an Address Delivered before the Society in April, 1833, Being a Synopsis of the History and Objects of the Union Society," in *Proceedings of the 108th Anniversary of the Union Society*, vol. 108, 39–40.
48. Mark Greenberg, "Creating Ethnic, Class, and Southern Identity in Nineteenth-Century America: The Jews of Savannah, Georgia, 1830–1880" (PhD diss., University of Florida, 1997), 1, 13. In 1878, there were over six hundred Jews living in Savannah, 2 percent of the population. See Hertzberg, *Strangers within the Gate City*, table 2, "Total and Estimated Jewish Population of Southern States and Selected Cities, 1878," 231.

49. Clive Webb, "Closing Ranks: Montgomery Jews and Civil Rights," *Journal of American Studies* 32:3 (December 1998), 466.
50. Selma S. Lewis, *A Biblical People in the Bible Belt: The Jewish Community of Memphis, Tennessee, 1840s–1960s* (Mercer: Mercer University Press, 1998), 22. See also Ellen Eisenberg, Ava Kahn, and William Toll, *Jews of the Pacific Coast: Reinventing Community on America's Edge* (Seattle: University of Washington Press, 2009).
51. Tobias, *The Hebrew Orphan Society of Charleston*, 9–10.
52. Ibid., 13.
53. Ibid., 14.
54. *Houston Telegraph*, March 7, 1855, cited in Stone, *The Chosen Folks*, 45.
55. On the "Cult of True Womanhood," see Nancy F. Cott, *The Bonds of Womanhood: "Woman's Sphere" in New England, 1780–1835* (New Haven: Yale University Press, 1977). For a more specific application to southern Jewish women, see Mark K. Bauman, "Southern Jewish Women and Their Social Service Organizations," *Journal of American Ethnic History* 22:3 (Spring 2003), 35.
56. See Ashton, *Rebecca Gratz*.
57. In his exploration of southern Jewish women's voluntary organizations, historian Mark Bauman has detailed the network of activism that spread from Gratz to her niece and several friends in the South. See "Southern Jewish Women and Their Social Service Organizations," 36.
58. Levy, 1834, 5, JHC.
59. Ibid.
60. Ibid.
61. Drew Gilpin Faust, *Mothers of Invention: Women of the Slaveholding South in the Civil War* (Chapel Hill: University of North Carolina Press, 1996); Margaret Ripley Wolfe, *Daughters of Canaan: A Saga of Southern Women* (Lexington: University Press of Kentucky, 1995).
62. Lewis, *A Biblical People in the Bible Belt*, 28.
63. Dale Rosengarten, "Ladies of the Lost Cause," public lecture at the College of Charleston, March 21, 2011.
64. Elliott Ashkenazi, ed., *The Civil War Diary of Clara Solomon: Growing Up in New Orleans, 1861–1862*, ed. Elliott Ashkenazi (Baton Rouge: Louisiana State University Press, 1995). See also Helen Jocbus Apte, *Heart of a Wife: The Diary of a Southern Jewish Woman*, ed. Marcus D. Rosenbaum (Wilmington, DE: Scholarly Resources Books, 1998).
65. Ashkenazi, *The Civil War Diary of Clara Solomon*, 61.
66. July 5, 1874, Meeting of the Ladies Purim Association. This group later became the Jewish Ladies Aid Society of Columbus, Georgia. See MS 109, BCA.
67. Faith Rogow, *Gone to Another Meeting: The National Council of Jewish Women, 1893–1993* (Tuscaloosa: University of Alabama Press, 1993); Beth S. Wenger, "Jewish Women of the Club: The Changing Public Role of Atlanta's Jewish Women (1870–1930)," *American Jewish History* 76:3 (March 1987), 311–333.

68. See Goldstein, *The Price of Whiteness*.
69. Levy, 1834, 9, JHC.
70. Jewish orphan homes were established in Brooklyn, New York, and Boston in 1822.
71. B. F. Jonas's Dedication Speech, 1856, New Orleans Jewish Widows and Orphans Home Microfilm, 14, AJA.
72. Goldstein, *The Price of Whiteness*, 11–31.
73. Jonas, 1856, 12, AJA. The New Orleans Home initially received $6,000 from the state, by far the most significant amount of public support the institution would receive.
74. Ibid., 8–9.
75. Ibid.
76. Kaplan, *The Making of the Jewish Middle Class*, 9–11, 31–35; Hyman, *Gender and Assimilation in Modern Jewish History*, 8, 27, 44–49. See also Judge Julian Mack's address to the 1906 National Conference of Jewish charities in which he remarked, "The hope for a betterment of the future is . . . in the Jewish women." *Fourth Biennial Session of the National Conference of Jewish Charities in the United States* (New York: National Conference of Jewish Charities, 1906), 31.
77. See Carol Smith-Rosenberg, *Disorderly Conduct: Visions of Gender in Victorian America* (New York: Knopf, 1985), 130, 173–176; Anne Firor Scott, "Women's Voluntary Associations: From Charity to Reform," in *Lady Bountiful Revisited: Women, Philanthropy, and Power*, ed. Kathleen D. McCarthy (New Brunswick: Rutgers University Press, 1990); Nancy Hewitt, *Women's Activism and Social Change: Rochester, New York, 1822–1872* (Ithaca: Cornell University Press, 1984); Keith Melder, "Ladies Bountiful: Organized Women's Benevolence in Early Nineteenth-Century America," *New York History* 48:3 (July 1967), 231–254; and June Sochen, *Consecrate Every Day: The Public Lives of Jewish Women, 1880–1980* (Albany: State University of New York Press, 1981), 46–48; and Ashton, *Rebecca Gratz*, 39, 111, 118.
78. Columbus, Georgia, "Daughters of Israel," Constitution and By-Laws, Sunday, October 4, 1874, MS 109, BCA.
79. Ibid.
80. New Orleans Jewish Children's Home Annual Report, 1879, 8, Louisiana Research Collection, Howard–Tilton Memorial Library, Tulane University, New Orleans, Louisiana (hereafter cited as LRC).
81. Ibid., 8–9.
82. Ibid., 9
83. Ibid., 34.
84. Ibid.
85. ARJWO Minutes, 229–30, AJA.
86. "Statistics of the Jews of the United States" (1880) included four Jewish Secret Societies, all providing "sick and endowment benefits" with a combined

membership of 44,267; five public Jewish hospitals; eleven orphan asylums; thirteen free schools "for religious instruction"; and "other Benevolent Institutions in almost every city in the Union, for dispensing charity, for free burial, etc." (56–57).

87. Gail Bederman, *Manliness and Civilization: A Cultural History of Gender and Race in the United States, 1880–1917* (Chicago: University of Chicago Press, 1995), 20–22. See Theodore Roosevelt's "The Strenuous Life," speech before the Hamilton Club, April 10, 1899, in *Roosevelt, the Strenuous Life: Essays and Addresses* (New York: The Century Co., 1905).

88. See, for example, Tom Watson's characterization of the dispassionate conduct of the men who lynched Leo Frank. Tom Watson, *Tom Watson's Jeffersonian*, August 1915.

89. Stern, 1883, 11, AJA.

90. Ibid.

91. See, for example, the serialized novel *The Jewess of Toledo*, by Franz Grillparzer, which appeared in *der Tageblatt* in 1901.

92. Henry L. Lazarus, March 26, 1882, New Orleans Orphans Home Anniversary, AJA.

93. Ibid.

94. 1880 Federal Census data on the nation's largest cities. This figure represents a significant decrease from 1870 when the city's foreign-born population was 25.3 percent.

95. Lazarus, 1882, AJA.

96. Bederman, *Manliness and Civilization*, 25, 31.

97. Zebulon Vance, *The Scattered Nation*, ed. Willis Bruce Dowd (New York: J. J. Little and Co., 1904), 11. Earlier versions of the speech were published in various southern newspapers, the content shifting over time to reflect changing conditions, such as the plight of Russian Jews in the 1880s.

98. Selig Adler, "Zebulon B. Vance and the 'Scattered Nation,'" *Journal of Southern Jewish History* 7:3 (August 1941), 357–377.

99. Vance, *The Scattered Nation*, 15, 30. See Scott Langston, "Interaction and Identity: Jews and Christians in Nineteenth-Century New Orleans," *Southern Jewish History* 3 (2000), 83–124.

100. Vance, *The Scattered Nation*, 25–26.

101. J. Barrett Cohen, *Judaism and the Typical Jew: An Address Delivered before the Jews of Charleston, S.C., on the Celebration of the Centennial Anniversary of the Birthday of Sir Moses Montefiore at the Hasel Street Synagogue, October 26, 1884* (Charleston: News and Courier Book Presses, 1884), 9.

102. Ibid., 20.

103. Ibid., 16.

104. Hertzberg, *Strangers within the Gate City*, 23.

105. Ibid., table 3, "Total, Native-Born White, Foreign-Born White, Negro, and Estimated Jewish Population of Atlanta, 1860–1910," 232. Approximately two thousand Russian immigrants arrived in Atlanta between the late 1880s and 1910,

making Jews Atlanta's largest foreign-born population. See table 4, "Foreign-Born White Population of Atlanta, 1870–1910," 232.
106. See Annual Reports, Container 2, Folder 1, BCA.
107. Rabbi Leo Reich, "Position of Woman: A Comparative Study," *The Magnet* 1:2 (April 1894), 82–91; Home Annual Reports, JELF, Series I, Container 2, Folder 1, BCA.
108. Ibid.
109. Ibid.
110. See Hall, "The Mind That Burns in Each Body," 336. On the image of white southern ladyhood see Hall, *Revolt against Chivalry: Jesse Daniel Ames and the Women's Campaign Against Lynching*, rev. ed. (New York: Columbia University Press, 1993); Anne Firor Scott, *The Southern Lady: From Pedestal to Politics, 1830–1930* (Chicago: University of Chicago Press, 1970); LeeAnn Whites, "'Stand by Your Man': The Ladies Memorial Association and the Reconstruction of Southern White Manhood," in *Women of the American South: A Multicultural Reader*, ed. Christie Farnham (New York: New York University Press, 1997), 133–149; Elizabeth Hayes Turner, "'White-Gloved Ladies' and 'New Women' in the Texas Woman Suffrage Movement," in *Southern Women: History and Identities*, ed. Virginia Bernhard, Betty Brandon, Elizabeth Fox-Genovese, and Theda Perdue (Columbia: University of Missouri Press, 1992); Suzanne Lebsock, "Woman Suffrage and White Supremacy," and Glenda Gilmore, "'But She Can't Find Her (V.O.) Key': Writing Gender and Race into Southern Political History," in *Taking Off the White Gloves: Southern Women and Women Historians*, ed. Michele Gillespie and Catherine Clinton (Columbia: University of Missouri Press, 1998).
111. Hertzberg notes in *Strangers within the Gate City* (38–40) that Jews were prevalent among "proprietors or managers" after the war.
112. Ibid., 233, 242.
113. Hertzberg estimates that Jews comprised one-fifth of the state's immigrant population. Ibid., 84.
114. See Seth Korelitz, "'A Magnificent Piece of Work': The Americanization Work of the National Council of Jewish Women," *American Jewish History* 83:2 (June 1995), 177.
115. Rogow explains that "social reform work would come to dominate the Council's activities to the exclusion of other pursuits" in *Gone to Another Meeting*, 20, 36. Karla Goldman notes that certain addresses at the Congress highlighted cultural differences between the middle-class, U.S.-born attendees and the "oppressed Russian exiles who find a home here." She cites Pauline Hanauer Rosenberg's speech on "American Jews of To-day." See Goldman, "Ambivalent Benevolence," 8.
116. Rogow, *Gone to Another Meeting*, see graph, appendix C, 241. See also Melissa Klapper's discussion of the NCJW's political influence in *Ballots, Babies, and Banners of Peace*, 52–54.
117. Wenger, "Jewish Women of the Club," 312.
118. Golden, *Our Southern Landsman*, 81.

NOTES TO CHAPTER 2

1. Numbers gleaned from the home's 1895 Annual Report, JELF, Series I, Container 2, Folder 1, BCA. The 1900 U.S. Census report indicates that all sixty-three inmates were the children of foreign-born parents, with all, except for seventeen sets of Russian parents, from Germany.
2. Wolf opens his study with his response to a December 1891 *North American Review* letter by a "Mr. Rogers," claiming that Jews did not serve in the military, save "in General Sherman's department," where they were "promptly ordered out . . . for speculating in cotton and carrying information to the Confederates." Whether Mr. Rogers intended General Grant's Order No. 11 is unclear, but Wolf's answer provided a detailed list of the many Jews who fought on the side of the Union. Quoted in Simon Wolf, *The American Jew as Patriot, Soldier and Citizen* (Philadelphia: The Levytype Company Publishers, 1895), 1.
3. While William Z. Ripley would not publish *The Races of Europe: A Sociological Study* until 1899, ethnologist Daniel Garrison Brinton had published *Races and Peoples* in 1890 and *The American Race* in 1891. Historian Nell Irvin Painter asserts that the nation's late nineteenth-century "obsession with race" provided fertile soil for new scientific engagements with human classificatory schemes to take root. See *The History of White People* (New York: Norton, 2010), 225–226. See also Beth Wenger's discussion of *The American Jew as Patriot, Soldier and Citizen* in *History Lessons*, 106–107.
4. Wolf, *The American Jew as Patriot, Soldier and Citizen*, 523.
5. Estimate drawn from Cyrus Adler and Henrietta Szold, eds., *American Jewish Yearbook*, vol. 1 (Philadelphia: American Jewish Committee, 1899–1900), 284; and Sarna, *American Judaism*, appendix "American Jewish Population Estimates, 1660–2000," 375; Marcus, *To Count a People*, 237–240.
6. Gerald Sorin estimates that 1,562,800 eastern European Jewish immigrants arrived in the United States by 1910. See *A Time for Building*, 42. See also Sachar, *A History of the Jews in America*, 151.
7. Rosen, *The Jewish Confederates*, 25; Sorin, *A Time for Building*, 7.
8. Hertzberg, *Strangers within the City Gate*, 3.
9. Golden, *Our Southern Landsman*, 20, 33; Hertberg, *Strangers within the Gate City*, 203.
10. See Ferris and Greenberg, eds., *Jewish Roots in Southern Soil*, 12.
11. Wolf, *The American Jew as Patriot, Soldier and Citizen*, 6.
12. Arthur T. Abernethy, *The Jew a Negro, Being a Study of the Jewish Ancestry from an Impartial Standpoint* (Moravian Falls, NC: Dixie Publishing, 1910).
13. Moses, 1806, 6, JHC.
14. For insight into European-descended people's categorization into different gradients of whiteness, see works by Jacobson, *Whiteness of a Different Color*; Painter, *The History of White People*; Neil Foley, *The White Scourge: Mexicans, Blacks, and Poor Whites in the Cotton Culture of Central Texas* (Berkeley: University of

California Press, 1997); and David Roediger, *The Wages of Whiteness: Race and the Making of the American Working Class* (New York: Verso Press, 1991).
15. Painter, *The History of White People*, 225–226.
16. Elnora Folkmar and Daniel Folkmar, "Dictionary of Races of Peoples" (Dillingham Report, United States Immigration Commission, Government Print Office, 1911), 1–2.
17. Ripley expressed amazement at Jewish immigrants' "tenacity of life," particularly their ability to thrive in overcrowded tenements and to labor in unhealthful sweatshop conditions. See Ripley, *The Races of Europe*, 383–384.
18. Commander, *The American Idea*, placed observant Jews at the top of the list of immigrant fecundity (82–83).
19. See Gail Bederman's account of Theodore Roosevelt (chapter 5 of *Manliness and Civilization*) and Thomas G. Dyer, *Theodore Roosevelt and the Idea of Race* (Baton Rouge: Louisiana State University Press, 1980). Some others who participated in the popularization of eugenic sciences and fears of "race suicide" include Myre St. Wald Iseman, *Race Suicide* (New York: Cosmopolitan Press, 1912); Charlotte Perkins Gilman, *The Crux: A Novel* (New York: Charlton Company, 1911); and Commander, *The American Idea*.
20. Commander, *The American Idea*, 232.
21. Ibid., 234; Iseman, *Race Suicide*, 129–131. See also Prescott F. Hall's definition of an "undesirable" immigrant as one who, among other proclivities, "tends to congregate in the slums of large cities." "Selection of Immigration," *Annals of the American Academy of Political and Social Science* 24 (July 1, 1904), 175.
22. On the ways the "Orient" took shape in the American imagination, see David Weir, *American Orient: Imagining the East From the Colonial Era through the Twentieth Century* (Amherst: University of Massachusetts Press, 2011); and Jun, *Race for Citizenship*.
23. David Philipson, "Human Brotherhood," *The Magnet* 1:2 (April 1894), BCA.
24. Wolf, *The American Jew as Patriot, Soldier and Citizen*, 551–552.
25. In 1880 California state law was amended to prohibit marriage between "Mongolians" and "white persons."
26. Efforts to engage Jewish people in agricultural pursuits originated decades before the late nineteenth-century influx of eastern Europeans, but few materialized into self-sustaining and durable farming communities. Leo Shpall, "Jewish Agricultural Colonies in the United States," *Agricultural History* 24:3 (July 1, 1950), 120–146, traces the first suggestion of an American Jewish agricultural community to a late eighteenth-century proposal asking the president to allow two thousand German Jews to settle on American soil.
27. Michael N. Dobkowski, ed., *Jewish American Voluntary Organizations* (Westport, CT: Greenwood Press, 1986), 88–89. See also Gabriel Davidson, *Our Jewish Farmers and the Story of the Jewish Agricultural Society* (New York: L. B. Fischer, 1943), 10–11.

28. Robert A. Rockaway, *Words of the Uprooted: Jewish Immigrants in Early Twentieth-Century America* (Ithaca: Cornell University Press, 1998), 1.
29. Bernard Marinbach, *Galveston: Ellis Island of the West* (Albany: State University of New York Press, 1983), xiii. See also Hasia R. Diner, *The Jews of the United States, 1654 to 2000* (Berkeley: University of California Press, 2004), 185.
30. Chris Monaco, "Moses E. Levy of Florida: A Jewish Abolitionist Abroad," *American Jewish History* 86:4 (1998), 377.
31. Ibid., 384–385.
32. Ellen Eisenberg, *Jewish Agricultural Colonies in New Jersey, 1882–1920* (Syracuse: Syracuse University Press, 1995), 26.
33. Esther L. Panitz, *Simon Wolf: Private Conscience and Public Image* (Madison: Fairleigh Dickinson University Press, 1987), 81.
34. In his 1857 address to the New Orleans Jewish Orphans Home, David C. Labatt urged his audience to channel poor coreligionists away from "ignoble employments" and "association with uncongenial occupations" such as money lending and peddling. ARJWO Microfilm, 15, AJA. Efforts to settle Jewish immigrants in agricultural communities originated during the earlier, primarily German wave of immigration. In 1855 Sigmund Waterman, the first Jewish professor at Yale, presented a speech titled "A Call to Establish a Hebrew Agricultural Society" to the national B'nai B'rith, arguing that farming communes would help fight anti-Semitism. (See the Encyclopedia of Southern Jewish Studies, http://www.isjl.org/history/archive/al/sandMountain.html). Jenna Weissman Joselit explains how "tilling the land had come to be seen as a way to normalize the Jew's traditional economic profile and ease his integration into European society" in "Land of Promise: The Eastern European Jewish Experience in South Carolina," in *A Portion of the People: Three Hundred Years of Southern Jewish Life*, ed. Theodore Rosengarten and Dale Rosengarten (Columbia: University of South Carolina Press, 2002), 23.
35. Vance, *The Scattered Nation*, 12.
36. Ibid., 25.
37. Walter L. Fleming, "Immigration to the Southern States," *Political Science Quarterly* 20:2 (June 1, 1905), 276.
38. Rowland T. Berthoff, "Southern Attitudes toward Immigration, 1865–1914," *Journal of Southern History* 17:3 (August 1, 1951), 328–329.
39. Fleming, "Immigration to the Southern States," 279; Berthoff, "Southern Attitudes toward Immigration, 1865–1914," 329.
40. Fleming, "Immigration to the Southern States," 279.
41. The Alliance Israelite Universelle received funding from German-born industrialist and philanthropist Baron Maurice de Hirsch.
42. Shpall, "Jewish Agricultural Colonies in the United States," 129.
43. A similarly unsuccessful agricultural colony settled in 1904 at Sand Mountain in northern Alabama. See Trudy G. Trivers, "Alabama's Sand Mountain and Early

Kibbutz," *Atlanta Jewish Times*, April 24, 1987. See also the Encyclopedia of Southern Jewish Communities entry for "Nat, Alabama," http://www.isjl.org/history/archive/al/sandMountain.html.
44. Wood, *Black Majority*.
45. Arnold Shankman, "Happyville, the Forgotten Colony," *American Jewish Archives* 30:1 (April 1978), 6.
46. Socialist Charles Weintraub purchased Sheffield Plantation in Montmorenci, South Carolina, and he and ten Jewish families moved there in December 1905.
47. In 1900, approximately 58 percent of South Carolina residents were black. Shankman, "Happyville, the Forgotten Colony," 5.
48. Kohn's address to the B'nai B'rith annual meeting on April 14, 1907, Cited in Joselit, "Land of Promise," 22.
49. Ibid., 22–23.
50. Settlers escaping the failure of Happyville moved to the nearby town of Aiken, South Carolina, which benefited from the infusion of new workers. See ibid., 22.
51. Eisenberg, *Jewish Agricultural Colonies in New Jersey, 1882–1920*, 90.
52. "The Attitude of the South toward Immigration," Immigration Restriction League, J. S. Patten, Secretary, March 2, 1908, Harvard University Archives, Open Collection Program. The League was created to support a "further restriction of elements undesirable for citizenship or injurious to our national character." Constitution, 1. See also Diner, *The Jews of the United States, 1654 to 2000*, 116; and Barbara Miller Solomon, *Ancestors and Immigrants: A Changing New England Tradition* (Cambridge: Harvard University Press, 1956).
53. "The Attitude of the South Toward Immigration," 1908.
54. See the introduction's discussion of the "nadir" in Logan, *The Negro in American Life and Thought*.
55. Joselit, "Land of Promise," 27.
56. Ibid.
57. Marcie Cohen Ferris, *Matzoh Ball Gumbo: Culinary Tales of the Jewish South* (Chapel Hill: University of North Carolina Press, 2005). For religious adaptations in Charleston, see Deborah Dash Moore, "Freedom's Fruits: The Americanization of an Old-Time Religion," in *A Portion of the People*, ed. Rosengarten and Rosengarten.
58. The 1900 Census indicates that one of the New Orleans home inmates was born in Austria and one from England, and one of the Russian children was born in Germany.
59. The other South-born children were from the following states: eighteen from Tennessee; two from Oklahoma; nine from Mississippi; twenty-nine from Louisiana; three from Florida; four from Arkansas; and seventeen from Alabama.
60. As in the Atlanta 1920 Census, there appears to have been little interest in carefully documenting the parentage of the institutionalized children.
61. Diana Pazicky claims that "a group or nation, like an individual, can experience

a sense of orphanhood and that its process of collective identity formation is also relational in nature." *Cultural Orphans in America* (Jackson: University Press of Mississippi, 1998), xii.
62. In *Special Sorrows*, Jacobson describes how Russian persecution cemented the sense of shared suffering that reinforced a Jewish nationalist investment in Zionism, 46–47.
63. Hale, *Making Whiteness*, 67–74.
64. "The Voice of the Fair Southland," *The State*, May 24, 1898, printed also in *The San Francisco Call*, 6.
65. Paul Gaston, *The New South Creed: A Study in Southern Mythmaking* (New York: Knopf, 1970), 83.
66. "The Voice of the Fair Southland," 1898.
67. Editor Rev. Edward B. M. Browne's "Salutatory," *Jewish South* (Atlanta), October 14, 1877, 4. The journal promised to develop a southern literary canon and to cultivate friendly relations between southern Jews and Christians.
68. "Special Notices," *Jewish South* (Atlanta), October 14, 1877, 2.
69. See, for example, an essay titled "Books and Authors by Artemidorus," *Jewish South* (Atlanta), October 14, 1877, 3.
70. In 1881 the paper transferred hands yet again, and its last issues were published in Houston, Texas. See Samuel S. Hill, Charles H. Lippy, and Charles Reagan Wilson, eds., *Encyclopedia of Religion in the South*, 2nd rev. ed. (Macon: Mercer University Press, 2005), 413.
71. "Our Greeting," *Jewish South* (Richmond), August 25, 1893, 2.
72. Ibid.
73. "A Question Answered," *Jewish South* (Richmond), September 15, 1893, 2.
74. Ibid.
75. Quoted in *Jewish Ledger*, New Orleans, January 11, 1895, 16.
76. Walter L. Fleming asserted in "Immigration to the Southern States" that "thousands of white farmers have moved away from their farms to villages and towns, because they do not feel safe with their wives and daughters in the midst of the black population. It is for these many reasons the South now wants white immigrants" (281).
77. See Freedman, *Redefining Rape*, 89–91; Hodes, *White Women, Black Men*, 176–77; Grace Hale, chapter 5, in *Making Whiteness*, "Deadly Amusements: Spectacle Lynchings, and the Contradictions of Segregation as Culture," 199–240; Hall, *Revolt against Chivalry*, 131, and "The Mind That Burns in Each Body"; Nancy MacLean, "The Leo Frank Case Reconsidered: Gender and Sexual Politics in the Making of Reactionary Populism," *Journal of American History* 78:3 (December 1991), 917–948.
78. See Edward J. Larson, *Sex, Race, and Science: Eugenics in the Deep South* (Baltimore: Johns Hopkins University Press, 1995); Nancy Ordover, *American Eugenics: Race, Queer Anatomy, and the Science of Nationalism* (Minneapolis: University of Minnesota Press, 2003); Alexandra Minna Stern, *Eugenic Nation: Faults and*

Frontiers of Better Breeding in Modern America (Berkeley: University of California Press, 2005).
79. Timothy A. Hasci, *Second Home: Orphan Asylums and Poor Families in America* (Cambridge: Harvard University Press, 1998), 13.
80. *Proceedings of the Conference on the Care of Dependent Children Held at Washington, DC, January 25, 26, 1909* (Washington, DC: GPO, 1909).
81. President Simon Wolf's 1909 Annual Report: 20th Anniversary Meeting, Vol. 1, 54, JELF Records, Annual Reports, Series I, Container 2, BCA.
82. Ibid., 55–56.
83. Reena Sigman Friedman explores the policies of three Jewish orphan homes—the Hebrew Orphan Asylum of New York, the Jewish Foster Home of Philadelphia, and Cleveland Jewish Orphan Asylum—in *These Are Our Children*.
84. Letter to Ralph Sonn, August 13, 1910, JELF, Series I, Container 21, Folder 17, BCA.
85. From the University South Caroliniana Society's description of the Emanuel Sternberger Manuscripts Collection, University of South Carolina, Columbia.
86. Emanuel Sternberger to Ralph Sonn, August 18, 1914, JELF, Series I, Container 21, Folder 17, BCA.
87. Ibid.
88. Issues of Watson's *Jeffersonian* magazine characterized Leo Frank as "lascivious" and a "moral pervert." See the January 1915 *Watson's Jeffersonian*, 146, 152.
89. Ralph Sonn to unnamed rabbi (handwriting illegible), April 30, 1915, JELF, Series I, Container 21, Folder 17, BCA.
90. Leonard Rogoff, *Down Home: Jewish Life in North Carolina* (Chapel Hill: University of North Carolina Press, 2010), 117–118.
91. Ralph Sonn to unnamed rabbi (handwriting illegible), April 30, 1915, JELF, Series I, Container 21, Folder 17, BCA.
92. Emanuel Sternberger to Ralph Sonn, May 9, 1915, JELF, Series I, Container 21, Folder 17, BCA.
93. March 13, 1917, ibid.
94. March 28, 1917, ibid.
95. Mrs. Gump of the North Carolina Children's Home Society to Weil, quoted in Weil's letter to Sonn, November 15, 1917, JELF, Series I, Container 21, Folder 17, BCA.
96. Sarah Weil to Ralph Sonn, November 15, 1917, ibid..
97. Becky Shulman to Sarah Weil, February 10, 1927, ibid.
98. See anonymous letter signed "Women and Men Who Are Trying to Keep Girls Straight, Eyes of a Thousand," October 10, 1922, Federation Files, Container 40, Folder 2, BCA. The letter may have come from the Ku Klux Klan—who frequently sent anonymous, threatening letters to individuals in an effort to regulate public morality—or from a member of the Jewish immigrant community, who would have seen the girls' behavior as threatening to collective ideals of Jewish respectability. See Nancy MacLean, *Behind the Mask of Chivalry: The Making of the Second Ku Klux Klan* (New York: Oxford University Press, 1994).

99. Tera Hunter describes Atlanta's Decatur Street, which was populated in the early twentieth century primarily by African Americans and poor whites, as a place for "colorful characters, violence, and illicit sex." *To 'Joy My Freedom: Southern Black Women's Lives and Labors after the Civil War* (Cambridge: Harvard University Press, 1997), 162. See also Hertzberg, *Strangers within the Gate City*, 187–189.
100. Case report, August 22, 1927, Federation Files, Container 40, Folder 2, BCA.
101. James Lebeau, "Profile of a Southern Jewish Community: Waycross, Georgia," *American Jewish Historical Quarterly* 58:4 (June 1969), 429–444. Al Jacobson, "Jews in Small Towns: Legends and Legacies," lists the bereaved children's uncle among the founding members of the Hebrew congregation. See http://www.museumoffamilyhistory.com/lia-jist-ga.htm.
102. Author's translation, Waycross citizens to Atlanta Hebrew Orphans Home, August 24, 1914. Composed on letterhead from the "Boston Shoe Factory, Dealer in New and Second-Hand Shoes" of Waycross, Georgia, with J. Rush, the proprietor, among the fifteen signatories. JELF, Series I, Container 22, Folder 1, BCA.
103. Ibid.
104. Ralph Sonn to the fifteen authors of the July 24 Waycross letter, August 28, 1914, JELF, Series I, Container 22, Folder 1, BCA.
105. Ibid.
106. Ibid.
107. Both the New Orleans and the Atlanta orphan homes tried to collect financial support from their constituent states, but some communities were more generous and consistent than others. In 1897, the Charleston Hebrew Orphan Society contributed $100 a yearly contribution that grew to $500 in 1906, as the Charleston community continued sending its orphans and half-orphans to the institution. See Tobias, *The Hebrew Orphan Society of Charleston*; and Hebrew Orphan Society Records, MS 1057-2 (Box 2, Folder 2), JHC.

NOTES TO CHAPTER 3

1. Oral interview with Jacob Blaustein, by Ray Ann Kremer, Jewish Oral History Project of Atlanta, October 24, 1991, 10, BCA.
2. 1910 and 1920 U.S. Census.
3. Oral interview with Blaustein, 10.
4. Hale, *Making Whiteness*, 87–88; Van Wormer, Jackson, and Sudduth, *The Maid Narratives*, 33.
5. Ritterhouse, *Growing Up Jim Crow*.
6. Ibid., 1.
7. Althusser, "Ideology and Ideological State Apparatuses," highlighted the role that institutions, like schools, play in teaching citizens how to follow and to emulate the "ruling ideologies" of a region.
8. New Orleans Jewish Orphan's Home *Golden City Messenger* (hereafter cited as GCM), April 1, 1923, 2, LRC.

9. Julie Newman, Blessing at the 40th Anniversary of the New Orleans Home, quoted in the *Jewish Ledger* (New Orleans), January 11, 1895, 16.
10. Theodore Roosevelt's Opening Address, January 25, 1909, in *Proceedings of the Conference on the Care of Dependent Children*, 35–36.
11. See note 3 in Marlene Trestman, "Fair Labor: The Remarkable Life and Legal Career of Bessie Margolin (1909–1996)," *Journal of Supreme Court History* 37:1 (March 2012), 42–74.
12. IOBB District Grand Lodge Seven began supporting the New Orleans home in 1875; IOBB District Grand Lodge Five supported the Atlanta home in its fundraising stages.
13. Joseph Magner, *The Story of the Jewish Orphans Home of New Orleans* (New Orleans: J. G. Hauser, 1905), 40–42.
14. Ralph Sonn to Charles Wilson, August 10, 1914, JELF, Series I, Container 22, Folder 1, BCA. See also the case of a father of five in Roanoke, Virginia, whose wife's death in 1911 drove him to seek the home's help. JELF, Series I, Container 7, Folders 15–18, BCA.
15. "Managing the Home: Cooperation Sought in Shaping Definite Admittance Policy," *GCM*, July 1923, 2, LRC.
16. ARJWO Constitution and By-Laws 1854, 11–12, AJA.
17. Moses Maimonides, "Eight Levels of Charity," Mishneh Torah, Laws of Charity, 10:7–14.
18. Shelly Tenenbaum, "Culture and Context: The Emergence of Hebrew Free Loan Societies in the United States," *Social Science History* 13:3 (Autumn 1989), 225.
19. Nathaniel Deutsch, *Inventing America's Worst Family: Eugenics, Islam, and the Fall and Rise of the Tribe of Ishmael* (Berkeley: University of California Press, 2009), 121.
20. Nancy Fraser and Linda Gordon, "A Genealogy of Dependency: Tracing a Keyword of the U.S. Welfare State," *Signs* 19:2 (Winter 1994), 316; Deutsch, *Inventing America's Worst Family*, 15; Robert Bremner, *From the Depths: The Discovery of Poverty in the United States* (New York: New York University Press, 1956), 123–124.
21. Jacob Furth, "Church, Charity, and Reform Work," *The Magnet* 2:2 (April 1895), JELF Files, Container 3, Folder 1, BCA.
22. Fraser and Gordon, "A Genealogy of Dependency," 316–318. See also Deutsch, *Inventing America's Worst Family*, 6.
23. Bremner, *From the Depths*, 124.
24. Ralph Sonn to Charles Wilson, August 10, 1914, JELF, Series I, Container 22, Folder 1, BCA.
25. See the hypothetical case of a needy family, described by President J. W. Newman of the New Orleans home, in the January 1925 *GCM*, 2, LRC.
26. See a 1908 case in Norfolk, Virginia, where a "worthless father's" criminal record and failure to provide financial support drove Superintendent Sonn to cut off correspondence with his children. JELF, Series I, Container 7, Folder 6, BCA.

27. Ralph Sonn to Charles N. Wilson, August 10, 1914, JELF, Series I, Container 22, Folder 1, BCA.
28. Isidore Blaustein to Ralph Sonn, August 24, 1914, JELF, Series I, Container 22, Folder 1, BCA.
29. Ibid.
30. Sonn to Blaustein, August 31, 1922, ibid.
31. Blaustein to Sonn, August 28, 1922, ibid.
32. Blaustein to Sonn, November 8, 1922, ibid.
33. Blaustein oral interview, 4.
34. New Orleans Annual Report, May 5, 1878, President Joseph Simon, 7, LRC.
35. "Certificate of Physician," JELF, Series I, Container 22, Folder 1, BCA.
36. President J. W. Newman, "Annual Report of the President: A Picture of the Daily Life of the Children," GCM, January 1925, 3, LRC.
37. Ibid., 3. Beginning in 1897, the New Orleans home placed sick children in an "isolated pavilion for the treatment of such diseases." See 1897 President's Annual Report in Magner, *The Story of the Jewish Orphans Home*, 74.
38. Medical Report to Herbert Haas and Victor Kriegshaber, February 24, 1922, JELF, Series I, Container 23, Folder 21, BCA.
39. Herbert Haas to Louis Fendig, March 21, 1922, JELF, Series I, Container 23, Folder 21, BCA.
40. February 5, 1899, Home Minutes, 25, JELF Series I, Container 3, Folder 2, BCA.
41. "Editorial," *American Jewess*, August 1897, 236.
42. *Jewish Sentiment*, 1898, quoted in Hertzberg, *Strangers within the Gate City*, 192.
43. Wiegman, *American Anatomies*, particularly chapter 3, "The Anatomy of Lynching."
44. "The Jewish Orphan Home: Resignation of the Matron—The Institution Being Managed by the Lady Commissioners," July 30, 1886, *Times-Picayune* (New Orleans), 3.
45. Joseph Magner described the board meeting of February 7, 1886, at which "the President announced that he had summarily discharged the Superintendent of the home." See *The Story of the Jewish Orphans Home*, 50.
46. President Edwin Kurdsheet, Annual Report to the New Orleans Home Board, March 21, 1886, 231–232, AJA.
47. Despite the home's efforts to keep the scandal secret, it leaked to a wider, non-Jewish audience, appearing in the *Times-Picayune*. See "Wandered Back: The Ex-Superintendent of the Jewish Orphan Home," July 28, 1886, *Times-Picayune* (New Orleans), 3.
48. President J. W. Newman's Address, May 1, 1923, GCM, 1, LRC.
49. Ibid., 1.
50. Friedman, *These Are Our Children*, 8, 34, 37.
51. Anna Berenson, "A Study of the Jewish Orphans Home," Tulane Master of the Arts Dissertation, 1933, 25, LRC.
52. Historian Juliette Landphair explains how wealthy citizens settled in the city's

western "uptown" area in large part because of its natural protection from flooding while poorer residents, including free people of color and immigrants, tended to gravitate to the lower flood-prone Ninth Ward. "'The Forgotten People of New Orleans': Community, Vulnerability, and the Lower Ninth Ward," *Journal of American History* 94:3 (December 2007), 837–845.
53. *GCM*, June 1923, 3, LRC.
54. Trestman, "Fair Labor," 42.
55. Oral interview with Joseph Green, by Lila Beth Young, Jewish Oral History Project of Atlanta, November 1, 1989, 10–11, BCA.
56. Friedman describes how chronic "understaffing, and the resulting neglect of basic hygiene" prevailed at the northern orphan homes. An accompanying photo dated in the 1920s shows a dismal scene of approximately ten young boys taking sponge baths at a long trough of water at the Cleveland home. *These Are Our Children*, 38–40.
57. Gary Polster, *Inside Looking Out: The Cleveland Jewish Orphan Asylum, 1868–1924* (Kent: Kent State University Press, 1990), 73–97.
58. Kahal Kodesh Beth Elohim in Charleston was among the first of the nation's synagogues to make adaptations to Reform modes of religious practice. See Moore, "Freedom's Fruits."
59. Gary P. Zola describes the relative "ideological unity" of southern rabbis as in part a result of their having lived "as a distinct minority far from any center of Jewish life and culture" and their need to develop "a Judaism that had planted its roots in a vast, non-Jewish landscape." "Southern Rabbis and the Founding of the First National Association of Rabbis," in *Dixie Diaspora*, ed. Bauman, 44–45, 49.
60. Berenson, "A Study of the Jewish Orphans Home," 149–150.
61. Mark K. Bauman and Arnold Shankman, "The Rabbi as Ethnic Broker: The Case of David Marx," *Journal of American Ethnic History* 2:2 (April 1, 1983), 53.
62. Ibid., 54.
63. Green oral interview, 14, BCA.
64. Blaustein oral interview, 36, BCA.
65. Ibid., 35.
66. Leon A. Jick, *The Americanization of the Synagogue, 1820–1870* (Hanover: University Press of New England for Brandeis University Press, 1992), 183, 191.
67. Green oral interview, 2, 16–17, BCA.
68. The southern orphans' opportunities for recreation as well as socializing with well-off neighbors also present a contrast with two of the northern institutions, the Cleveland home and the Hebrew Orphans Asylum of New York. The relatively smaller Philadelphia Jewish Foster Home sent their inmates to public school and allowed children to forge friendships with peers living outside the institution. See Friedman, *These Are Our Children*, 43, 47.
69. Green oral interview, 18–19, BCA.
70. In 1919 the Hebrew Orphan Asylum of Brooklyn, New York, established two summer camps, "Wakitan" for boys and "Wehaha" for girls.

71. *GCM*, September 1923, 1, LRC.
72. Ibid., 1, 3.
73. Gail Bederman, "'Teaching Our Sons to Do What We Have Been Teaching the Savages to Avoid': G. Stanley Hall, Racial Recapitulation, and the Neurasthenic Paradox," in *Manliness and Civilization*.
74. Jacob Blaustein spoke fondly of his relationship with Superintendent Sonn, whom he described as "compassionate" but "strict." Blaustein oral interview, 11, BCA.
75. Bederman, *Manliness and Civilization*, 119–120.
76. Hasci, *Second Home*, 36–39.
77. Theodore Roosevelt's Opening Address, January 25, 1909, in *Proceedings of the Conference on the Care of Dependent Children*, 5.
78. Dr. Lee K. Frankel, Fiftieth Anniversary Address, Jewish Orphans Home of New Orleans January, 1905, LRC.
79. Thomas Nelson Page, *The Negro: The Southerner's Problem* (New York: C. Scribner's Sons, 1904), 81. For similarly racist depictions of African Americans, see Thomas Dixon Jr.'s best-selling trilogy *The Leopard's Spots: A Romance of the White Man's Burden, 1865–1900* (1902; New York: A. Wessels, 1906), *The Clansman: An Historical Romance of the Ku Klux Klan* (New York: A. Wessels, 1907), and *The Traitor: A Story of the Fall of the Invisible Empire* (New York: Doubleday, Page & Company, 1907). *The Clansman* would later be adapted into the popular film *The Birth of a Nation* in 1915.
80. Photographs of inmates suggest that uniforms had fallen out of use before the Margolin and Blaustein children entered their respective institutions. While Green refers to a "uniform" of coveralls for playtime, he described wearing "normal clothing" to school. Green oral interview, 15–16, BCA. By contrast, Jules Doneson describes how wards of the Philadelphia Jewish Foster Home wore uniforms and were identified by numbers rather than by names. A former inmate, Doneson quipped that he was "unaware of having a name until reaching the age of nine or ten." *Deeds of Love: A History of the Jewish Foster Home and Orphan Asylum of Philadelphia—America's First Jewish Orphanage* (New York: Vintage Press, 1996), 43.
81. Blaustein oral interview, 36; Green oral interview, 15–16, BCA.
82. In "Charity within the Bounds of Race and Class: Female Benevolence in the Old South," *South Carolina Historical Magazine* 96:1 (January 1995), Gail S. Murray argues that, even prior to the Civil War, "the strict discipline and military-style routine many practiced [in northern institutions] was unfamiliar to southern institutions" (65).
83. Perhaps ironically, this system of self-governance was modeled on a structure first tested at a prison. See Berenson, "A Study of the Jewish Orphans Home," 16–17, and note 10.
84. Each child would begin the week with a certain amount of money in his or her account, and each infraction would result in a "check" against the child's record. A certain number of "checks" would result in a loss of money.

85. Both Green and Blaustein discuss this instance of "uncalled for" punishment in an institution that was otherwise moderate on discipline. Green described Strauss, the home's superintendent from 1923 to 1928, as a "frustrated German bachelor" who was a strict disciplinarian. See Blaustein oral interview, 14; and Green oral interview, 4–5, BCA.
86. Blaustein oral interview, 8, BCA.
87. Annual Address of President J. W. Newman, May 1, 1923, *GCM*, 1, LRC.
88. Ibid.
89. Berenson, "A Study of the Jewish Orphans Home," 27, LRC.
90. Ibid.
91. Golden, *Our Southern Landsman*, 20, 33; Hertzberg, *Strangers within the Gate City*, 203. On the location of Atlanta's black community, see Hunter, *To 'Joy My Freedom*, 100–105; and Ronald H. Bayor, *Race and the Shaping of Twentieth-Century Atlanta* (Chapel Hill: University of North Carolina Press, 1996).
92. Emanuel Sternberger to Ralph Sonn, August 18, 1914, JELF, Series I, Container 21, Folder 17, BCA.
93. Hale, *Making Whiteness*, 88.
94. Berenson, "A Study of the Jewish Orphans Home," 46–47, LRC.
95. Superintendent Sonn, 1903 Home Annual Report, 31, JELF, Series I, Container 2, Folder 1, BCA.
96. On the practice of apprenticing poor Jewish girls as servants in private northern homes, see Friedman, *These Are Our Children*, 114; and Prell, *Fighting to Become Americans*, 35. In *From Slavery to Poverty*, Gunja SenGupta discusses the practice of placing young African American wards of the Howard Orphanage and Industrial School of New York as domestic servants in the homes of well-off whites (207). It appears that the (non-Jewish) municipal orphanage in Charleston, which only accepted white children, also apprenticed its female charges as domestic workers during the antebellum period. However, John E. Murray observes that work was often difficult to find due to widespread use of enslaved African American women to perform domestic service. See Murray, "Charity within the Bounds," 54; and John E. Murray, *The Charleston Orphan House*, 81, 186–187.
97. Superintendent Sonn, 1903 Home Annual Report, 32, JELF, Series I, Container 2, Folder 1, BCA.
98. Lisa Krissoff Boehm, *Making a Way Out of No Way: African American Women and the Second Great Migration* (Jackson: University Press of Mississippi, 2009); Hunter, *To 'Joy My Freedom*; Elizabeth Clark-Lewis, "'This Work Had a End': African-American Domestic Workers in Washington, DC, 1910–1940," in *To Toil the Livelong Day: America's Women at Work, 1780–1980*, ed. Carol Groneman and Mary Beth Norton (Ithaca: Cornell University Press, 1987), 198; David Katzman, *Seven Days a Week: Women and Domestic Service in Industrializing America* (New York: Oxford University Press, 1978); and Van Wormer, Jackson, and Sudduth, *The Maid Narratives*.

99. Dolores Janiewski asserts that racial understandings formed through slavery caused "labor itself [to] function as a mark of degradation." "Southern Honor, Southern Dishonor: Managerial Ideology and the Construction of Gender, Race, and Class Relations in Southern Industry," in *Work Engendered: Toward a New History of American Labor*, ed. Ava Baron (Ithaca: Cornell University Press, 1991), 74.
100. Superintendent Report to the Board, February 6, 1898, JELF Minutes, Container 3, Folder 2, BCA.
101. Hale, *Making Whiteness*, 94.
102. Ibid., 102.
103. 1920 U.S. Census lists Fannie Young as "cook" and George Kendrick, born in 1860, as "yardman."
104. Magner, *The Story of the Jewish Orphans Home*, 68. While the report did not indicate the nurses' race, it was common practice at that time for whites to hire African American "nurses" to care for small children, and the 1925 Child Welfare League of America's "Report on the Jewish Children's Home of New Orleans, Louisiana," clearly describes these nurses as "colored maids."
105. *GCM*, August 1923, 4, LRC.
106. *GCM*, April 1923, 4, LRC.
107. Rebecca Sharpless, *Cooking in Other Women's Kitchens: Domestic Workers in the South, 1865–1960* (Chapel Hill: University of North Carolina Press, 2010), 169; and Van Wormer, Jackson, and Sudduth, *The Maid Narratives*, 34–38.
108. Allison Owen, Chairman, and Fred W. Ellsworth, Vice Chairman, Child Welfare League of America, "Report on the Jewish Children's Home of New Orleans, Louisiana," 1925, 7, LRC.
109. Hale, *Making Whiteness*, 101.
110. Friedman, *These Are Our Children*, 94–131; Polster, *Inside Looking Out*, 98–133; Howard Goldstein, *The Home on Gorham Street and the Voices of Its Children* (Tuscaloosa: University of Alabama Press, 1996); Hyman Bogen, *The Luckiest Orphans: A History of Hebrew Orphan Asylum of New York* (Urbana: University of Illinois Press, 1992).
111. Michael Heymann, 1894 Annual Report, New Orleans Jewish Children's Home, 320, AJA.
112. Wendy Bessman, "The 'Typical Home Kid Overachievers': Instilling a Success Ethic in the Jewish Children's Home of New Orleans," *Southern Jewish History* 8 (2005), 121–159.
113. Mary McCune, "Social Workers in the *Muskeljudentum*: 'Hadassah Ladies,' 'Manly Men,' and the Significance of Gender in the American Zionist Movement, 1912–1928," *American Jewish History* 86:2 (June 1998), 135–165.
114. David C. Labatt, 1857 Address to the ARJWO, Microfilm, 15, AJA.
115. 1883 New Orleans Annual Report, "Statement D, continued," 33, LRC.
116. Magner, *The Story of the Jewish Orphans Home*, 78.
117. See Magner, describing the Annual Meeting on March 19, 1893. Max Frishman,

alumnus of the New Orleans home, "made a strong appeal to all the Jewish people in the fair Southland for the establishment of a training school wherein the orphans could be taught useful and needed trades and professions." *The Story of the Jewish Orphans*, 67. See also the January 12, 1896, Annual Meeting, quoted in ibid., 71–72.

118. 1898 Home Annual Report, 40, JELF, Series I, Container 2, Folder 1, BCA.
119. Superintendent Sonn, 1903 Annual Report, 31, ibid.
120. 1889 Minutes, ARJWO, 265, AJA.
121. Rabbi Isadore Lewinthal, 1904 Address at the Isidore Newman School, New Orleans Jewish Orphans Home Annual Report, 1904, LRC.
122. Bessman, "The 'Typical Home Kid Overachievers,'" 128.
123. *GCM*, July 1923, 1, LRC.
124. Ibid.
125. Berenson, "A Study of the Jewish Orphans Home," 25, LRC.
126. See Trestman, "Fair Labor," 45–47.
127. See "The Home News," August 1927 (Vol. 1), 3, JELF, Series I. Container 2, Folder, 1, BCA.
128. Ibid.
129. Ibid., 7.
130. Isidore Blaustein to Ralph Sonn, November 8, 1922, JELF, Series I, Container 22, Folder 3, BCA.
131. Ibid.
132. Sonn to Blaustein, November 13, 1922, ibid.
133. Home records reveal that Annie paid off her school loans in 1967. Ibid.
134. Details courtesy of Marlene Trestman.
135. See Trestman, "Fair Labor," 46.
136. Jack J. Margolin's obituary in the *Times-Picayune* (New Orleans), November 21, 1991.
137. Isidore Blaustein to Armand Wyle, May 12, 1929, JELF, Series I, Container 22, Folder 2, BCA.
138. Sally Blaustein to Isidore Blaustein, May 7, 1929, ibid.
139. Armand Wyle to Isidore Blaustein, May 8, 1929, ibid.
140. Ibid.
141. Ibid.
142. Blaustein oral interview, 81.
143. Ibid., 80.
144. Sally and Annie Blaustein to Viola Wyle, June 13, 1929, JELF, Series I, Container 22, Folder 1, BCA.
145. Armand and Viola Wyle to Sally Blaustein, June 17, 1929, ibid.
146. Armand Wyle to Sally Blaustein, July 19, 1929, ibid.
147. Sally Blaustein to Viola Wyle, August 10, 1934, ibid.
148. Viola Wyle to Sally Wyle, August 11 1934, ibid. Mrs. Wyle followed up the next month with fifty dollars from the home's Dowry Fund.

NOTES TO CHAPTER 4

1. Some material in this chapter is updated and revised from an article of mine titled "'A Predominant Cause of Distress': Gender, Benevolence, and the *Agunah* in Regional Perspective," *American Jewish History* 98:2 (April 2013), 159–182.
2. Morris Harris to Ralph Sonn, July 1, 1914, JELF, Series I, Container 22, Folder 20, BCA.
3. Morris Harris (et al.) to Ralph Sonn, May 1915, ibid.
4. Ibid.
5. Anna R. Igra, *Wives without Husbands: Marriage, Desertion, and Welfare in New York, 1900–1935* (Chapel Hill: University of North Carolina Press, 2006).
6. For recent efforts to address the *agunah* problem, see Rabbi Adam Mintz, "A Courageous Proposal: The First Heter Agunah in America," *Jewish Orthodox Feminist Alliance Journal* 6:4 (Summer 2007), 14–15; and Rabbi Shlomo Riskin, "The Tragedy of the Agunah: A Proposed Solution," *Jewish Orthodox Feminist Alliance Journal* 5:4 (Summer 2005), 13–14.
7. Sylvia Barack Fishman, *A Breath of Life: Feminism in the American Jewish Community* (New York: Free Press, 1993), 35; Honey Rackman, "Getting a *Get*," in *Women in Chains: A Sourcebook on the Agunah*, ed. Jack Nusan Porter (Northvale, NJ: Jason Aronson Inc., 1995), 220. Fishman notes the irony that children of unmarried Jewish women are considered legitimate Jews, with all the rights of other Jewish children. On *mamzerut*, see Moshe Chigier, "Ruminations over the *Agunah* Problem," and Rackman, "Getting a *Get*."
8. Shlomo Riskin, "A Modern Orthodox Perspective," in *Women in Chains*, ed. Porter, 188.
9. Naomi Seidman, "Theorizing Jewish Patriarchy *in extremis*," in *Judaism since Gender*, ed. Miriam Peskowitz and Laura Levitt (New York: Routledge, 1997), 45.
10. Gur Alroey, *Bread to Eat and Clothes to Wear: Letters from Jewish Migrants in the Early Twentieth Century* (Detroit: Wayne State University Press, 2011), 63–78; Mark Baker, "The Voice of the Deserted Woman, 1867–1870," *Jewish Social Studies* 2:1 (Autumn 1995), 98–123.
11. Alroey, *Bread to Eat and Clothes to Wear*, 69.
12. Polish immigrant Loena Tamarkin described how the village rabbi convinced her parents to divorce before her father could migrate to the United States in the 1910s. See Tamarkin, *Dear Lizzie: Memoir of a Jewish Immigrant Woman*, ed. Elizabeth Reis (Bloomington: Xlibris, 2000), 12, 25.
13. Igra, *Wives without Husbands*; and "Male Providerhood and the Public Purse: Anti-desertion Reform in the Progressive Era," in *The Sex of Things: Gender and Consumption in Historical Perspective*, ed. Victoria de Grazia and Ellen Furlough (Berkeley: University of California Press, 1996).
14. Judge Julian W. Mack, May 1906 Opening Address to the National Conference of Jewish Charities, in *Proceedings of the National Conference of Jewish Charities* (New York: Stettiner Bros., 1907), 29.
15. Reena Sigman Friedman, "'Send Me My Husband Who Is in New York City':

Husband Desertion in the American Jewish Community, 1900–1926," *Jewish Social Studies* 44:1 (Winter 1982), 1. On what appeared to be higher rates of desertion among Jewish immigrants, see Ari Lloyd Fridkis, "Desertion in the American Jewish Immigrant Family: The Work of the National Desertion Bureau in Cooperation with the Industrial Removal Office," *American Jewish History* 71:2 (December 1981), 287.

16. Frankel, May 1906 Opening Address to the National Council of Jewish Charities, 56. See also Baker, "The Voice of the Deserted Jewish Woman," on the reach of the Yiddish press.
17. Fridkis, "Desertion in the American Jewish Immigrant Family," 289.
18. Igra, "Male Providerhood and the Public Purse," 190.
19. Igra, *Wives without Husbands*, 36–38, 96–97.
20. Federation Case File, Container 61, Folder 10, JELF, Series I, BCA.
21. Ibid.
22. Rabbi Tobias Geffen, unpublished manuscript titled "Autobiography of Rabbi Tobias Geffen," translated from Yiddish in 1951 by Rabbi Samuel Geffen, typed by Phyllis Simon Berner, mimeographed by Joel Ziff, edited by Ruth Adler and Rita Geffen in June 2007.
23. Rabbi Tobias Geffen (1870–1970), "the dean of Orthodox Jewish rabbis in the South," was one of very few rabbis in the region who could grant a halakhically legitimate *get* during the early twentieth century. See Joel Ziff, ed., *Lev Tuviah: On the Life and Work of Rabbi Tobias Geffen* (Newton, MA: Rabbi Tobias Geffen Memorial Fund, 1988).
24. Geffen, "Autobiography," 23–24.
25. E-mail correspondence with Joel Ziff, Rabbi Geffen's grandson. Geffen's autobiography states that he was the only European-trained Orthodox rabbi within a four-state area.
26. Geffen "Autobiography," 25.
27. Ibid.
28. September 6, 1896, Hebrew Orphans Home Minutes, 256, JELF, Series I, Container 3, Folder 1, BCA.
29. Chairman D. Kaufman's 1905 Report of the Committee of Indenture and Discharge, Annual Reports, JELF, Series I, 28, Container 2, Folder 1, BCA.
30. Ibid., 29.
31. Ibid., 30–31. See Frasier and Gordon's "A Genealogy of Dependency," for a discussion of the emergence of dependency-as-pathology in the industrializing nation.
32. Friedman, "Send Me My Husband Who Is in New York City," 1.
33. Joseph Kohn, President's Report, 58th Annual Report, March 30, 1913, New Orleans Jewish Orphans Home, 25, LRC.
34. Superintendent Sonn's 1905 Annual Report, Home Annual Reports, 33, JELF, Series I, Container 2, Folder 1, BCA.
35. Figure 1, "Mothers' Pensions Laws: Dates of Enactment," in Theda Skocpol et al., "Women's Associations and the Enactment of Mothers' Pensions in the United

States," *American Political Science Review* 87:3 (September 1993), 687, indicates that most northern and western states passed mothers' pensions between 1911 and 1913, while most of the South passed them after 1918.

36. The Hebrew Orphan Asylum of Brooklyn depended on state funding for its mothers' subsidies after passage of New York's 1915 Child Welfare Act. As a result of state funding, the population of the state's orphan homes shrank considerably as more children were able to remain at home with their mothers.
37. Mrs. J. B. Lowenberg to Ralph Sonn, May 14, 1920, JELF, Series I, Container 20, Folders 9–10, BCA.
38. Ibid.
39. Ibid.
40. Ralph Sonn to Mrs. J. B. Lowenberg, May 24, 1920, ibid.
41. Igra, *Wives without Husbands*, 100–101.
42. JELF, Series I, Container 7, Folder 32, BCA.
43. Ibid.
44. Prell, *Fighting to Become Americans*, 25–26.
45. Eva L. Stern, "To Mothers in Israel," *Tageblatt*, February 27, 1901.
46. See, for example, a letter to the *Tageblatt* by Louie Millensohn; and a 1910 letter to "A Bintel Brief" from "thirty-seven inmates of Blackwell's Island Prison workhouse," cited in Igra, "Male Providerhood and the Public Purse," 188.
47. Igra, *Wives without Husbands*, 2.
48. Prell, *Fighting to Become Americans*, 7.
49. Glenn, *Daughters of the Shtetl*, 12.
50. Reis, introduction to *Dear Lizzie*, 16.
51. For examples of this clash between Old World and American gender ideals, see Anzia Yezierska's portrayal of the father in *The Bread Givers* (New York: Doubleday, 1925).
52. Fredrickson, *The Black Image in the White Mind*, 256–282; Freedman, *Redefining Rape*, 92.
53. Harold Miller (pseudonym) to Ralph Sonn, June 13, 1920, JELF, Series I, Container 9, Folder 1, BCA.
54. The Census of 1920 indicates that the street on which the family lived was populated primarily by African American and Russian families.
55. Harold Miller to Ralph Sonn, July 22, 1920, JELF, Series I, Container 9, Folder 1, BCA.
56. See Jacobson, *Whiteness of a Different Color*.
57. Gwendolyn Mink, *The Wages of Motherhood: Inequality in the Welfare State, 1917–1942* (Ithaca: Cornell University Press, 1995), 28–33.
58. Superintendent Sonn's Report to the Board, 1904, Home Annual Reports, 33, JELF, Series I, Container 2, Folder 1, BCA.
59. Board of Directors Report, 1909, Home Annual Reports, 33, ibid.
60. President Wolf's 1909 Annual Report, 54, ibid.
61. Mink, *The Wages of Motherhood*, 21.

62. Morris Harris to Ralph Sonn, July 1, 1914, JELF, Series I, Container 22, Folder 20, BCA.
63. Ibid.
64. Jonathan Stearn to Ralph Sonn, June 1, 1915, ibid.
65. Ibid.
66. Ibid.
67. The elder brother was over the age limit and so remained with his mother.
68. Morris Harris to Ralph Sonn, May 1915, JELF, Series I, Container 22, Folder 20, BCA.
69. Jonathan Stearn to Ralph Sonn, June 1, 1915, ibid.
70. Ibid.
71. Hyman S. Jacobs to Ralph Sonn, May 8, 1918, ibid.
72. Ibid.
73. Ralph Sonn to Hyman S. Jacobs, May 9, 1918, ibid.
74. Jonathan Stearn to Ralph Sonn, October 7. 1918, ibid.
75. Ralph Sonn to Marcus Endel and Louis Fendig, June 21, 1921, ibid.
76. Marcus Endel to Ralph Sonn, July 5, 1921, ibid.
77. Minnie Rosenberg to Ralph Sonn, January 9, 1912, JELF, Series I, Container 12, Folder 18, BCA.
78. Ibid.
79. Mrs. Levy to Ralph Sonn, July 24, 1913, ibid.
80. Minnie Rosenberg to Ralph Sonn, March 17, 1912, ibid.
81. It appears that the other child's unspecified disability prohibited his admission to the home.
82. Libby Spiegel to Ralph Sonn, January 3, 1917, JELF, Series I, Container 5, Folder 21, BCA.
83. Ibid.
84. Ibid.
85. Mary Hardy to Feist Strauss, October 23, 1924, JELF, Series I, Container 7, Folder 38, BCA.
86. The home's collaborations with non-Jewish social workers were a necessary adaptation in remote regions with small Jewish communities like Petersburg.
87. Feist Strauss to Mary Hardy, October 27, 1924, ibid.
88. Feist Strauss to Mrs. V. H. Nussbaum, November 13, 1924, ibid.
89. Ibid.
90. Ibid.
91. Mrs. V. H. Nussbaum to Feist Strauss, November 17, 1924, ibid.
92. Mrs. J. B. Lowenberg to Ralph Sonn, May 14, 1920, JELF, Series I, Container 20, Folder 9, BCA.
93. March 15, 1922, ibid.
94. JELF, Series I, Container 20, Folder 10, BCA.
95. Undated case report, Federation Files, Container 62, Folder 1, BCA.
96. Ibid.

97. Case report, October 24, 1929, ibid.
98. Charles Zunser to Ed Kahn, November 6, 1929, ibid.
99. Ibid. A case report dated March 14, 1934, suggests that Mr. Kellerman never succeeded in obtaining a *get* from his first wife, but the MRA social worker deemed it best to "let the matter drop for the present."
100. Ed Kahn to Charles Zunser, October 30, 1929, and a case report dated October 16, 1929, ibid.
101. Ed Kahn to National Desertion Bureau, November 18, 1929, ibid.

NOTES TO CHAPTER 5

1. Rebecca Weiss to Viola Wyle, August 23, 1935, JELF, Series II (MS 205), Container 12, Folder 4, BCA.
2. July 4, 1935, ibid.
3. August 23, 1935, ibid.
4. Ibid.
5. August 8, 1935, ibid.
6. August 23, 1935, ibid.
7. R. Weiss/Blakeney to V. Wyle, November 15, 1929, ibid.
8. Ibid.
9. Board President Victor Kriegshaber's Annual Address, January 1929, JELF. Series I, Annual Reports, Container 2, Folder 1, BCA.
10. Victor Kriegshaber to Leopold Haas, president of Atlanta Federation of Jewish Charities, October 15, 1925, Federation Files, Container 22, Folder 7, BCA.
11. The 1930 U.S. Census shows the twenty-eight-year-old Bolotin working as a social worker in an unnamed Chicago charity.
12. See Ed Kahn's letter to George Hand, director of Atlanta's Red Cross, July 27, 1954, Rose Goldstein (Anderson)'s Personnel Series I, File, Federation Files, Container 45, Folder 2, BCA.
13. On the professionalization of social work, see Lubove, *The Professional Altruist*, 18–23; Walter Trattner, *From Poor Law to Welfare State: A History of Social Welfare in America* (New York: Free Press, 1974), 219–238. On women's involvement in building a "maternalist state," see Theda Skocpol, *Protecting Soldiers and Mothers: The Political Origins of Social Policy in the United States* (Cambridge: Belknap Press of Harvard University Press, 1992), 317–372.
14. Wyle reported that only ten children remained in the home; three had been "placed with relatives," twenty-three fostered in Atlanta homes, and the remaining fifty-one subsidized in their own homes. Viola Wyle's 1930 Annual Report to the Local and General Board, Federation Files, Container 22, Folder 7, BCA.
15. Karen W. Tice, *Tales of Wayward Girls and Immoral Women: Case Records and the Professionalization of Social Work* (Urbana: University of Illinois Press, 1998), 85–86.
16. SenGupta, *From Slavery to Poverty*, 19.

17. R. Weiss to V. Wyle, August 8, 1935, JELF, Series II (MS 205), Container 12, Folder 4, BCA.
18. Lubove, *The Professional Altruist*, 16.
19. Case report from V. Wyle's November 6, 1929, visit, JELF, Series II (MS 205), Container 12, Folder 4, BCA.
20. Ibid.
21. Ibid.
22. Ibid.
23. Ibid.
24. See Trattner, *From Poor Law to Welfare State*, 201–203; Linda Gordon, *Pitied but Not Entitled: Single Mothers and the History of Welfare, 1890–1935* (New York: Free Press, 1994); and Bremner, *From the Depths*.
25. Immigration records reveal that the couple left from the port of Southampton, indicating Galveston as their final destination. Even after the Galveston Plan ended, the city served as an Industrial Removal Office base for helping Jewish immigrants acclimate to their new home and boasted a vibrant and transnationally diverse Jewish community. See Marinbach, *Galveston*.
26. For a comprehensive history of Poland's partitioning, see Norman Davies, *God's Playground: A History of Poland in Two Volumes*, vol. 2 (New York: Oxford University Press, 2005).
27. Case report, JELF, Series II (MS 205), Container 16, Folder 5, BCA.
28. Little did Rebecca know that her social worker was herself the Ohio-born daughter of a Czechoslovakian mother.
29. Ralph Sonn's 1904 Annual Report to the Board, JELF, Series I, Container 2, Folder 1, BCA. At the 1909 Anniversary Address, President Simon Wolf urged that "children when found with mothers should not be taken from the mother but kept with the parent, and that whatever amount of money the child should cost per capita should be given to the mother in aid of not only educating and caring for the child, but also in caring for herself." 1909 Annual Report, ibid.
30. Ed Kahn, "Your Federation," Federation Files, Container 33, Folder 1, BCA. See also Max C. Gettinger, *Coming of Age: The Atlanta Jewish Federation, 1962–1982* (Hoboken, NJ: Ktav Publishing, 1994); and Mark K. Bauman, "The Transformation of Jewish Social Services in Atlanta, 1928–1948," *American Jewish Archives* 53:1–2 (2001), 83–111.
31. Kahn, "Your Federation."
32. Leo Hexter to Ludwig Bernstein, March 11, 1924, Federation Files, Container 22, Folder 7, BCA.
33. Leo Hexter to Ralph Sonn, April 29, 1924, ibid.
34. Leo Hexter to Victor Kriegshaber, November 10, 1925, ibid.
35. Skocpol et al., "Women's Associations and the Enactment of Mothers' Pensions in the United States."
36. Gordon, *Pitied but Not Entitled*, 45, 49.

37. Case report, August 26, 1930, Series II (MS 205), Container 16, Folder 5, BCA.
38. Superintendent Armand Wyle's Address to the Board, January 25, 1931, JELF, Series I, Container 4, Folder 2, BCA.
39. Annual Report to the Board, "Report of the Social Service Worker," ibid.
40. Molly Ladd-Taylor and Lauri Umansky, eds., *"Bad" Mothers: The Politics of Blame in Twentieth-Century America* (New York: New York University Press, 1997), 2–3.
41. Undated case report, JELF, Series I, Container 6, Folder 2, BCA.
42. Case report, March 16, 1926, JELF, Series I, Container 9, Folder 5, BCA.
43. See case reports about a "feeble-minded" immigrant mother in Fitzgerald, Georgia, in the 1920s, JELF, Series I, Container 9, Folders 1–2; and a 1926 visit to the home of a "course, uncouth" subsidized Polish widow in Atlanta, JELF, Series I, Container 10, Folders 1–2, BCA.
44. See Joyce Antler, *You Never Call, You Never Write! A History of the Jewish Mother* (New York: Oxford University Press, 2007).
45. Donald Weber, "The Jewish American World of Gertrude Berg: *The Goldbergs* on Radio and Television, 1930–1950," in *Talking Back*, ed. Adler, 91. See also Antler's chapter 2, "Molly Goldberg: 'The Prototype of the Jewish Mother' in the Twentieth Century."
46. See Gilman, "Feminism, College Education, and the Birth Rate"; "The Sanctity of Human Life"; "A Suggestion on the Negro Problem," *American Journal of Sociology* 14:1 (July 1908), 78–85; and her novel *The Crux*; and Margaret Sanger, *The Pivot of Civilization* (New York: Brentano's, 1922); and "Birth Control and Racial Betterment," *Birth Control Review*, February 1919.
47. Hale, *Making Whiteness*, 74.
48. In a letter dated September 30, 1929, to Lois Dobrin of the Jewish Welfare Bureau in Florida, Viola Wyle inquired about Weiss's ability to work and reminded the worker "that we are not a family welfare organization, and all that we can do is to subsidize the two children, not Mrs. Weiss." JELF, Series II, Container 12, Folder 4, BCA.
49. Tice, *Tales of Wayward Girls and Immoral Women*, 24–26.
50. R. Weiss to V. Wyle, October 14, 1929, JELF, Series II, Container 12, Folder 4, BCA.
51. Gordon and Fraser, "A Genealogy of Dependency," 316. See also Sonya Michel, "The Limits of Maternalism: Policies toward American Wage-Earning Women during the Progressive Era," in *Mothers of a New World: Maternalist Politics and the Origins of Welfare States*, ed. Sonya Michel and Seth Koven (New York: Routledge, 1993), 283.
52. R. Weiss to V. Wyle, February 13, 1930, JELF, Series II, Container 12, Folder 4, BCA.
53. Ibid.
54. See case report written by Viola Wyle following her first visit to the Weiss home in November 1929, ibid.
55. R. Weiss to V. Wyle, February 13, 1930, ibid.

56. V. Wyle's letters to R. Weiss, November 27, 1929, and June 11, 1930, ibid.
57. R. Weiss to V. Wyle, October 14, 1929, ibid.
58. R. Weiss to V. Wyle, June 22, 1930, ibid.
59. See Viola Wyle's November 6, 1929, visit to Fort Pierce, ibid.
60. R. Weiss to V. Wyle, February 13, 1930, ibid.
61. Edward Kahn, "Facing the Situation: A Statement of Social Work Experience during 1930," presented at the Federation meeting on June 27, 1931, Federation Files, Container 24, Folder 3, BCA.
62. V. Wyle to R. Weiss, February 10, 1930, JELF, Series II, Container 12, Folder 4, BCA.
63. R. Weiss to V. Wyle, February 13, 1930, ibid.
64. Ibid.
65. See chapter 3's discussion of the southern orphan homes' resistance to placing their female inmates out as domestic servants. This practice represents a sharp distinction from northern homes, which actively sought "household assistant" positions for their wards. See Friedman, *These Are Our Children*, 114–115.
66. Hunter, *To 'Joy My Freedom*, 29, 49–53.
67. Riv-Ellen Prell describes how the opposite was true for Jewish benevolent workers at the Clara De Hirsch Home for Working Girls in New York. See *Fighting to Become Americans*, 35. Case files from the Atlanta home and the MRA reveal that social workers often encouraged subsidized mothers to earn money by taking in boarders or performing work at home such as sewing or mending.
68. Armand Wyle's February 25, 1931, case report, JELF, Series II, Container 12, Folder 4, BCA.
69. R. Weiss to V. Wyle, March 21, 1931, ibid.
70. Polly Stone Buck, *The Blessed Town: Oxford, Georgia, at the Turn of the Century* (Chapel Hill: University of North Carolina Press, 1986), 115, quoted in Hunter, *To 'Joy My Freedom*, 109.
71. Case report, Series II (MS 205), Container 16, Folder 5, BCA..
72. Joanne Meyerowitz, *Women Adrift: Independent Wage Earners in Chicago, 1880–1930* (Chicago: University of Chicago Press, 1988), 18. See also Kathy Peiss, *Cheap Amusements: Working Women and Leisure in Turn-of-the-Century New York* (Philadelphia: Temple University Press, 1986); Elizabeth Rose, "Taking on a Mother's Job: Day Care in the 1920's and 1930's," in *"Bad" Mothers*, ed. Ladd-Taylor and Umansky.
73. Armand Wyle's report of his February 25, 1932, discussion with Weiss's brother-in-law, JELF, Series II, Container 12, Folder 4, BCA.
74. See Andrew Heinz's chapter titled "The Parlor and the Piano," in *Adapting to Abundance: Jewish Immigrants, Mass Consumption, and the Search for American Identity*, ed. Andrew R. Heinze (New York: Columbia University Press, 1990).
75. V. Wyle to Mrs. Myers, July 1,1935, JELF, Series II, Container 12, Folder 4, BCA.
76. R. Weiss/Blakeney to V. Wyle via Mrs. Myers, July 4, 1935, ibid.

77. Ibid.
78. Levitt, "Impossible Assimilations, American Liberalism, and Jewish Difference," 812.
79. Jacobson, *Whiteness of a Different Color*, 129. See also Peggy Pascoe, "Miscegenation Law, Court Cases, and Ideologies of 'Race' in Twentieth-Century America," *Journal of American History* 83:1 (June 1996), 47–48.
80. See Jeffrey Gurock, *Orthodox Jews in America* (Bloomington: Indiana University Press, 2009).
81. This was the last letter placed in her file: any others she sent to Viola Wyle were likely kept as personal mail, as her case was closed on July 10.
82. R. Weiss/Blakeney to V. Wyle, August 23, 1935, JELF, Series II, Container 12, Folder 4, BCA.
83. In *From Slavery to Poverty*, Gunja SenGupta shows how "the alleged pathology of 'pauperism'" was "steeped in the imagery of blackness" (8).
84. Martha Gardner, *The Qualities of a Citizen: Women, Immigration, and Citizenship, 1870–1965* (Princeton: Princeton University Press, 2005), 87–88.
85. MacLean, "The Leo Frank Case Reconsidered," 929–931.
86. R. Weiss/Blakeney to V. Wyle via Mrs. Myers, August 23, 1935, JELF, Series II, Container 12, Folder 4, BCA.
87. R. Weiss/Blakeney to Wyle, August 23, 1935, ibid.
88. Ibid.

NOTES TO CHAPTER 6

1. The first Jews to arrive in America as early as the mid-1600s, western Sephardim were generally wealthier and better educated than the later wave of Sephardic immigrants, and they established a network of cemeteries and synagogues along the eastern seaboard. See Ben-Ur, *Sephardic Jews in America*, 2, 14; Francesco Cordasco, *Dictionary of American Immigration History* (Metuchen, NJ: Scarecrow Press, 1990), 657–662; Bobbie S. Malone, "As Told to Memoirs, Ruth and Rosalie: Two Tails of Jewish New Orleans," *Southern Jewish History* 1 (1998), 121.
2. New immigrant Sephardim migrated from regions as varied as Salonika, Rhodes, Yanina, Kastoria, Monastir, Turkey, Aleppo, Damascus, Iran, Iraq, Egypt, Morocco, and Yemen.
3. Diane Matza, "Sephardic Jews Transmitting Culture across Three Generations," *American Jewish History* 79:3 (Spring 1990), 337; Paloma Diaz-Mas, *Sephardim: The Jews from Spain* (Chicago: University of Chicago Press, 1992), 64; Ben-Ur, *Sephardic Jews in America*, 30.
4. Louis M. Hacker, "The Communal Life of the Sephardic Jews in New York City," *Jewish Social Service Quarterly* 3:2 (December 1926), 32.
5. Ibid., 33.
6. Ben-Ur, *Sephardic Jews in America*, 108–112. Paloma Diaz-Mas describes how Ladino was "used to 'translate' religious texts in holy languages into the vernacular" in *Sephardim*, 75. See also Yitzchak Kerem, "The Settlement of Rhodian and

Other Sephardic Jews in Montgomery and Atlanta in the Twentieth Century," *American Jewish History* 85:4 (1997), 378.
7. Hacker, "The Communal Life of the Sephardic Jews in New York City," 32, 33, 39.
8. Kerem, "The Settlement of Rhodian and Other Sephardic Jews." See also Cordasco, *Dictionary of American Immigration History*, 60.
9. Kerem, "The Settlement of Rhodian and Other Sephardic Jews," 377.
10. Sol Beton, *Sephardim and a History of Or V'Shalom* (Atlanta: Congregation Or V'Shalom, 1981), 101.
11. Kerem, "The Settlement of Rhodian and Other Sephardic Jews," 390.
12. Beton, *Sephardim*, 101.
13. Hertzberg, *Strangers within the Gate City*, 96.
14. Kerem, "The Settlement of Rhodian and Other Sephardic Jews," 386, 391.
15. Ibid., 386.
16. MRA Minutes, August 12, 1929, and December 23, 1929, Federation Files, Container 25, Folder 17, BCA. Also cited in Kerem, "The Settlement of Rhodian and Other Sephardic Jews," 386.
17. When Tourial's brother died from influenza in 1923, his family received support from both the MRA and the orphan home, and Tourial helped the institutions provide support to his widowed sister-in-law and her children. See case report in Federation Files, Container 72, Folder 21, BCA.
18. Federation Files (MS 82), Container 55, Folder 4, BCA.
19. See the 1920 Census, where the couple is listed as having been born in New York, even though the 1930 Census confirms their Turkish origins.
20. Beton, *Sephardim*, 116.
21. Ibid., 117.
22. See 1930 U.S. Census. Most of the Ferreras' neighbors rented their homes and were engaged in working-class occupations like stonecutting, dry cleaning, and construction.
23. The couple probably sought counsel from the city's Sephardic rabbi, Joseph I. Cohen. See Kerem, "The Settlement of Rhodian and Other Sephardic Jews," 380.
24. Kahn, "Your Federation."
25. See Edward Kahn's January 16, 1950, letter to Albert A. Hutler, recommending Rose Goldstein Anderson for a social worker position at the United Jewish Fund of San Diego. Federation Files, Container 45, Folder 2, BCA.
26. U.S. Census of 1930.
27. Jacobson, *Whiteness of a Different Color*, 9.
28. Case report, July 22, 1929, Federation Files, Container 55, Folder 4, BCA.
29. Undated MRA case report, likely Spring 1930, Federation File, Container 42, Folder 10, BCA.
30. Undated MRA case report, likely February 15, 1929, when the case opened, Federation Files, Container 57, Folder 23, BCA.
31. Similar assumptions about Sephardic clients' inferior intelligence can be observed in a 1924 Atlanta orphan home case where two sons of a widowed Turkish

immigrant were characterized as "imbeciles" and sent to the Georgia Training School for Mental Defectives. In 1927, the children's uncles enlisted the help of Congregation Or V'Shalom to pressure the home for the boys' release. JELF, Series I, Container 7, Folder 2, BCA.
32. Undated MRA case report, likely February 15, 1929, when the case opened, Federation Files, Container 57, Folder 23, BCA.
33. Case report, February 21, 1929, ibid.
34. Case report, February 26, 1929, ibid.
35. Case report, December 31, 1930, ibid.
36. Case report, November 24, 1933, ibid.
37. See Melissa Klapper's discussion of the shifting expectations for young Jewish women's courtship and sexuality in *Jewish Girls Coming of Age in America, 1860–1920* (New York: New York University Press, 2007), 225–228.
38. Case report, July 22, 1929, Federation Files, Container 55, Folder 4, BCA.
39. Case report, October 31, 1929, ibid.
40. Ibid.
41. Case report, September 1930, ibid.
42. Case reports, September 15, 1930, June 18, 1931, and June 26, 1931, ibid.
43. Case report, June 26, 1931, ibid.
44. Case report, April 16, 1930, ibid.
45. Case report, June 14, 1937, ibid.
46. Case report, January 9, 1932, ibid.
47. Case report, June 26, 1931, ibid.
48. Case report, February 1935, page 17, Federation Files, Container 63, Folder 4, BCA.
49. Ibid.
50. Case report, February 28, 1935, Federation Files, Container 63, Folder 4, BCA.
51. Case report, October 31, 1929, Federation Files, Container 55, Folder 4, BCA.
52. Case report, July 22, 1929, ibid.
53. Case report, September 1930, ibid.
54. Case report, July 13, 1931, ibid.
55. Ibid.
56. Case report, June 11, 1937, Federation Files, Container 55, Folder 4, BCA.
57. Case report, May 5, 1930, ibid.
58. Case report, September 3, 1929, Federation Files, Container 72, Folder 18, BCA.
59. Webb, *Fight against Fear*, 29; Hertzberg, *Strangers within the City Gate*, 183, 187.
60. Case report, September 4, 1929, Federation Files, Container 72, Folder 18, BCA.
61. Tera Hunter describes Decatur Street's reputation for "colorful characters, violence, and illicit sex." See *To 'Joy My Freedom*, 145, 162.
62. Case report, October 16, 1929, Federation Files, Container 72, Folder 18, BCA.
63. Ibid.
64. Case report, October 20, 1929, ibid.
65. Mary Douglas, *Purity and Danger: An Analysis of Concepts of Pollution and Taboo* (New York: Praeger, 1966), 41.

66. Case report, September 29, 1930, Federation Files, Container 42, Folder 10, BCA.
67. Case report, January 21, 1930, Container 55, Folder 4, BCA.
68. See Federation Files, Container, 63, Folder 4, BCA. The cost of the family's maid service declined over the time that the MRA oversaw the case: from $3.50 or $4.00 per week in 1928 to $3.00 in 1935. This may have been a result of shifts in the kinds of work the maid was expected to perform—in 1928 including child care as well as general cleaning, while chiefly laundry in 1935—or a result of wage fluctuations during the Depression.
69. Hunter, *To 'Joy My Freedom*, 3, 34, 50–51; Van Wormer, Jackson, and Sudduth, *The Maid Narratives*; Sharon Harley, "When Your Work Is Not Who You Are: The Development of a Working-Class Consciousness among Afro-American Women," in *We Specialize in the Wholly Impossible: A Reader in Black Women's History*, ed. Darlene Clark Hine, Wilma King, and Linda Reed (New York: Carlson Publishing, 1995); Clark-Lewis, "This Work Had a' End."
70. Phyllis Palmer, *Domesticity and Dirt: Housewives and Domestics in the United States, 1920–1945* (Philadelphia: Temple University Press, 1989), 4, 146–147.
71. Case report, June 24, 1932, Federation Files, Container 57, Folder 23, BCA.
72. Case report, July 22, 1929, Federation Files, Container 55, Folder 4, BCA.
73. Case report, September 19, 1929, ibid.
74. Ibid.
75. Case report, October 16, 1929, ibid. This information conflicted with Victor's assertion on November 25, 1930, that the maid's services cost five dollars a week.
76. Case report, February 20, 1931, ibid.
77. Ibid.
78. Case report, April 29, 1931, ibid.
79. Case report, January 21, 1930, ibid.
80. See Steven Hertzberg's chapter in *Strangers within the Gate City* on "Jews and Blacks" (181–201) for a discussion of the ways in which Jewish business owners often relied on African American patronage.
81. Micki McElya, *Clinging to Mammy: The Faithful Slave in Twentieth-Century America* (Cambridge: Harvard University Press, 2007); Patricia Morton, "'My Ole Black Mammy' in American Historiography," *Southern Women*, ed. Caroline Matheny Dillman (New York: Hemisphere, 1988), and *Disfigured Images: The Historical Assault on Afro-American Women* (New York: Greenwood Press, 1991); Kenneth Goings, *Mammy and Uncle Mose: Black Collectibles and American Stereotyping* (Bloomington: Indiana University Press, 1994), 8–11; Patricia A. Turner, *Ceramic Uncles and Celluloid Mammies: Black Images and Their Influence on Culture* (New York, Anchor Books, 1994), 24–25, 43–45, 53. See also Grace Hale's chapter titled "Domestic Reconstruction: White Homes, 'Black Mammies,' and 'New Women,'" in *Making Whiteness*, 85–119.
82. Case report, February 4, 1931, Federation Files, Container 55, Folder 4, BCA.
83. Case report, February 11, 1931, ibid.
84. Case report, May 12, 1931, ibid.

85. Ibid., and again on January 18, 1932.
86. Case report, May 12, 1931, ibid.
87. Ibid.
88. Case report, November 19, 1925, Federation Files, Container 72, Folder 18, BCA.
89. Case report, May 1936 Case File, Federation Files, Container 51, Folder 3, BCA.
90. See 1930 U.S. Census.
91. The MRA and JELF case files contain many similar examples of subsidized Jewish immigrants refusing to seek medical care at Grady Hospital. Another Sephardic mother refused to give birth at Grady (Federation Files, Container 39, Folder 15, BCA), and yet another would not return to the hospital after being mistreated by doctors "owing to the fact that she could not speak English" (Federation Files, Container 39, Folder 14, BCA).
92. Case report, May 1936, Federation Files, Container 51, Folder 3, BCA.
93. Their names and some of their photographs appear in Beton, *Sephardim*, 152–153.

NOTES TO THE CONCLUSION

1. Mark Ottoni-Wilhelm, "Giving to Organizations That Help People in Need: Differences across Denominational Identities," *Journal for the Scientific Study of Religion* 49:3 (September 2010), 389–412. The study found that Jewish families are 8 percent more likely to give to charity and give 20 percent more than families of other denominations.
2. Levitt, "Impossible Assimilations, American Liberalism, and Jewish Difference," 808–809.
3. Ibid., 809.

SELECTED BIBLIOGRAPHY

ARCHIVES
AJA Jacob Rader Marcus Center of the American Jewish Archives, Hebrew Union College, Cincinnati, Ohio
BCA Ida Pearle & Joseph Cuba Archives and Genealogy Center, William Breman Museum, Atlanta, Georgia
JHC Jewish Heritage Collection at the College of Charleston, Addlestone Library, Charleston, South Carolina
LRC Louisiana Research Collection, Howard–Tilton Memorial Library, Tulane University, New Orleans, Louisiana

NEWSPAPERS
American Jewess
Atlanta Jewish Times
Jewish Daily Forward / der Forverts
Jewish Daily News / der Yiddishes Tageblatt
Jewish Ledger
Jewish South
New York Age
New York Times
Times-Picayune
Tom Watson's Jeffersonian

PUBLISHED PRIMARY SOURCES
Abernethy, Arthur T. *The Jew a Negro, Being a Study of the Jewish Ancestry from an Impartial Standpoint*. Moravian Falls, NC: Dixie Publishing, 1910.
Adler, Cyrus, and Henrietta Szold, eds. *American Jewish Yearbook*. Vol. 1. Philadelphia: American Jewish Committee, 1899–1900.
Cohen, J. Barrett. *Judaism and the Typical Jew: An Address Delivered before the Jews of Charleston, S.C., on the Celebration of the Centennial Anniversary of the Birthday of Sir Moses Montefiore at the Hasel Street Synagogue, October 26, 1884* Charleston: News and Courier Book Presses, 1884.
Commander, Lydia Kingsmill. *The American Idea*. New York: A. S. Barnes and Co., 1907.

Croxton, Frederick C. "Statistical Review of Immigration, 1820–1910: Distribution of Immigrants, 1850–1900." In *Reports of the Immigration Commission*. Washington: GPO, 1911.
Daly, Charles P. *The Settlement of the Jews in North America*. New York: P. Cowen, 1893.
Davidson, Gabriel. *Our Jewish Farmers and the Story of the Jewish Agricultural Society*. New York: L. B. Fischer, 1943.
Dixon, Thomas. *The Clansman: An Historical Romance of the Ku Klux Klan*. New York: A. Wessels, 1907.
———. *The Leopard's Spots: A Romance of the White Man's Burden, 1865–1900*. 1902; New York: A. Wessels, 1906.
———. *The Traitor: A Story of the Fall of The Invisible Empire*. New York: Doubleday, Page & Company, 1907.
DuBois, William Edward Burghardt. *Black Reconstruction in America, 1860–1880*. New York: Free Press, 1998
"Editorial." *American Jewess*, August 1897.
Elzas, Barnett A. *The Jews of South Carolina, from the Earliest Times to the Present Day*. Philadelphia: J. B. Lippincott, 1905.
———. *Story of a Long Lost Seal: Proves the Age of the Hebrew Benevolent Society*. n.p., 1900.
Fleming, Walter L. "Immigration to the Southern States." *Political Science Quarterly* 20:2 (June 1, 1905), 276–297.
Folkmar, Elnora, and Daniel Folkmar. "Dictionary of Races of Peoples." Dillingham Report, United States Immigration Commission, Government Print Office, 1911.
Gilman, Charlotte Perkins. *The Crux: A Novel*. New York: Charlton Company, 1911.
———. "Feminism, College Education, and the Birth Rate." *Forerunner* 6 (October 1915), 259–261.
———. "A Suggestion on the Negro Problem." *American Journal of Sociology* 14:1 (July 1908), 78–85.
Grillparzer, Franz. *The Jewess of Toledo: Esther*. Yarmouth Port, MA: Register Press, 1953.
Hacker, Louis M. "The Communal Life of the Sephardic Jews in New York City." *Jewish Social Service Quarterly* 3:2 (December 1926), 32.
Hall, Prescott F. "Selection of Immigration." *Annals of the American Academy of Political and Social Science* 24 (July 1, 1904), 169–184.
History of the Jews of Louisiana: Their Religious, Civic, Charitable and Patriotic Life. Jewish Historical Publishing Company of Louisiana, 1903.
Iseman, Myre St. Wald. *Race Suicide*. New York: Cosmopolitan Press, 1912.
Magner, Joseph. *The Story of the Jewish Orphans Home of New Orleans*. New Orleans: J. G. Hauser, 1905.
Page, Thomas Nelson. *The Negro: The Southerner's Problem*. New York: C. Scribner's Sons, 1904.
Philipson, David. "Human Brotherhood." *The Magnet* 1:2 (April 1894), n.p.

Proceedings of the Conference on the Care of Dependent Children Held at Washington, DC, January 25, 26, 1909. Washington, DC: GPO, 1909.

Proceedings of the National Conference of Jewish Charities. New York: Stettiner Bros., 1907.

Roosevelt, Theodore. "The Strenuous Life." Speech before the Hamilton Club, April 10, 1899, in *Roosevelt, the Strenuous Life: Essays and Addresses.* New York: The Century Co., 1905.

Sanger, Margaret. "Birth Control and Racial Betterment." *Birth Control Review*, February 1919.

———. *The Pivot of Civilization.* New York: Brentano's, 1922.

Vance, Zebulon Baird. *The Scattered Nation.* Edited by Willis Bruce Dowd. New York: J. J. Little and Co., 1904.

"The Voice of the Fair Southland." *The State*, May 24, 1898.

Wells, Ida B. "Southern Horrors: Lynch Law in All Its Phases." *New York Age*, June 25, 1892.

Wolf, Simon. *The American Jew as Patriot, Soldier and Citizen.* Philadelphia: The Levytype Company Publishers, 1895.

Woodhull, Victoria. "To Women Who Have an Interest in Humanity, Present and Future: Personal Greeting." *Woodhull and Claflin's Weekly*, October 31, 1874.

Yezierska, Anzia. *The Bread Givers.* New York: Doubleday, 1925.

UNPUBLISHED PRIMARY SOURCES

Geffen, Tobias. "Autobiography of Rabbi Tobias Geffen." Unpublished manuscript, translated by Samuel Geffen, 1951.

Jewish Oral History Project of Atlanta. Histories from 1989 and 1991, BCA.

SECONDARY SOURCES

Abrams, Jeanne E. *Jewish Women Pioneering the Frontier Trail: A History in the American West.* New York: New York University Press, 2007.

Adler, Selig. "Zebulon B. Vance and the 'Scattered Nation.'" *Journal of Southern History* 7:3 (August 1, 1941), 357–377.

Alroey, Gur. *Bread to Eat and Clothes to Wear: Letters from Jewish Migrants in the Early Twentieth Century.* Detroit: Wayne State University Press, 2011.

Althusser, Louis. "Ideology and Ideological State Apparatuses (Notes towards an Investigation)." In *Lenin and Philosophy, and Other Essays*, translated by Ben Brewster. London: New Left Books, 1971.

Antler, Joyce, ed. *The Journey Home: How Jewish Women Shaped Modern America.* New York: Free Press, 1997.

———, ed. *Talking Back: Images of Jewish Women in American Popular Culture.* Hanover: University Press of New England for Brandeis University Press, 1998.

———. *You Never Call! You Never Write! A History of the Jewish Mother.* New York: Oxford University Press, 2007.

Apte, Helen Jacobus. *Heart of a Wife: The Diary of a Southern Jewish Woman*, edited by Marcus D. Rosenbaum. Wilmington, DE: Scholarly Resources Books, 1998.

Ashton, Dianne. *Rebecca Gratz: Women and Judaism in Antebellum America*. Detroit: Wayne State University Press, 1997.

Baker, Mark. "The Voice of the Deserted Jewish Woman, 1867–1870." *Jewish Social Studies* 2:1 (Autumn 1995), 98–123.

Bass, Jack. *The Palmetto State: The Making of Modern South Carolina*. Columbia: University of South Carolina Press, 2009.

Baum, Charlotte. *The Jewish Woman in America*. New York: Dial Press, 1976.

Bauman, Mark K. "Southern Jewish Women and Their Social Service Organizations." *Journal of American Ethnic History* 22:3 (2003), 34.

———. *The Southerner as American: Jewish Style*. Cincinnati: American Jewish Archives, 1996.

———. "The Transformation of Jewish Social Services in Atlanta, 1928–1948." *American Jewish Archives* 53:1–2 (2001), 83–111.

Bauman, Mark K., and Arnold Shankman. "The Rabbi as Ethnic Broker: The Case of David Marx." *Journal of American Ethnic History* 2:2 (April 1, 1983), 51–68.

Bayor, Ronald H. *Race and the Shaping of Twentieth-Century Atlanta*. Chapel Hill: University of North Carolina Press, 1996.

Bederman, Gail. *Manliness and Civilization: A Cultural History of Gender and Race in the United States, 1880–1917*. Chicago: University of Chicago Press, 1995.

Ben-Ur, Aviva. *Sephardic Jews in America: A Diasporic History*. New York: New York University Press, 2009.

Berthoff, Rowland T. "Southern Attitudes toward Immigration, 1865–1914." *Journal of Southern History* 17:3 (August 1, 1951), 328–360.

Bessman, Wendy. "The 'Typical Home Kid Overachievers': Instilling a Success Ethic in the Jewish Children's Home of New Orleans." *Southern Jewish History* 8 (2005), 121–159.

Beton, Sol. *Sephardim and a History of Or V'Shalom*. Atlanta: Congregation Or V'Shalom, 1981.

Boehm, Lisa Krissoff. *Making a Way Out of No Way: African American Women and the Second Great Migration*. Jackson: University Press of Mississippi, 2009.

Bogen, Hyman. *The Luckiest Orphans: A History of the Hebrew Orphan Asylum of New York*. Urbana: University of Illinois Press, 1992.

Bornstein, George. *The Colors of Zion: Blacks, Jews, and Irish from 1845 to 1945*. Cambridge: Harvard University Press, 2011.

Bourdieu, Pierre. *Distinction: A Social Critique of the Judgment of Taste*, translated by Richard Nice. New York: Routledge Press, 1984.

Bourdieu, Pierre, and Jean-Claude Passeron. "Cultural Reproduction and Social Reproduction." In *Knowledge, Education, and Cultural Change: Papers in the Sociology of Education*, edited by Richard K. Brown. London: Tavistock, 1973.

Bremner, Robert Hamlett. *From the Depths: The Discovery of Poverty in the United States*. New York: New York University Press, 1956.

Brodkin, Karen. *How Jews Became White Folks and What That Says about Race in America*. New Brunswick: Rutgers University Press, 1998.
Brundage, W. Fitzhugh. *Lynching in the New South: Georgia and Virginia, 1880–1930*. Urbana: University of Illinois Press, 1993.
———. *Where These Memories Grow: History, Memory, and Southern Identity*. Chapel Hill: University of North Carolina Press, 2000.
Buck, Polly Stone. *The Blessed Town: Oxford, Georgia, at the Turn of the Century*. Chapel Hill: University of North Carolina Press, 1986.
Cash, Wilber J. *The Mind of the South*. New York: Knopf, 1941.
Chigier, Moshe. "Ruminations over the *Agunah* Problem." In *Women in Chains: A Sourcebook on the Agunah*, edited by Jack Nusan Porter. Northvale, NJ: Jason Aronson Inc., 1995.
Clark-Lewis, Elizabeth. "'This Work Had a End': African-American Domestic Workers in Washington, DC, 1910–1940." In *To Toil the Livelong Day: America's Women at Work, 1780–1980*, edited by Carol Groneman and Mary Beth Norton. Ithaca: Cornell University Press, 1987.
Cordasco, Francesco. Dictionary of American Immigration History. Metuchen, NJ: Scarecrow Press, 1990.
Coser, Rose Laub, Laura S. Anker, and Andrew J. Perrin, eds. Women of Courage: Jewish and Italian Immigrant Women in New York. Contributions in Women's Studies no. 173. Westport, CT: Greenwood Press, 1999.
Cott, Nancy F. *The Bonds of Womanhood: "Woman's Sphere" in New England, 1780–1835*. New Haven: Yale University Press, 1977.
Davies, Norman. God's Playground: a History of Poland in Two Volumes. Vol. 2. New York: Oxford University Press, 2005.
Davila, Arlene. Latino Spin: Public Image and the Whitewashing of Race. New York: New York University Press, 2008.
Deutsch, Nathaniel. Inventing America's Worst Family: Eugenics, Islam, and the Fall and Rise of the Tribe of Ishmael. Berkeley: University of California Press, 2009.
DeWitt, Michael. Dir. "Delta Jews." Film. PBS, 1999.
Diaz Mas, Paloma. Sephardim: The Jews from Spain. Chicago: University of Chicago Press, 2007.
Dillman, Caroline Matheny, ed. "'My Ole Black Mammy' in American Historiography." In Southern Women. New York: Hemisphere, 1988.
Diner, Hasia R. The Jews of the United States, 1654 to 2000. Berkeley: University of California Press, 2004.
Dinnerstein, Leonard and Mary Dale Palsson, eds. Jews in the South. Baton Rouge, LA: Louisiana State University Press, 1973.
Dobkowski, Michael N., ed. *Jewish American Voluntary Organizations*. Westport, CT: Greenwood Press, 1986.
Doneson, Jules. *Deeds of Love: A History of the Jewish Foster Home and Orphan Asylum of Philadelphia—America's First Jewish Orphanage*. New York: Vintage Press, 1996.

Douglas, Mary. *Purity and Danger: An Analysis of Concepts of Pollution and Taboo.* New York: Praeger, 1966.
Dyer, Thomas G. *Theodore Roosevelt and the Idea of Race.* Baton Rouge: Louisiana State University Press, 1980.
Eisenberg, Ellen. *Jewish Agricultural Colonies in New Jersey, 1882–1920.* Syracuse: Syracuse University Press, 1995.
Eisenberg, Ellen, Ava F. Kahn, and William Toll. *Jews of the Pacific Coast: Reinventing Community on America's Edge.* Seattle: University of Washington Press, 2009.
Ewen, Elizabeth. *Immigrant Women in the Land of Dollars: Life and Culture on the Lower East Side, 1890–1925.* New York: Monthly Review Press, 1985.
Faust, Drew Gilpin. *Mothers of Invention: Women of the Slaveholding South in the American Civil War.* Chapel Hill: University of North Carolina Press, 1996.
Feld, Marjorie N. *Lillian Wald: A Biography.* Chapel Hill: University of North Carolina Press, 2008.
Ferris, Marcie Cohen. "Dining in the Dixie Diaspora: A Meeting of Region and Religion." In *Jewish Roots in Southern Soil: A New History*, edited by Marcie Cohen Ferris and Mark I. Greenberg. Waltham: Brandeis University Press, 2006.
———. *Matzoh Ball Gumbo: Culinary Tales of the Jewish South.* Chapel Hill: University of North Carolina Press, 2005.
Finkelman, Paul. "How the Jews Won the Right to Remain in New Netherland." In *New Essays in American Jewish History: Commemorating the Sixtieth Anniversary of the Founding of the American Jewish Archives*, edited by Jacob Rader Marcus. Cincinnati: American Jewish Archives of Hebrew Union College–Jewish Institute of Religion, 2010.
Fishman, Sylvia Barack. *A Breath of Life: Feminism in the American Jewish Community.* New York: Free Press, 1993.
Foley, Neil. *The White Scourge: Mexicans, Blacks, and Poor Whites in the Cotton Culture of Central Texas.* Berkeley: University of California Press, 1997.
Fox, Cybelle. *Three Worlds of Relief: Race, Immigration, and the American Welfare State from the Progressive Era to the New Deal.* Princeton: Princeton University Press, 2012.
Franklin, John Hope, and Charles Grier Sellers. *The Southerner as American.* Chapel Hill: University of North Carolina Press, 1960.
Fraser, Nancy, and Linda Gordon. "A Genealogy of Dependency: Tracing a Keyword of the U.S. Welfare State." *Signs* 19:2 (Winter 1994), 309–336.
Fredrickson, George M. *The Black Image in the White Mind: The Debate on Afro-American Character and Destiny, 1817–1914.* New York: Harper Torchbooks, 1971.
Freedman, Estelle B. *Redefining Rape: Sexual Violence in the Era of Suffrage and Segregation.* Cambridge: Harvard University Press, 2013.
Fridkis, Ari Lloyd. "Desertion in the American Jewish Immigrant Family: The Work of the National Desertion Bureau in Cooperation with the Industrial Removal Office." *American Jewish History* 71:2 (December 1981), 285–299.
Friedman, Reena Sigman. "'Send Me My Husband Who Is in New York City':

Husband Desertion in the American Jewish Immigrant Community, 1900–1926." *Jewish Social Studies* 44:1 (Winter 1982), 1–18.

———. *These Are Our Children: Jewish Orphanages in the United States, 1880–1925*. Hanover: University Press of New England for Brandeis University Press, 1994.

Friedman-Kasaba, Kathie. *Memories of Migration: Gender, Ethnicity, and Work in the Lives of Jewish and Italian Women in New York, 1870–1924*. Albany: State University of New York Press, 1996.

Gaines, Kevin Kelly. *Uplifting the Race: Black Leadership, Politics, and Culture in the Twentieth Century*. Chapel Hill: University of North Carolina Press, 1996.

Gardner, Martha. *The Qualities of a Citizen: Women, Immigration, and Citizenship, 1870–1965*. Princeton: Princeton University Press, 2005.

Gaston, Paul M. *The New South Creed: A Study in Southern Mythmaking*. New York: Knopf, 1970.

Gettinger, Max C. *Coming of Age: The Atlanta Jewish Federation, 1962–1982*. Hoboken, NJ: Ktav Publishing, 1994.

Gilmore, Glenda. "'But She Can't Find Her (V.O.) Key': Writing Gender and Race into Southern Political History." In *Taking Off the White Gloves: Southern Women and Women Historians*, edited by Michele Gillespie and Catherine Clinton. Columbia: University of Missouri Press, 1998.

Glenn, Susan A. *Daughters of the Shtetl: Life and Labor in the Immigrant Generation*. Ithaca: Cornell University Press, 1990.

Goings, Kenneth W. *Mammy and Uncle Mose: Black Collectibles and American Stereotyping*. Bloomington: Indiana University Press, 1994.

Golden, Harry. *Our Southern Landsman*. New York: Putnam, 1974.

Goldman, Karla. "The Ambivalence of Reform Judaism: Kaufmann Kohler and the Ideal Jewish Woman." *American Jewish History* 79:4 (Summer 1990), 477–499.

———. *Beyond the Synagogue Gallery: Finding a Place for Women in American Judaism*. Cambridge: Harvard University Press, 2000.

Goldstein, Eric L. "How Southern is Southern Jewish History?" Biennial Scholars' Conference in American Jewish History. Charleston, SC, 2006.

———. *The Price of Whiteness: Jews, Race, and American Identity*. Princeton: Princeton University Press, 2006.

Goldstein, Howard. *The Home on Gorham Street and the Voices of Its Children*. Tuscaloosa: University of Alabama Press, 1996.

Gordon, Linda. *The Great Arizona Orphan Abduction*. Cambridge: Harvard University Press, 1999.

———. *Pitied but Not Entitled: Single Mothers and the History of Welfare, 1890–1935*. New York: Free Press, 1994.

Greenberg, Mark I. "Creating Ethnic, Class, and Southern Identity in Nineteenth-Century America: The Jews of Savannah, Georgia, 1830–1880." PhD diss., University of Florida, 1997.

Greeson, Jennifer Rae. *Our South: Geographic Fantasy and the Rise of National Literature*. Cambridge: Harvard University Press, 2010.

Gurock, Jeffrey S. *Orthodox Jews in America*. Bloomington: Indiana University Press, 2009.

Hagy, James. "This Happy Land." In *A Portion of the People: Three Hundred Years of Southern Jewish Life*, edited by Dale Rosengarten and Theodore Rosengarten. Columbia: University of South Carolina Press in association with McKissick Museum, 2002.

Hale, Grace Elizabeth. *Making Whiteness: The Culture of Segregation in the South, 1890–1940*. New York: Pantheon Books, 1998.

Hall, Jacqueline Dowd. "'The Mind That Burns in Each Body': Women, Rape, and Racial Violence." In *Powers of Desire: The Politics of Sexuality*, edited by Sharon Thompson, Christine Stansell, and Ann Barr Snitow. New York: Monthly Review Press, 1983.

———. *Revolt against Chivalry: Jessie Daniel Ames and the Women's Campaign against Lynching*. Rev. ed. New York: Columbia University Press, 1993.

Handlin, Oscar. *Adventure in Freedom: Three Hundred Years of Jewish Life in America*. New York: McGraw-Hill, 1954.

Harley, Sharon. "When Your Work Is Not Who You Are: The Development of a Working-Class Consciousness among Afro-American Women." In *We Specialize in the Wholly Impossible: A Reader in Black Women's History*, edited by Darlene Clark Hine, Wilma King, and Linda Reed. New York: Carlson Publishing, 1995.

Hasci, Timothy A. *Second Home: Orphan Asylums and Poor Families in America*. Cambridge: Harvard University Press, 1998.

Heinze, Andrew R. "The Parlor and the Piano." In *Adapting to Abundance: Jewish Immigrants, Mass Consumption, and the Search for American Identity*, edited by Andrew R. Heinze. New York: Columbia University Press, 1990.

Hertzberg, Steven. *Strangers within the Gate City: The Jews of Atlanta, 1845–1915*. Philadelphia: Jewish Publication Society of America, 1978.

Hewitt, Nancy. *Women's Activism and Social Change: Rochester, New York, 1822–1872*. Ithaca: Cornell University Press, 1984.

Higginbotham, Evelyn Brooks. "African-American Women's History and the Metalanguage of Race." *Signs* 17:2 (January 1, 1992), 251–274.

———. *Righteous Discontent: The Women's Movement in the Black Baptist Church, 1880–1920*. Cambridge: Harvard University Press, 1993.

Hill, Samuel S., Charles H. Lippy, and Charles Reagan Wilson, eds. *Encyclopedia of Religion in the South*. 2nd ed. rev. Macon: Mercer University Press, 2005.

Hine, Darlene Clark. "Rape and the Inner Lives of Black Women in the Middle West: Preliminary Thoughts on the Culture of Dissemblence." In *Unequal Sisters: A Multicultural Reader in U.S. Women's History*, edited by Vicki Ruíz and Ellen Carol DuBois. New York: Routledge, 1994.

Hodes, Martha E. *White Women, Black Men: Illicit Sex in the Nineteenth-Century South*. New Haven: Yale University Press, 1997.

Huginnie, A. Yvette. "A New Hero Comes to Town: The Anglo Mining Engineer and

'Mexican Labor' as Contested Terrain in Southeastern Arizona, 1880–1920." *New Mexico Historical Review* 69:4 (October 1994), 323–344.

Hunter, Tera W. *To 'Joy My Freedom: Southern Black Women's Lives and Labors after the Civil War*. Cambridge: Harvard University Press, 1997.

Hyman, Paula. *Gender and Assimilation in Modern Jewish History: The Roles and Representation of Women*. Seattle: University of Washington Press, 1995.

Hyman, Paula, and Deborah Dash Moore, eds. *Jewish Women in America: An Historical Encyclopedia*. New York, Routledge Press, 1997.

Igra, Anna R. "Male Providerhood and the Public Purse: Anti-desertion Reform in the Progressive Era." In *The Sex of Things: Gender and Consumption in Historical Perspective*, edited by Victoria de Grazia and Ellen Furlough. Berkeley: University of California Press, 1996.

———. *Wives without Husbands: Marriage, Desertion, and Welfare in New York, 1900–1935*. Chapel Hill: University of North Carolina Press, 2007.

Jacobson, Matthew Frye. *Special Sorrows: The Diasporic Imagination of Irish, Polish, and Jewish Immigrants in the United States*. Cambridge: Harvard University Press, 1995.

———. *Whiteness of a Different Color: European Immigrants and the Alchemy of Race*. Cambridge: Harvard University Press, 1998.

Janiewski, Dolores. "Southern Honor, Southern Dishonor: Managerial Ideology and the Construction of Gender, Race, and Class Relations in Southern Industry." In *Work Engendered: Toward a New History of American Labor*, edited by Ava Baron. Ithaca: Cornell University Press, 1991.

Jick, Leon A. *The Americanization of the Synagogue, 1820–1870*. Hanover: University Press of New England for Brandeis University Press, 1992.

Joselit, Jenna Weissman. "Land of Promise: The Eastern European Jewish Experience in South Carolina." In *A Portion of the People: Three Hundred Years of Southern Jewish Life*, edited by Theodore Rosengarten and Dale Rosengarten. Columbia: University of South Carolina Press, 2002.

Jun, Helen Heran. *Race for Citizenship: Black Orientalism and Asian Uplift from Preemancipation to Neoliberal America*. New York: New York University Press, 2011.

Kaplan, Marion A. *The Making of the Jewish Middle Class: Women, Family, and Identity in Imperial Germany*. New York: Oxford University Press, 1991.

Katzman, David M. *Seven Days a Week: Women and Domestic Service in Industrializing America*. New York: Oxford University Press, 1978.

Kerem, Yitzchak. "The Settlement of Rhodian and Other Sephardic Jews in Montgomery and Atlanta in the Twentieth Century." *American Jewish History* 85:4 (1997), 373–391.

Klapper, Melissa. *Ballots, Babies, and Banners of Peace: American Jewish Women's Activism, 1890–1940*. New York: New York University Press, 2013.

———. *Jewish Girls Coming of Age in America, 1860–1920*. New York: New York University Press, 2007.

Korelitz, Seth. "'A Magnificent Piece of Work': The Americanization Work of the National Council of Jewish Women." *American Jewish History* 83:2 (1995), 177–203.

Ladd-Taylor, Molly, and Lauri Umansky, eds. *"Bad" Mothers: The Politics of Blame in Twentieth-Century America*. New York: New York University Press, 1998.

Landphair, Juliette. "'The Forgotten People of New Orleans': Community, Vulnerability, and the Lower Ninth Ward." *Journal of American History* 94:3 (December 1, 2007), 837–845.

Langston, Scott. "Interaction and Identity: Jews and Christians in Nineteenth-Century New Orleans." *Southern Jewish History* 3 (2000), 83–124.

Larson, Edward J. *Sex, Race, and Science: Eugenics in the Deep South*. Baltimore: Johns Hopkins University Press, 1996.

Lebsock, Suzanne. "Woman Suffrage and White Supremacy." In *Taking Off the White Gloves: Southern Women and Women Historians*, edited by Michele Gillespie and Catherine Clinton. Columbia: University of Missouri Press, 1998.

Levitt, Laura. "Impossible Assimilations, American Liberalism, and Jewish Difference: Revisiting Jewish Secularism." *American Quarterly* 59:3 (September 2007), 807–832.

———. *Jews and Feminism: The Ambivalent Search for Home*. New York: Routledge, 1997.

Lewis, Selma S. *A Biblical People in the Bible Belt: The Jewish Community of Memphis, Tennessee, 1840s–1960s*. Macon: Mercer University Press, 1998.

Light, Caroline E. "'A Predominant Cause of Distress': Gender, Benevolence, and the *Agunah* in Regional Perspective." *American Jewish History* 97:2 (2013), 159–182.

Logan, Rayford Whittingham. *The Negro in American Life and Thought: The Nadir, 1877–1901*. New York: Dial Press, 1954.

Lowe, Lisa. *Immigrant Acts: On Asian American Cultural Politics*. Durham: Duke University Press, 1996.

Lubove, Roy. *The Professional Altruist: The Emergence of Social Work as a Career, 1880–1930*. Cambridge: Harvard University Press, 1965.

MacLean, Nancy. *Behind the Mask of Chivalry: The Making of the Second Ku Klux Klan*. New York: Oxford University Press, 1994.

———. "The Leo Frank Case Reconsidered: Gender and Sexual Politics in the Making of Reactionary Populism." *Journal of American History* 78:3 (December 1991), 917–948.

Malamed, Sandra Cumings. *The Jews in Early America: A Chronicle of Good Taste and Good Deeds*. McKinleyville, CA: Fithian Press, 2003.

Malone, Bobbie S. "As Told to Memoirs, Ruth and Rosalie: Two Tails of Jewish New Orleans." *Southern Jewish History* 1 (1998), 121–134.

Marcus, Jacob Rader. *To Count a People: American Jewish Population Data, 1585–1984*. Lanham, MD: University Press of America, 1990.

Marinbach, Bernard. *Galveston: Ellis Island of the West*. Albany: State University of New York Press, 1983.

Markovitz, Jonathan. *Legacies of Lynching: Racial Violence and Memory*. Minneapolis: University of Minnesota Press, 2004.

Matza, Diane. "Sephardic Jews Transmitting Culture across Three Generations." *American Jewish History* 79:3 (Spring 1990), 336–354.
McCandless, Peter. *Slavery, Disease, and Suffering in the Southern Lowcountry*. New York: Cambridge University Press, 2011.
McCune, Mary. "Social Workers in the *Muskeljudentum*: 'Hadassah Ladies,' 'Manly Men,' and the Significance of Gender in the American Zionist Movement, 1912–1928." *American Jewish History* 86:2 (June 1998), 135–165.
McElya, Micki. *Clinging to Mammy: The Faithful Slave in Twentieth-Century America*. Cambridge: Harvard University Press, 2007.
Melder, Keith. "Ladies Bountiful: Organized Women's Benevolence in Early Nineteenth-Century America." *New York History* 48:3 (1967), 231–254.
Meyerowitz, Joanne J. *Women Adrift: Independent Wage Earners in Chicago, 1880–1930*. Chicago: University of Chicago Press, 1988.
Michel, Sonya. *Children's Interests/Mothers' Rights: The Shaping of America's Child Care Policy*. New Haven: Yale University Press, 1999.
———. "The Limits of Maternalism: Policies toward American Wage-Earning Women during the Progressive Era." In *Mothers of a New World: Maternalist Politics and the Origins of Welfare States*, edited by Seth Koven and Sonya Michel. New York: Routledge, 1993.
Mink, Gwendolyn. *The Wages of Motherhood: Inequality in the Welfare State, 1917–1942*. Ithaca: Cornell University Press, 1995.
Mintz, Adam. "A Courageous Proposal: The First Heter Agunah in America." *Jewish Orthodox Feminist Alliance Journal* 6:4 (Summer 2007), 14–15.
Monaco, Chris. "Moses E. Levy of Florida: A Jewish Abolitionist Abroad." *American Jewish History* 86:4 (1998), 377–396.
Moore, Deborah Dash. *B'nai B'rith and the Challenge of Ethnic Leadership*. Albany: State University of New York Press, 1981.
———. "Freedom's Fruits: The Americanization of an Old-Time Religion." In *A Portion of the People: Three Hundred Years of Southern Jewish Life*, edited by Dale Rosengarten and Theodore Rosengarten. Columbia: University of South Carolina Press in association with McKissick Museum, 2002.
Morton, Patricia. *Disfigured Images: The Historical Assault on Afro-American Women*. New York: Greenwood Press, 1991.
Murray, Gail S. "Charity within the Bounds of Race and Class: Female Benevolence in the Old South." *South Carolina Historical Magazine* 96:1 (January 1995), 54–70.
Murray, John E. *The Charleston Orphan House: Children's Lives in the First Public Orphanage in America*. Chicago: University of Chicago Press, 2013.
Omi, Michael, and Howard Winant. *Racial Formation in the United States: From the 1960s to the 1990s*. New York: Routledge and Kegan Paul, 1986.
Oney, Steve. *And the Dead Shall Rise: The Murder of Mary Phagan and the Lynching of Leo Frank*. New York: Pantheon, 2003.
Ong, Aihwa. "Cultural Citizenship as Subject-Making: Immigrants Negotiate Racial

and Cultural Boundaries in the United States." *Current Anthropology* 37:5 (December 1996), 737–762.
Ordover, Nancy. *American Eugenics: Race, Queer Anatomy, and the Science of Nationalism.* Minneapolis: University of Minnesota Press, 2003.
Painter, Nell Irvin. *The History of White People.* New York: Norton, 2010.
Palmer, Phyllis M. *Domesticity and Dirt: Housewives and Domestic Servants in the United States, 1920–1945.* Philadelphia: Temple University Press, 1989.
Panitz, Esther L. *Simon Wolf: Private Conscience and Public Image.* Madison: Fairleigh Dickinson University Press, 1987.
Pazicky, Diana Loercher. *Cultural Orphans in America.* Jackson: University Press of Mississippi, 1998.
Peiss, Kathy. *Cheap Amusements: Working Women and Leisure in Turn-of-the-Century New York.* Philadelphia: Temple University Press, 1986.Polster, Gary Edward. *Inside Looking Out: The Cleveland Jewish Orphan Asylum, 1868–1924.* Kent: Kent State University Press, 1990.
Prell, Riv-Ellen. *Fighting to Become Americans: Jews, Gender, and the Anxiety of Assimilation.* Boston: Beacon Press, 1999.
Rabinowitz, Howard. "Nativism, Bigotry, and Anti-Semitism in the South." In *Dixie Diaspora: An Anthology of Southern Jewish History*, edited by Mark K. Bauman. Tuscaloosa: University of Alabama Press, 2006.
Rackman, Honey. "Getting a Get." In *Women in Chains: A Sourcebook on the Agunah*, edited by Jack Nusan Porter. Northvale, NJ: Jason Aronson Inc., 1995.
Reznikoff, Charles. *The Jews of Charleston: A History of an American Jewish Community.* Philadelphia: Jewish Publication Society of America, 1950.
Ripley, William Zebina. *The Races of Europe: A Sociological Study.* New York: D. Appleton and Co., 1899.
Riskin, Shlomo. "A Modern Orthodox Perspective." In *Women in Chains: A Sourcebook on the Agunah*, edited by Jack Nusan Porter. Northvale, NJ: Jason Aronson Inc., 1995.
———. "The Tragedy of the Agunah: A Proposed Solution." *Jewish Orthodox Feminist Alliance Journal* 5:4 (Summer 2005), 13–14.
Ritterhouse, Jennifer. *Growing Up Jim Crow: How Black and White Southern Children Learned Race.* Chapel Hill: University of North Carolina Press, 2006.
Rockaway, Robert A. *Words of the Uprooted: Jewish Immigrants in Early Twentieth-Century America.* Ithaca: Cornell University Press, 1998.
Roediger, David. *The Wages of Whiteness: Race and the Making of the American Working Class.* New York: Verso Press, 1991.
Rogoff, Leonard. *Down Home: Jewish Life in North Carolina.* Chapel Hill: University of North Carolina Press, 2010.
———. "Is the Jew White? The Racial Place of the Southern Jew." *American Jewish History* 85:3 (1997), 195–230.
Rogow, Faith. *Gone to Another Meeting: The National Council of Jewish Women, 1893–1993.* Tuscaloosa: University of Alabama Press, 1993.

Rosaldo, Renato. "Cultural Citizenship." Hemispheric Institute Encuentro. http://hemisphericinstitute.org/.
———. "Cultural Citizenship and Educational Democracy." *Cultural Anthropology* 9:3 (August 1994), 402–411.
Rose, Elizabeth. "Taking on a Mother's Job: Day Care in the 1920's and 1930's." In *"Bad" Mothers: The Politics of Blame in Twentieth-Century America*, edited by Molly Ladd-Taylor and Lauri Umansky. New York: New York University Press, 1998.
Rosen, Robert N. "Jewish Confederates." In *Jewish Roots in Southern Soil: A New History*, edited by Marcie Cohen Ferris and Mark I. Greenberg. Waltham: Brandeis University Press, 2006.
———. *The Jewish Confederates*. Columbia: University of South Carolina Press, 2000.
Rosengarten, Dale, and Theodore Rosengarten, eds. *A Portion of the People: Three Hundred Years of Southern Jewish Life*. Columbia: University of South Carolina Press in association with McKissick Museum, 2002.
Ryan, Mary M. *The Grammar of Good Intentions: Race and the Antebellum Culture of Benevolence*. Ithaca: Cornell University Press, 2003.
Sachar, Howard M. *A History of the Jews in America*. New York: Knopf, 1992.
Sarna, Jonathan D. *American Judaism: A History*. New Haven: Yale University Press, 2004.
Scott, Anne Firor. *The Southern Lady: From Pedestal to Politics, 1830–1930*. Chicago: University of Chicago Press, 1970.
———. "Women's Voluntary Associations: From Charity to Reform." In *Lady Bountiful Revisited: Women, Philanthropy, and Power*, edited by Kathleen D. McCarthy. New Brunswick: Rutgers University Press, 1990.
Seidman, Naomi. "Theorizing Jewish Patriarchy *in extremis*." In *Judaism since Gender*, edited by Miriam Peskowitz and Laura Levitt. New York: Routledge, 1997.
SenGupta, Gunja. *From Slavery to Poverty: The Racial Origins of Welfare in New York, 1840–1918*. New York: New York University Press, 2009.
Shankman, Arnold. "Happyville, the Forgotten Colony." *American Jewish Archives* 30:1 (April 1978), 3–19.
Sharpless, Rebecca. *Cooking in Other Women's Kitchens: Domestic Workers in the South, 1865–1960*. Chapel Hill: University of North Carolina Press, 2010.
Shpall, Leo. "Jewish Agricultural Colonies in the United States." *Agricultural History* 24:3 (July 1, 1950), 120–146.
Skocpol, Theda. *Protecting Soldiers and Mothers: The Political Origins of Social Policy in the United States*. Cambridge: Belknap Press of Harvard University Press, 1992.
Skocpol, Theda, Marjorie Abend-Wein, Christopher Howard, and Susan Goodrich Lehmann. "Women's Associations and the Enactment of Mothers' Pensions in the United States." *American Political Science Review* 87:3 (September 1993), 686–701.
Smith-Rosenberg, Carroll. *Disorderly Conduct: Visions of Gender in Victorian America*. New York: Knopf, 1985.
Sochen, June. *Consecrate Every Day: The Public Lives of Jewish American Women, 1880–1980*. Albany: State University of New York Press, 1981.

Solomon, Barbara Miller. *Ancestors and Immigrants: A Changing New England Tradition*. Cambridge: Harvard University Press, 1956.

Solomon, Clara. *The Civil War Diary of Clara Solomon: Growing Up in New Orleans, 1861–1862*, edited by Elliott Ashkenazi. Baton Rouge: Louisiana State University Press, 1995.

Sorin, Gerald. *A Time for Building: The Third Migration, 1880–1920*. Baltimore: Johns Hopkins University Press, 1992.

Stepick, Alex, Terry Rey, and Sarah J. Mahler, eds. *Churches and Charity in the Immigrant City: Religion, Immigration, and Civic Engagement in Miami*. New Brunswick: Rutgers University Press, 2009.

Stern, Alexandra. *Eugenic Nation: Faults and Frontiers of Better Breeding in Modern America*. Berkeley: University of California Press, 2005.

Stone, Bryan Edward. *The Chosen Folks: Jews on the Frontiers of Texas*. Austin: University of Texas Press, 2010.

Tamarkin, Leona. *Dear Lizzie: Memoir of a Jewish Immigrant Woman*, edited by Elizabeth Reis. Bloomington: Xlibris, 2000.

Tenenbaum, Shelly. "Culture and Context: The Emergence of Hebrew Free Loan Societies in the United States." *Social Science History* 13:3 (October 1, 1989), 211–236.

Tice, Karen W. *Tales of Wayward Girls and Immoral Women: Case Records and the Professionalization of Social Work*. Urbana: University of Illinois Press, 1998.

Tobias, Thomas J. *The Hebrew Orphan Society of Charleston, S.C., Founded 1801: An Historical Sketch*. Charleston: The Society, 1957.

Trattner, Walter I. *From Poor Law to Welfare State: A History of Social Welfare in America*. New York: Free Press, 1974.

Trestman, Marlene. "Fair Labor: The Remarkable Life and Legal Career of Bessie Margolin (1909–1996)." *Journal of Supreme Court History* 37:1 (March 2012), 42–74.

Trivers, Trudy G. "Alabama's Sand Mountain and Early Kibbutz." *Atlanta Jewish Times*, April 24, 1987.

Turner, Elizabeth Hayes. "'White-Gloved Ladies' and 'New Women' in the Texas Woman Suffrage Movement." In *Southern Women: Histories and Identities*, edited by Virginia Bernhard, Betty Brandon, Elizabeth Fox-Genovese, and Theda Perdue. Columbia: University of Missouri Press, 1992.

Turner, Patricia A. *Ceramic Uncles and Celluloid Mammies: Black Images and Their Influence on Culture*. New York: Anchor Books, 1994.

Van Wormer, Katherine, David W. Jackson, and Charletta Sudduth. *The Maid Narratives: Black Domestics and White Families in the Jim Crow South*. Baton Rouge: Louisiana State University Press, 2012.

Webb, Clive. "Closing Ranks: Montgomery Jews and Civil Rights." *Journal of American Studies* 32:3 (December 1998), 463–481.

———. *Fight against Fear: Southern Jews and Black Civil Rights*. Athens: University of Georgia Press, 2001.

Weber, Donald. "The Jewish American World of Gertrude Berg: *The Goldbergs* on Radio and Television, 1930–1950." In *Talking Back: Images of Jewish Women in*

American Popular Culture, edited by Joyce Antler. Hanover: University Press of New England for Brandeis University Press, 1998.

Weinberg, Sydney Stahl. *The World of Our Mothers: The Lives of Jewish Immigrant Women*. Chapel Hill: University of North Carolina Press, 1988.

Weir, David. *American Orient: Imagining the East From the Colonial Era through the Twentieth Century*. Amherst: University of Massachusetts Press, 2011.

Wenger, Beth S. *History Lessons: The Creation of American Jewish Heritage*. Princeton: Princeton University Press, 2010.

———. "Jewish Women of the Club: The Changing Public Role of Atlanta's Jewish Women (1870–1930)." *American Jewish History* 76:3 (March 1987), 311–333.

Whites, LeeAnn. "'Stand by Your Man': The Ladies Memorial Association and the Reconstruction of Southern White Manhood." In *Women of the American South: A Multicultural Reader*, edited by Christie Farnham. New York: New York University Press, 1997.

Wiegman, Robyn. *American Anatomies: Theorizing Race and Gender*. Durham: Duke University Press, 1995.

Wilhelm, Cornelia. *The Independent Orders of B'nai B'rith and True Sisters: Pioneers of a New Jewish Identity, 1843–1914*, translated by Alan L. Nothnagle and Sarah Wobick-Segev. Detroit: Wayne State University Press, 2011.

Wolfe, Margaret Ripley. *Daughters of Canaan: A Saga of Southern Women*. Lexington: University Press of Kentucky, 1995.

Wood, Peter H. *Black Majority: Negroes in Colonial South Carolina from 1670 through the Stono Rebellion*. New York: Knopf, 1974.

Woodward, C. Vann. *Origins of the New South, 1877–1913*. Vol. 9, *A History of the South*. Baton Rouge: Louisiana State University Press, 1951.

Ziff, Joel David, ed. *Lev Tuviah: On the Life and Work of Rabbi Tobias Geffen*. Newton, MA: Rabbi Tobias Geffen Memorial Fund, 1988.

Zola, Gary P. "The Ascendancy of Reform Judaism in the American South." In *Jewish Roots in Southern Soil: A New History*, edited by Marcie Cohen Ferris and Mark I. Greenberg. Waltham: Brandeis University Press, 2006.

———. "Southern Rabbis and the Founding of the First National Association of Rabbis." In *Dixie Diaspora: An Anthology of Southern Jewish History*, edited by Mark K. Bauman. Tuscaloosa: University of Alabama Press, 2006.

INDEX

Abernethy, Arthur T., 11, 55, 57, 58n12
Abi Yetomim Ubne Ebyonim (Father of Orphans). *See* Charleston Hebrew Orphans Society
African Americans, 46, 199; African American women and domestic labor, 16, 18, 22, 81–84, 108–109, 172, 174–175, 182–183, 199, 202–204, 209; Jews socializing with, 16, 73, 81–82, 208; and lynching, 18, 65, 70, 93; and mythologies of rape, 18, 58, 70–71, 92–93, 135, 141; stereotypes of, 63, 104, 206
agriculture, 31, 60–64, 112, 116, 135
agunah (deserted woman), 14, 21, 123–149, 165, 183, 189
Am Olam, 62
American Jewess (newspaper), 92
Andrews, Joseph, 34
Antin, Mary, 12–13, 214
anti-Semitism, 3, 5, 10, 47, 57, 61–62, 171. *See also* Frank, Leo
Atlanta Hebrew Orphans Asylum. *See* Hebrew Orphans Home of Atlanta; orphan homes
authenticity: and anxieties about Christian conversion, 38; and benevolence, 3–4, 23, 25, 70; and domesticity, 54; and desertion, 125–126, 136; and immigration, 51–52, 62; and intermarriage, 176–177; and orphan homes, 9; and racial difference, 185, 187, 194; and womanhood, 17, 53, 134, 166

Baron de Hirsch Fund, 61
Bauman, Mark, 5n15, 32n40, 35n55, 35n57, 98n59, 98n61, 160n30

Bederman, Gail, 47, 44n87, 59n19, 102n73, 103n75
Ben-Ur, Aviva, 185
Big Sisters, 84, 96, 101, 104–106, 120, 163
Bourdieu, Pierre, 10, 16n47

Calhoun, John C., 34
Cash, Wilbur, 9
charity, 3–5, 8, 13–14, 22, 25, 27, 32–33, 39, 42–43, 47, 152, 185, 211–212; as pauperizing, 87–88, 133, 151–152, 179–182; woman as symbol of, 35–37, 40–41, 45, 53. *See also gemilut hasadim*
Charleston Hebrew Orphans Society, 4, 28–30
Child Welfare League of America, 84, 110n104, 111
chivalry, 9, 19, 44–51, 136, 141. *See also* honor; masculinity
Christian Lady Bountiful, 40–41
Christianity, and anxieties about conversion, 76, 82, 178
citizenship: African American, 12, 17, 54; and benevolence, 3–6, 8, 44, 57–58, 152; and contamination, 72, 91–92; cultural, 3, 6–7, 33, 58–59, 67–68, 104, 122, 152, 156–159, 167–176, 181, 183, 188, 209, 211, 213; and gender, 37, 41, 45, 48, 50–51, 88, 93, 166; and immigration, 57–59; and labor, 135, 173; and maternal subsidies, 138, 152; and nationality, 158; and orphan uplift, 67, 72, 79, 83, 85, 121; and pauperism, 170; and race, 15–16, 25, 38, 43, 52, 138, 167, 185; and region, 14, 26, 70, 121; and sectionalism, 45–46

Civil War, 6, 10, 25, 36, 38, 44–46, 49, 56, 65, 69. *See also* Lost Cause; Reconstruction
cleanliness, 82, 97, 110–111, 157, 183, 191–192, 196, 200, 210. *See also* domesticity; respectability
Cleveland Jewish Orphan Asylum. *See* orphan homes
Cohen, J. Barrett, 48–50
color line, 3, 7, 10–11, 15, 25, 57, 136, 167, 184, 199–200, 213; as means of policing sex, 18, 20, 50–53. *See also* Jim Crow
Confederacy, 5–6, 8–9, 16, 36–37, 44, 56–57, 65, 71
congregations: Ahavath Achim, Atlanta, 99, 198; Beth Israel, Houston, 43; Gates of Prayer, New Orleans, 98; Hebrew Benevolent Congregation (the Temple), Atlanta, 49, 95, 98–99; Kahal Kadosh Mikveh Israel, Savannah, 26; Kahal Kadosh Beth Elohim, Charleston, 27, 48; Ohavai Sholom, Nashville, 115; Or V'Shalom, Atlanta, 187, 189, 198; Shearith Israel, Atlanta, 129; Temple Emanu-El, San Francisco, 43; Temple Sinai, New Orleans, 98; Touro Synagogue, New Orleans, 98
consumption. *See* cultural capital
cultural capital: and class mobility, 155–156; as domain of propertied men, 30; and domestic service, 16, 174–175, 182; and orphan homes, 82–83, 92–95, 115, 121, 124, 137–138, 148; and motherhood, 152, 163–165; and nationality, 158–159; and taste, 165, 196, 209. *See also* Bourdieu, Pierre

Daly, Charles P., 26
de Hirsch, Baron Maurice, 61
Decatur Street, 77, 199–200
Depression (economic), 21, 49, 51, 57, 151–156, 160–163, 166, 170–175, 179, 184, 198, 202, 211
desertion. *See* agunah
Dillingham, William P., 58
Dillingham Report, 58–59
domesticity, 82, 103, 158, 165; Victorian ideals of, 52–53. *See also* femininity; motherhood
DuBois, W. E. B., 15

education: manual, 111–114; secular, 112–113
Eisenberg, Ellen, 64; eugenics, 17, 59, 71, 138, 167. *See also* race
Ezekiel, Herbert Tobias, 69

Family Service League of Petersburg, 144
farming communities, 61–65; Am Olam, 62; Happyville, South Carolina, 63–65; Louisiana, 63; Sicily Island, 63. *See also* agriculture
Federal Emergency Relief Association, 168
Federation of Jewish Charities, Atlanta, 77, 154, 160, 187–189
femininity: ideals of, 9, 17–18, 20, 40–41, 45, 50, 172–173, 182; and virtuous sexuality, 19, 35, 51, 70–71, 77, 92, 179–180, 193. *See also* respectability
Folkmar, Elnora C., and Daniel, 59
Frank, Leo, 2, 13–14, 56, 58, 73
Frankel, Lee K., 103, 128
French Alliance Israelite Universelle, 63. *See also* farming communities
Friedman, Rena Sigman, 94, 97
Furth, Jacob, 88

Gaines, Kevin, 12
Galveston Plan, 61, 157
Gaston, Paul, 68
Geffen, Rabbi Tobias, 123, 129, 147–148
gemilut hasadim (loving kindness), 3, 8, 19–20, 33, 37, 43, 54, 57, 67, 82, 152, 185–186, 212; as evidence of Jewish patriotism, 56–58, 213; as path to good citizenship, 6, 13, 16–17, 157, 213
gender. *See* chivalry; femininity; masculinity; respectability
get (Jewish divorce), 123, 126, 129, 189
Glenn, Susan, 135
The Goldbergs (radio show), 166
Golden, Harry, 1, 3, 53
Golden City Messenger (newspaper), 101, 106, 110, 116
Golden City Plan, 104
Goldstein, Eric, 6, 32, 37–39, 42
Goldstein, Rose, 154, 188–211

Grady Memorial Hospital, 208–209
Gratz, Rebecca, 35

Hacker, Louis, 183–187
Hale, Grace E., 108–110
Hebrew Benevolent Societies, 9, 24; Atlanta, Georgia, 9, 49; Charleston, 24, 27, 34–36, 212; Hebrew Ladies Benevolent Societies, 41–42; Houston, 35; Memphis, 34. *See also* Jewish women's organizations
Hebrew Immigrant Aid Society, 63
Hebrew Orphan Society, Charleston, South Carolina, 28, 38, 48
Hebrew Orphans Home of Atlanta. *See also* orphan homes
Hertzberg, Steven, 24n2, 187
Heymann, Michael, 112
Higginbotham, Evelyn Brooks, 4n10, 12
honor: collective Jewish claims to, 20, 54, 58, 68, 78–79, 213; and southern culture, 19–20, 44, 46, 52–54, 68–69, 70, 74, 78. *See also* chivalry
Hunter, Tera, 77n99, 172, 174

Igra, Anna R. 124, 127n13, 128n18, 129n19, 135n47
immigration, 1, 3–4, 19, 26, 33, 51–52, 55–56; and acculturation, 168–170, 176, 181, 213, 215; ; and desertion, 129–130; eastern European, 4–5, 25, 51, 54, 56–57, 61–62, 87, 79, 127; and impact on orphan homes, 55, 66–67; and nativism, 47, 56, 64–65, 87; racial politics of, 58–60; restriction of, 58–60, 65, 184; Sephardic, 25–26, 183–184, 186–189, 194; and social tensions among coreligionists, 4, 15, 21, 65–66, 79, 88, 159; southern views of, 62–66
Immigration Restriction League, 65
Independent Order of B'nai B'rith, 33, 41, 62n34, 73, 75, 86, 97, 120, 168
Industrial Removal Office, 61
Isidore Newman Manual Training School, 85, 115–118

Jacobson, Matthew Frye, 11, 24, 178, 183, 191
Jewish Colonization Association, 61
Jewish Educational Loan Fund (JELF), 19. *See also* orphan homes: Hebrew Orphans Home of Atlanta
Jewish South, The (newspaper), 9, 68–69
Jewish Welfare Bureau, Florida, 156, 167n48, 168
Jewish women's club movement, 52
Jewish women's organizations: Council of Jewish Women, 53, 75, 96, 142, 168; Daughters of Israel (Jewish Ladies Aid Society) of Columbus, Georgia, 37, 40–41; Female Association for the Relief of Women and Children in Reduced Circumstances, 35; Female Hebrew Benevolent Society, Philadelphia, 35; Hebrew Ladies Benevolent Society, Albany, Georgia, 41; Ladies Aid and Sewing Circle, New Orleans, 42; Ladies Hebrew Benevolent Association, Norfolk, 142, 146; Ladies Hebrew Benevolent Associations (of Shreveport, Louisiana; Mobile, Alabama; Vicksburg, Mississippi; and Bastrop, Louisiana), 42; Ladies Hebrew Benevolent Society, Victoria, Texas, 42
Jim Crow, 3, 5, 10, 16–17, 57, 81–82, 135–137, 186, 206, 213. *See also* color line; white supremacy
Johnson Reed Act (National Origins Act) of 1924, 184
Jonas, Benjamin Franklin, 8, 38–40, 43, 212
Joselit, Jenna Weissman, 62n34, 64n47, 65
Jun, Helen Heran, 15

Kahn, Ed, 148, 160, 190
kashrut (dietary laws), 66
Kerem, Yitzchak, 186
Klapper, Melissa, 21n53, 53n116, 193n37
Kohn, August, 64

Lazarus, Henry L., 46
Leucht, Isaac L., 114
Levitt, Laura, 1, 15, 126n9, 177, 212
Levy, Jacob Clavius, 28, 35–36, 43, 45

Logan, Rayford, 4
Lost Cause, 7, 9, 19, 54, 71, 206. *See also* Civil War; nostalgia
loving kindness. See *gemilut hasadim*
Lowe, Lisa, 6n18, 7
lynching, 2, 4, 18, 65, 70–71, 92–93. *See also* white supremacy

Maimonides, Moses, 87
Margolin, Bessie, 84–86, 90–91, 97, 116, 118
Marx, David, 98
masculinity, 44, 47, 49, 58, 102, 112, 184; and breadwinning obligations, 21, 89, 135–137; and chivalry, 9, 17–19, 51, 83, 135, 213; and citizenship, 88; and manual labor, 55, 60, 112, 116. *See also* honor
maternal subsidies, 21, 72, 122, 125, 131–134, 137–138, 143–145, 159–168, 174, 190, 210
miscegenation, 11, 60, 70. *See also* race; white supremacy
miscarriage, 194, 198, 204
mitzvot (good deeds), 8
Montefiore, Moses, 48
Montefiore Relief Association (MRA), 22, 77, 129, 147–149, 154, 160, 187–211
Moses, Mordecai, 34
motherhood: and consumption, 14, 106, 134–135, 152, 158, 165 171–177, 181, 183–211, 215; and eugenics, 17; ideals of, 72, 163, 166, 174; and race, 137–138. *See also* maternal subsidies

"nadir" of southern race relations, 4, 19. *See also* lynching; white supremacy
National Council of Jewish Women. *See* Jewish women's organizations
National Desertion Bureau, 124, 128, 133, 147–148
New Orleans Jewish Orphans Home (New Orleans Society for the Relief of Hebrew Widows and Orphans). *See* orphan homes
New York Jewish Federation, 184
Newman, Isidore, 115

Newman, Joseph W., 93–94, 106
nostalgia, 6, 9, 16, 25, 46, 54, 58, 70–71. *See also* Lost Cause; chivalry

orphan homes, 4, 66; Cleveland Jewish Orphan Asylum, 33, 97, 153; Hebrew Orphans Home of Atlanta, 1–4, 12, 19–21, 41, 44, 49–51, 55–56, 59, 66–67, 73–80, 122–123, 129–133, 137–138, 142, 146–149, 150–151, 160–161, 163–164, 166, 181, 189–190, 199, 208; New Orleans Jewish Orphans Home, 4, 8, 20, 38, 42–44, 46, 66, 70–72, 75, 83, 85, 89–122, 130–131, 137–138, 148–149, 163; Philadelphia Orphan Asylum, 35
orphans, 2, 10, 67, 71, 79, 82–83, 104, 108; and education, 20, 76, 113–118, 120–122; and innocence, 71, 92; and need for maternal figure, 84, 96, 105, 163. *See also* uplift
Orthodoxy, 66, 97, 99, 126, 129, 156, 158, 178, 182, 186, 198

Page, Thomas Nelson, 103–104
Painter, Nell Irvin, 56n3, 58
Palmer, Phyllis, 203
Pazicki, Diana, 67
Pember, Phoebe Yates, 36
Philipson, Rabbi David, 59
poverty, 3, 209–210, 215; and dependency on the public purse, 1, 26, 40, 44, 54, 73, 77, 127, 141, 149, 152, 169; and the stigma of pauperism, 10, 67, 71, 87–88, 133, 157, 169–170, 179; and worthiness, 13, 72, 88–89, 122, 125, 134, 141–146, 152, 157, 163–170, 188
progressive movement, 52

race: and anxieties about mixing, 18, 21, 70; as contamination, 6, 10, 18–19, 58, 72, 108, 135, 120, 200–202; as culture, 11, 39, 214; as Jewish particularity, 37–42, 47–52; racial science, 3–4, 20, 38, 56–58, 71; and segregation, 92, 110, 181. *See also* chivalry; respectability; uplift; white supremacy
Reconstruction, 3–5, 7–9, 14–17, 22, 25, 42–43,

46, 52–53, 58, 62, 65, 68–70, 108–109, 152, 206; and "Redemption" of the South, 19, 47, 52, 68. *See also* Civil War; Lost Cause

Reform Judaism, 5, 48, 66, 95, 97–99, 115, 186

Reich, Rabbi Leo, 98

Reis, Elizabeth, 127n12, 135

respectability, 46, 57, 77, 148, 152, 162, 170, 177, 190, 199, 210, 215; and gender, 17–18, 21, 41, 77–79, 114, 120, 133, 141, 168, 180, 213. *See also* femininity; masculinity

Ripley, William Z., 55, 56n2, 58

Roosevelt, Theodore, 59, 71, 103, 164

Rosaldo, Renato, 6

Russia: Pale of Settlement in, 25, 51, 85, 158–159; as space of Jewish persecution, 46–47, 56, 67n62

Schiff, Jacob H., 61

segregation. *See* color line; Jim Crow

SenGupta, Gunja, 155, 241n96

Sephardim: and immigration, 25–26, 184–187, 201; and perceived difference from Ashkenazim, 22, 185–187, 190–195, 197–198, 200, 202, 208, 211, 208–209

Sheftall, Benjamin, 34

slavery: Jewish involvement in, 30, 61; and the southern economy, 32

social Darwinism, 87, 131

social workers, 6–7, 13–16, 19–22, 61, 71, 77, 84, 103, 106, 120, 124–125, 134, 138, 144–154, 159, 163, 168, 177, 183–184, 188–210, 214; and case files, 4, 19, 22, 155; and professionalization, 13, 20, 153–155, 163. *See also* surveillance

Solomon, Clara, 36

Sonn, Ralph A., 73, 83, 109, 114–115, 138, 141–143, 168

SS Aquitania, 157–158

Stern, George, 44–45

Strauss, Feist, 76, 106, 117, 122, 144, 153

Stuyvesant, Peter, 26

surveillance, 13–14, 106–107, 167–168, 180

Talented Tenth, 12

the Temple. *See* congregations: Hebrew Benevolent Congregation (the Temple), Atlanta

Tourial, Ezra, 187–188

Trestman, Marlene, 84–85, 97n54, 116n126, 118n134–136

tzedakah (justice to the poor), 13, 87. *See also gemilut hasadim*

Union Society, Savannah, 34

United Hebrew Charities, New York, 128

United States Children's Bureau, 138

uplift, 3, 11–14, 42, 87, 162; and orphans, 20, 67, 83, 109. *See also* cultural capital

Vance, Zebulon, 48, 62

Voorsanger, Rabbi Jacob, 43

Watson, Ebbie Julian, 63

Watson, Thomas E., 74

Weber, Donald, 166

Weil, Sarah, 75–76

Wenger, Beth, 5n12, 24, 37n67, 53

White House Conference on the Care of Dependent Children, 71, 103, 131, 137, 161, 164

white supremacy, 4–5, 11, 18, 22, 52, 65, 68, 202. *See also* color line; Jim Crow; lynching; slavery

Wolf, Simon, 55–60, 72n81, 114, 137, 160n29

womanhood. *See* femininity

Wyle, Armand, 151, 173–174, 176

Wyle, Viola, 150–151, 153–157, 174, 176–178, 181, 199

yellow fever, 27, 34, 38, 41

ABOUT THE AUTHOR

Caroline E. Light is Director of Undergraduate Studies at Harvard University's Program in Studies of Women, Gender, and Sexuality. She has a doctorate in history and teaches courses in gender and ethnic studies; transnational feminist history; immigration; consumer culture; and intersections of citizenship, race, and sexuality in the United States.